Thought
for
the
Day

Thought for the Day

CHRISTINE
MORGAN

BBC Books, an imprint of Ebury Publishing
20 Vauxhall Bridge Road,
London SW1V 2SA

BBC Books is part of the Penguin Random House group of companies
whose addresses can be found at global.penguinrandomhouse.com

Penguin
Random House
UK

This book is published to accompany the radio programme
entitled *Thought for the Day*, broadcast on BBC Radio 4.

First published by BBC Books in 2022

www.penguin.co.uk

A CIP catalogue record for this book is available from the British Library

ISBN 9781785947698

Printed and bound in Great Britain by Clays Ltd, Elcograf S.p.A.

Penguin Random House is committed to a sustainable future for
our business, our readers and our planet. This book is made from
Forest Stewardship Council® certified paper.

MIX
Paper from
responsible sources
FSC
www.fsc.org   FSC® C018179

CONTENTS

Chapter Six: People 233

For Mum and Dad
Brenda and Gerry

Christine Morgan was Head of Religion & Ethics at BBC Radio until 2020. For over 30 years she was a producer and editor in both radio and television. Throughout that time she worked on *Thought for the Day*, of which she was Editor for over a decade. Every morning it delivered Britain's most high-profile religious broadcast to the six million listeners of Radio 4's *Today* programme.

INTRODUCTION

Thought for the Day is unique. Its place in the middle of the nation's most influential news programme means it is the highest-profile religious broadcast in the country – with over six million listeners every day. Sitting at the heart of Radio 4's *Today* programme it speaks to a general audience of people of all faiths and none.

For the last 50 years *Thought for the Day* has offered a different lens through which to see the world. In the cut and thrust of the news and politics, it offers a different perspective on the events of the day. In the words of one of *Thought*'s most distinguished contributors, the late Rabbi Lord Jonathan Sacks: 'The news is about today, but the great faiths remind us of yesterday and tomorrow. They're our living dialogue with the past and the future; those two essential things called memory and hope.'

There are those who have argued that religion was fading away in the modern world and would soon become a thing of the past. But in recent generations waves of immigration – from *Windrush* to the influx of people from the Indian subcontinent to work in the textile mills of the north – have seen Britain become a multi-faith society. Yet it's not simply a process of counting the numbers who attend worship services every week; it is much more complex. A diverse range of initiatives, demonstrating good relations between various faiths – many examples of which appear in *Thought for the Day* – have shown us that, far from being a barrier to social cohesion, religion can be a bridge. To some that may be considered Reithian, but in today's world religion is far more than that; it is bound up in identity, community, culture, the common good and a search for the spiritual. *Thought* is an interface between religion and society and the voice it gives to religion is increasingly important in multi-faith Britain.

As we know, it's not the daily good that religion does that grabs the headlines. Religion tends to do its good in private and its bad in public. Globally, the terror of 9/11 created a seismic shift in geopolitics and shattered the idea that religion was fading away. International events have made clear that faith is a political and ideological driving force that cannot be ignored. *Thought* does not shy away from the harm done in the name of religion but it also seeks to explain how religion is practised with goodwill by billions across the world. In the words of another contributor, Nick Baines, Anglican Bishop of Leeds: 'Over 85 per cent of the world's population hold an individual or social/communal religious commitment. In order to understand the world, we need to look through their eyes.'

Over the past half-century, *Thought* has evolved hugely. It grew out of two predecessors. *Lift Up Your Hearts* was a devotional slot, first broadcast on the BBC Home Service in 1939 just after the start of the Second World War. This was followed, from 1965, by *Ten to Eight*, a more substantial, five-minute sequence. Anglican clerics such as Richard Harries became key contributors but, as Bishop Richard testifies, it was a different world then. He describes the talks as being more prayerful and sermon-like, and most of the time there was no production process. He just wrote a script and then read it out on air.

Then in 1970 the *Today* programme – including the morning religion slot – was relaunched. It was transformed from a magazine-type programme to full-on news and current affairs. The religion slot stayed in the schedule at 7.47am but was renamed *Thought for the Day*. The range of contributors was widened and the brief was changed 'to reflect the worship, thought and action of the principal religious traditions represented in Britain'. An early Jewish contributor, Rabbi Lionel Blue, broadcast every Monday morning while Richard Harries broadcast every Friday: a powerful way to bookend the week.

From this point on, *Thought* was no longer a sermon but rather a reflection on the news from the perspective of one of the major faith traditions. For a while, all the producers remained male white Christians, as did most of the presenters, albeit with some very distinguished names, described by Richard Harries as 'the establishment personified'. Women were gradually admitted to the production process. I joined in 1987 and worked on the slot as a production assistant, producer and then editor, 33 years in all.

Over that period *Thought for the Day* evolved, as did the *Today* programme, the wider news agenda, and the cultural mores of British society. Technology got faster, relationships more open, family life freed up on a different kind of weekly schedule with both parents working. *Thought* was now going much further than merely reminding us of the prospect of eternity; it started to tell us a lot about the world in which we live.

Thought for the Day sits inside the *Today* programme but it is produced by the BBC's Religion & Ethics department. It has always been broadcast live. During COVID, it had to be recorded the night before, but thankfully the vigour and immediacy of live broadcasting with contributors in the studio are now back. In my time, I have worked with nine different *Today* editors and respected them all. But it was a sensitive relationship – I was very aware of our responsibility to match the quality of the rest of the programme. I was also conscious of occasional tensions between the values of news and of religion.

The theology of social justice – to feed the hungry and welcome the stranger – is integral to all the world's major religions. As *Thought* contributors aren't challenged on air, maintaining a strict editorial balance across our contributors, and within scripts on particular subjects, such as foodbanks and refugees, was very important to avoid sounding politically partisan.

Some critics said we should have more radical voices on to 'de-sanitise' our offering. I even remember one occasion where I was sitting at a media dinner next to a columnist who told me: 'You should put Abu Hamza on *Thought for the Day*.' Hamza was the extremist, Islamist preacher and agitator whose image was filling front pages at the time (he was later jailed for life, without parole, for terrorism). I laughed and said he would disqualify himself on several grounds: he'd never be prepared to work with a producer, his message fell foul of fairness, impartiality and not denigrating other faiths, and most of all he was completely unrepresentative of the vast majority of Muslims in this country. It has always been important that *Thought* finds people who have things to say from within their communities, who can offer an authentic view of how they live and what they believe – and who would seldom get the chance to be heard on a mainstream news programme. As longstanding *Thought* contributor Bishop James Jones puts it: 'There is no other national institution that has so affirmed the place of ethnic voices for the last 30 years.'

Such representation has continued to be a central part of the brief, and building that has been a long process. It wasn't until March 1992 that Umar Hegedus became the first Muslim speaker on *Thought for the Day*, but Professor Mona Siddiqui, who began in 1997 as our first female Muslim contributor, is still making important contributions to the slot 25 years later. Today our Hindu, Buddhist and Sikh contributors continue to educate us with new insights from ancient faiths and throw light from new directions on to the issues of contemporary life. And as Mona Siddiqui has said: 'It is important that we talk about religious language and religion in ways that the whole world can actually identify with.'

How right she is. At their best all our regular contributors write from the heart with intelligence and humanity and speak to people way beyond their own communities. The experience of the global pandemic proved that. Everyone stepped up to produce extraordinary contributions. And that's where producer and contributor working together through a 24-hour period is key. The writer has to have something they really want to say and the producer is the sounding board in a collaborative process that makes for the best writing. It could be very strange at times to have such an intense telephone relationship with people you seldom meet in person. I remember with great affection those first production conversations with the contributors each morning to choose the subject; I count myself very fortunate to have shared their wisdom, creative ideas and hard work to get them ready for broadcast. For those starting out, the watchwords were don't preach but include theology, aim to sound like yourself, don't use 'we' as if you can speak for everyone and, crucially, what is the one thought you want them to take away?

BBC editorial guidelines requiring impartiality can be constraints, and compliance has been tightened over the years. But platitudinous was a dangerous place for us to be. It is possible to say strong things on *Thought* without getting in hot water if you work at it. Indeed, I remember my first boss, David Winter, rightly warning me it was the only programme in the Religion portfolio that would get me sacked. Wise words. Though it was also David who said that the best *Thoughts* were the ones that made him cut himself shaving! News doesn't stand still and it's invariably built around controversy and conflict. Our writers had to be skilful at introducing a theological idea to unpack events in a way which wouldn't be heard elsewhere in this overwhelmingly secular news environment. It often brought great feedback from the fabulous Radio 4 audience. It's easy to underestimate how the intellectually curious will happily grapple with different ideas and those not formally religious will connect with a spiritual message.

There have long been those who have suggested that if *Thought for the Day* is to be truly representative it should include atheists among its contributors. Secularists and humanists have campaigned for decades for non-religious voices to be included. We have resisted the idea, with the support of successive Controllers of Radio 4 and the BBC Governors and Board, in order to maintain the distinctively religious nature of the broadcast – an oasis of a few minutes of faith-based reflection. Richard Dawkins is right that religious people do not have a monopoly on ethics, but *Thought* is not an ethical reflection; it's a religious one. As the former Bishop of Southwark, Tom Butler, told a House of Lords committee that raised the subject of *Thought for the Day* when considering BBC Charter renewal: 'It is like asking why the sports news is always about sport. Why can they not have somebody on there who is going to be talking about some other hobby such as birdwatching? They could, but it would no longer be the sporting slot.'

I believe we also tapped into something of an unconscious cultural void. I remember a distinguished journalist from a leading paper telling me how he had ditched the faith of his Anglican upbringing in his early twenties. So his daughters, aged nine and seven, had never been exposed to Christianity on any level. He had begun to feel really worried that he was depriving them of core themes and stories that were part of their national heritage in the same way Shakespeare is still threaded through our culture and language. He felt he was denying them a rich source in their formation – something he had benefitted from.

I hope *Thought* offered a way of filling some of those gaps for many listeners.

In the end, every programme starts with the audience – with listeners of all shades of belief and unbelief. *Thought* needs to reach hearts and minds with a different kind of wisdom to help keep those themes and stories alive and interwoven with the concerns of the day – or maybe to simply offer relief to the gloom and rancour of so much of the news. It's a tough call for just under three minutes of radio. I do know we reached one particular listener; when Richard Harries was the Bishop of Oxford he was welcomed to Chequers by Prime Minister Margaret Thatcher with the opening words: 'I listen to you on the radio. Sometimes I agree with you, and sometimes you make me mad!'

When I began to think how this book should chart the history of this unique broadcast over five decades, my instinct was to try to capture every big event and moment, every social change and debate. But the more I gathered and sorted, the more I realised this would have to be a series of snapshots that bring out the colour, time and place of the kind of stories and people that have been part of our response on this great *Thought for the Day* journey. So this book includes national and international milestones, great writing and listener favourites – of those who wrote to tell us how profoundly they had been affected by an individual *Thought*. There were particular scripts that brought back memories for me of wars, natural disasters, political mael-stroms and extraordinary scientific developments. Then there was the tension of the election night, when we needed a script for each party and one for a hung Parliament, and the fright of hearing Rabbi Lionel Blue struggling on air to speak properly with three paragraphs to go. As I listened, I feared he had been taken ill and then realised he was trying to work from memory – he'd lost the second page of his script. Every broadcast brought its own mix of terrors, excitement and even jubilation at an editorial development not just successfully registered but nailed. It was also down to the inventiveness and experience of our contributors that, as we marked the religious rituals and festivals of the liturgical year, we connected to the seasons of the natural world, the continuity of the faiths, and the depth of commitment among individuals who live their lives in relationship with God. *Thought* is a challenge but it is also the most wonderful, rewarding piece of religious current affairs to be had anywhere.

The selection of contributors to this book is a fraction of the number who have written for the slot over those 50 years, and not all the *Thoughts* I would have liked to include were still available. But what we have is an amazing variety of faiths, men and women from all walks of life, people of all colours, heritage and sexualities, whose voices have enriched and delighted – and deepened the integration of the different faiths into the life of the nation. This book tries to represent a little of all that. Looking back on quite how versatile and responsive we've been has been both exciting and humbling – I am indebted to all the dedicated and amazing contributors we've worked with, as well as the talented production team I've asked so much of. They have been exceptional in more ways than I can say. It has been a fascinating journey through half a century in which *Thought for the Day* quietly told the story of a changing Britain back to itself. The whole thing has been an honour and a privilege.

Christine Morgan

July 2022

Chapter One

National

REV. DR COLIN MORRIS

Immigration and our patron saints

Rev. Dr Colin Morris was one of the foremost thinkers, writers and broadcasters of his generation. Ordained a Methodist minister, he began as a missionary in Zambia and became a trusted adviser to President Kenneth Kaunda. He spoke with passion about dignity for ordinary people and racial equality, even when it made him unpopular. He returned to the UK to be president of the Methodist Conference followed by a BBC career as Head of Religious Broadcasting and Controller of Northern Ireland at the end of the Troubles. His strengths as a communicator and consummate broadcaster attracted universal admiration, but he was always solidly grounded in his faith and never lost his mischievous sense of fun in the face of the pompous or absurd.

The furore this script set off happened when Thought for the Day *was just a year old in 1971. Colin took exception to the government's draft Immigration Bill, which proposed to classify British residents as patrials or non-patrials – the latter being without a father or grandfather born in Britain, which would remove their right to remain in the UK. The government protested to the BBC and Colin found himself 'dropped' for a while. And although the producer responsible, Roy Trevivian, defended the script, he left the BBC shortly after.*

1 March 1971

Today is St David's Day. A great man, St David, but I do hope that all Welsh men realise how fortunate he was to have lived before the proposed Immigration Bill becomes law. According to its terms, people who wish to come and live here will be divided into patrials and non-patrials, according to whether or not you have a father or grandfather born in Britain. Now you can see St David's problem: he was born in France.

However, the Welsh are in no worse a plight than the rest of us. St George probably wasn't a historical character at all, but if by any chance he was, he'd give the immigration people a headache because he came from Libya. Thus he was not only a non-patrial but also black. Then Saint Andrew was born in Galilee, so he's out. There's something a bit Irish about the fact that the only genuine patrial patron saint we've got is St Patrick of Ireland.

We may have to take a look at some of our national heroes in the light of this new Bill. Sir Winston Churchill was a patrial, but his mother was American, so perhaps we need a new companion volume to that admirable reference work, *Who's Who*; we could call it *Who's Half-Who*. At least this terminology is going to solve the perpetual problem of the correct name of certain public places – 'Men' and 'Women' is a bit stark; 'Ladies' and 'Gentlemen' is snobbish. We can now label them 'Patrials' and 'Matrials'. Old rhymes will take on a new significance:

Ten little black boys going down the mine
One forgot his pass card, then there were nine;
Nine little black boys trying to pull their weight
One was non-patrial so now there are eight.

All good clean fun, but for Christians there is the additional problem that we shall have to extend that one-sentence manifesto of the apostle Paul which forms the basis of our judgement of human beings: 'There is neither Jew nor Gentile, bond nor free, male or female, patrial or non-patrial. All are one in Christ.'

I don't subscribe to the view that any government which proposes legislation with which I cannot agree is composed of fiends incarnate. I'm sure they are honourable and compassionate men and women, so I hope they'll think again about this Bill if for no other reason than that it is alien to the spirit of the greatest non-patrial of them all, Jesus of Nazareth.

BISHOP JIM THOMPSON

Faith in the City

Faith in the City *was a milestone for the Church of England and the government in the Thatcher era. It was a hard-hitting report published by a commission set up by the Archbishop of Canterbury in 1983 to examine the problems of the nation's inner cities and housing estates, and report on how the Church, government and other bodies should respond. After two years of taking evidence in the depressed inner cities, the Commission made a series of recommendations for action by both Church and government on unemployment, education, policing, social work and more. Its recommendations were widely seen as criticisms of the Thatcher government and the report provoked a storm of outrage in some quarters for being 'too political'.*

Bishop Jim Thompson had a rare talent for conveying the warmth of his physical presence in his voice. A Thought for the Day *contributor for 20 years, he wasn't on the Commission but his determination to act as a voice for the poor and marginalised in his diocese of Stepney routinely brought criticisms that he was a 'leftie'. To Jim, living by gospel values needed no apology. But his advocacy for the poor was such that Margaret Thatcher blocked his elevation to Bishop of Birmingham.* Thoughts *like this wouldn't have helped.*

7 March 1984

A leading politician once suggested that the clergy should give up politics for Lent. It's a time when Christians remember that Jesus went out into the wilderness and prayed about the role he was going to live out in Palestine. After 40 days he embarked on a very public ministry, which was to take him right to the centre of his country's capital city – to the heart of the political arena in Jerusalem, where he was put to death by the occupying forces.

The difficulty about giving up political issues for Lent – which would in itself be a relief – is that we would have to give up praying as well. Concern about the special socio-political issues of our day grows out of prayer. Involvement is what counts to people and lends urgency to our need to pray.

To give an example: if I pray for my children at school I ask God to take care of them, that they may grow into civilised educated Christian adults. But the Lord's commandment was to love my neighbour as myself. My neighbours in Stepney also have children, so I start praying about our schools, the pressures on staff, and the children.

That leads me to think about the future of the Inner London Education Authority and the effects it will have on the children in the poorer areas of London.

Nor do my thoughts stop there, because I think of the schools in Namibia, which I visited last October. Children there have to walk many dangerous miles to school. They cannot learn after lunch because there is no lunch. They cannot write because there are no pencils or paper. I think of children and teachers being abducted and never arriving at school at all.

So, as soon as I pray for my own children, I am into prayer about my neighbours' children and the political issues which affect their education – whether in inner London or southern Africa.

It's not that I believe that any party political manifesto would be the same as Jesus's manifesto – nor do I believe it's the task of the clergy to use their position to score party political points. Christians who pray and read their bibles may come to different political conclusions.

But to suggest that there is part of God's world which is spiritual and another part which is political is to ghettoise religion, and de-moralise politics.

BISHOP LORD RICHARD HARRIES

The Death of Diana, Princess of Wales

The news of the death of Diana, Princess of Wales on that August morning in 1997 was so shocking and unexpected it was hard to take in, let alone process. How could anyone sum up the thoughts and reactions to this enormous loss – the loss of someone so young and vital, who so dominated our public life and media?

It fell to Richard Harries, Bishop of Oxford, to do just that. He was already a long-standing and highly respected contributor to Thought for the Day. *With the instinctive response of a man of God and church leader, he spoke of the grieving family and the nature of the person taken so suddenly – and then offered prayers, which came from the depth and practice of his Christian faith to find words to console in the midst of this terrible news.* Thought for the Day *is not a devotional slot but there are very rare occasions when the cadence of the Prayer Book is a profound connector for many more than just those who would go to church. Bishop Richard got the tone exactly right.*

31 *August 1997*

At a time like this we all reach for the same inadequate words. We have a sense of shock, of deep sadness, especially for the two princes – young boys who have lost their mother so suddenly. The prayers of all who pray will be with them today.

Princess Diana was the best known, the most sought after, the most photographed figure in the world, combining the glamour of a superstar with the aura of royalty and her own personal magnetism. But in the end, like each of us, she was a person with her own thoughts and struggles, her own hopes and despairs.

The real Diana, who, despite the media attention and even the friendship of her closest friends, was someone whom only she really knew – that inner person, with the scars left by her own parents' divorce, her struggles to overcome bulimia, her unhappy marriage. How tempting it must have been for her to just not bother, to give up, to despair. But instead she made something of her life, emerging as a person in her own right – above all, drawing on the well of her own suffering to feel for others who were in pain.

Few of us are fully aware of why we do what we do, or of the range of motives that drive us. But the simple fact is that Princess Diana reached out from her own vulnerability to those in distress – to those suffering from AIDS, to children mutilated by mines – willing to touch, hold and hug both young and old. That, in a cold and cynical world, is something for which we should be profoundly thankful.

In her inner struggles it was clear too that the princess was trying to make sense of life, trying to find some meaning and purpose in it all. How far she got I don't know. But I do know that the God to whom she goes is good and just and gentle. He is a God who knows her better than she knew herself, who desires her wellbeing more passionately than she desired it herself.

That is why, like many other Christians, I want to pray: 'Rest eternal, grant unto them, O Lord; let light perpetual shine upon them' – for her and for the others who were killed in the car crash. For as Saint Paul wrote, 'I am sure that neither death nor life, nor things present, nor things to come, nor anything else in all creation, will be able to separate us from the love of God in Christ Jesus our Lord.'

The fairy story has turned into a Greek tragedy. There is an inescapable tragic element to human existence. But through the cross and resurrection of Christ, tragedy does not have to be the last word. We commend her to a faithful God.

ABDAL HAKIM MURAD

The other side of Sharia law

In 2008 the Archbishop of Canterbury, Rowan Williams, unwittingly lit a fire under the subject of Sharia law in Britain. At least, that was the inter-pretation of tabloid newspapers who were horrified at the prospect of what they saw as legal separateness for Britain's largest minority. In a lecture on civil and religious law at the Royal Courts of Justice, Dr Williams said that giving Islamic law official status in the UK would help achieve social cohesion because some Muslims did not relate to the British legal system. Some, like Baroness Warsi, said the comments were 'unhelpful and may add to the confusion that already exists in our communities'. But other Muslim groups supported Dr Williams's views, which set out a broad code of conduct for all aspects of life, from diet to the wearing of the hijab.

This was a big story and Abdal Hakim Murad was exactly the right person to put it into context. A respected academic, known as Tim Winter before he converted to Islam, he is the Founder and Dean of the Cambridge Muslim College and also Director of Studies for Theology at Wolfson College Cambridge. He studied at the Al-Azhar Mosque in Cairo which is renowned as the most prestigious university in the Islamic world and is critical of extremists such as Osama bin Laden and al-Qaeda.

11 February 2008

The controversy over the archbishop's remarks on Sharia rumbles on. Tabloid newspapers and far-right pundits in partic-ular have vented much rancour, horrified at the prospect of what they see as legal separateness for Britain's largest minority.

As the weekend wore on, however, the mood seemed slowly to shift. There were signs that more people were actually reading the archbishop's lecture, which was written as a subtle reflection on the right relationship between faith, law and citizenship in the modern state. And the criticisms grew more muted.

Some took the view that Dr Williams was probably right but should have expressed himself in a way that could not have been misquoted by the tabloids.

Others worked through his admittedly difficult argument, and concluded that he had been utterly misunderstood. So the Bishop of Hulme said: 'The way he has been ridiculed, lampooned and treated by some people and indeed some of the media … is quite disgraceful.' Similar words came from Britain's senior woman priest, June Osborne, and the Catholic prelate, Cardinal Murphy-O'Connor.

It is now clear to most that Dr Williams, far from recommending some kind of parallel law for Muslims, was pointing out that informal religious tribunals, which already adjudicate on a limited number of civil – never criminal – matters, in a way which is entirely legal under arbitration laws, should be more systematically brought under the regulation of the legal system. He was not commending greater separateness, or an expansion of Muslim courts – quite the opposite.

Although his prose is sometimes dense, I know he thinks this because a few weeks ago I was with him in Singapore, where we were shown how many of the city's religious minorities, including the Muslims, have their own courts to deal with civil matters such as marriage and divorce. He is interested in the challenge that religious diversity poses to a secular legal system. But he is sure that social cohesion is best served when there is a mechanism by which arbitration conducted within communities can be formally related to national law.

A storm in a teacup, then? Not quite. The issue of how faith is acknowledged in law will continue to be a tricky one, and not just for Muslims. For instance, one recent poll showed that 9 per cent of Americans think that the Bible should be their country's only source of law, and the percentage is growing.

For me, my major reaction to this dispute has been a sadness that we are so quick to judge. There is something un-British, and certainly un-religious, about the way in which nowadays we suddenly shout and panic without ascertaining the facts.

In the Quran itself, we read: 'O people of faith! If a person brings you some news, inquire into it carefully, lest you should harm others unwittingly and afterwards be sorry for what you did.'

CANON DR ALAN BILLINGS

The MPs' expenses scandal

The MPs' expenses scandal ripped through all political parties in the Houses of Parliament in 2009. Extravagant and manipulative claims made by MPs and peers were exposed by a series of leaks to the Daily Telegraph *– with one of the most outlandish claims being a request that taxpayers' money be used to pay for a floating duck island in a pond at an MP's home. The scandal was on a serious scale and everyone knew that things would have to change. One MP confessed that MPs had 'lost the confidence of the public and we need to get that back'.*

The thoughtful style of Anglican priest Canon Dr Alan Billings made him a popular contributor. He brought to the slot his expertise as a former Director of the Centre for Ethics and Religion at Lancaster University. He had also taught the ethics of war to chaplains to the forces at the Defence Academy of the United Kingdom. And he had a very useful background in politics as a former deputy leader of Sheffield City Council. All of which was just perfect in this Thought *on the ethics of MPs' expenses.*

11 May 2009

The moral high ground has become a lot less crowded in recent days as a number of former occupants have been catapulted from it. As the hapless MPs departed they left two phrases ringing in our ears. The first was, 'I can understand the public's anger' and the second was 'in good faith'. But we became angry because we found out what was going on; which begs the question, if they knew what was going on, why hadn't they been angry too? And we didn't doubt they acted in good faith. What made us cross was that they never seemed to query the rules by which, in good faith, they acted.

If only they had acknowledged earlier the need for a wider scrutiny and a greater transparency. And perhaps there is something in the idea of transparency that we can all reflect on for the living of our own lives.

Among the many threads that, woven together, form the Christian faith is the idea of Last Judgement. 'Nothing is covered up', said Jesus, 'that will not be revealed; neither hid, that shall not be known. Whatever you have said in the darkness shall be heard in the light, and what you have whispered in private rooms shall be proclaimed upon the housetops.'

We shouldn't misunderstand this. The Last Judgement is not the idea that after death we are all going to be cruelly tripped up or caught out – in the way the MPs no doubt feel they have been tripped up. It's the endpoint of a life that is understood as transparent at all times, because it is transparent to God.

As the psalmist said: 'O Lord, thou hast searched me and known me. Thou knowest when I sit down and when I rise up … Even before a word is on my tongue … thou knowest it altogether.'

At one time, the idea of being transparent to God, and a last or definitive judgement, would have been a significant part of Christian faith, and many would have lived their lives in the light of it. One reason for it receding is because some have said that if you act out of fear and not because this is how you freely want to behave, that is hardly morality.

But this misses the point. In seeking to live a moral life we need all the help we can get – all the incentives and disincentives going – because the way is narrow and we are easily blown off course.

Which brings us back to public life. If believing that our lives are transparent to God is no longer at the forefront of our minds, no longer as potent an idea as it once was, then we shall just have to rely on the Freedom of Information Act – a sort of secular equivalent of the Last Judgement!

CLIFFORD LONGLEY

The Chilcot Inquiry and a 'Just War'

The public inquiry into the nation's role in the Iraq War, the Chilcot Inquiry, began in 2009. Among those it questioned were the former prime minister Tony Blair and former government officials, including Alastair Campbell, the PM's director of communications. They defended their decision to join the US invasion of Iraq as a necessary pre-emptive action to forestall the use of 'weapons of mass destruction' by the Iraqi dictator Saddam Hussein. Other witnesses took a different view. The former international development secretary Clare Short repeatedly criticised Tony Blair and Attorney General Peter Goldsmith, alleging they had deceived MPs to obtain consent for the invasion of Iraq. Foreign Office lawyers were quizzed on the legality of the war.

Clifford Longley is a distinguished journalist who has covered British and international religious affairs for almost six decades. He has been a leader writer for The Times *and* Daily Telegraph, *a panellist on Radio 4's* Moral Maze, *and he now writes for the Catholic weekly paper* The Tablet. *His extensive knowledge of ethical principles – together with his clarity of thought and engaging style in unpacking the arguments – were particularly helpful when it came to analysing the workings of the Chilcot Inquiry.*

1 *February 2010*

At the start of the Falklands War, the editor of *The Times* asked me to give him a clear outline of St Thomas Aquinas's theory of the 'Just War'. He later defended Margaret Thatcher's policy in those terms. I've read in several places recently that Tony Blair also immersed himself in Thomas Aquinas as he came to his decision to join the US invasion of Iraq. He did so despite the grave doubts of the archbishops of Canterbury and Westminster on whether the invasion could satisfy the Just War criteria. The Pope and the Vatican were even more forthright, as were a large group of leading American churchmen.

When critics complain that the Iraq War was not only illegal but immoral, this must be what they are talking about. Yet the Chilcot Inquiry's questioning of Tony Blair last Friday kept off the subject. They concentrated on the legality, as they had done with previous witnesses and no doubt will again. We can be pretty sure that had he been asked, Mr Blair could have mounted a stout defence of his policy based on the principles Thomas Aquinas set out. And there would be plenty of people ready to try to shoot holes in his arguments, including the two archbishops.

Thomas Aquinas was trying to answer the question: How do you apply Christ's command to 'love your enemies' to an international conflict, and how should you treat your enemy – including non-combatants – on and off the battlefield? Thus the Just War principles apply both to the reasons for going to war and the way the war is conducted. The first question boils down to four main tests – asking, essentially, when is war the lesser of two evils:

- The damage inflicted by the aggressor on the nation or community of nations must be lasting, grave and certain.
- All other means of putting an end to it must have been shown to be impractical or ineffective.
- There must be serious prospects of success.

- And the use of arms must be proportionate, and not produce evils and disorders graver than the evil to be eliminated.

All four tests have to be passed with a reasonable degree of certainty, and they say nothing I can see that would justify pre-emptive action. There are scholars who would like Just War theory developed to take account of terrorism and weapons of mass destruction, and also the issues of humanitarian intervention and of risk assessment. There is undoubtedly a case for them to argue, as one would expect Mr Blair to do. But this lies beyond the terms of reference of the Chilcot Inquiry, evidently.

It says something about our culture that we turn to lawyers for answers to our big ethical questions rather than to philosophers or religious teachers. Yet does anybody seriously think the legal issues are more important than the moral ones?

BISHOP JAMES JONES

The Queen's Diamond Jubilee

James Jones is widely known for his extraordinary leadership of the independent panel into the deaths of 97 football fans at Hillsborough during his time as Bishop of Liverpool. But he has also been involved in many other areas over the decades and has had many dealings with HM The Queen and, indeed, with HRH Prince Charles. The insights he gained working with the royal family informed this Thought *on the anniversary of the monarch's 60 years on the throne. The Diamond Jubilee celebrations took place at a time of austerity and so were scaled back to avoid excessive cost to taxpayers; something the Queen sensitively matched with a visibly pared-down family group on the balcony. The Duke of Edinburgh had been hospitalised for a few days with an infection, but, overall, the celebrations were a huge success and a lift for the whole country and beyond.*

As Bishop James points out, the importance of the Queen's Christian faith can sometimes get lost amid all the general coverage – until she attends the church service of Thanksgiving for her strength, wisdom and dedicated service. But it's through such public participation that she signals to every community, and to believers from every faith tradition, that she is Defender of the Faith for them too.

6 June 2012

Although Her Majesty became Queen 60 years ago in 1952 the coronation was delayed to the following year for Winston Churchill felt the post-war economic crisis was too severe to allow anyone a day off and declared: 'Can't have Coronations with bailiffs in the house'!

I don't suppose the Queen ever imagined she would be on the throne for six decades. Her father's reign lasted only a quarter of that. In her accession speech she compared herself with the King saying: 'My heart is too full for me to say anything more to you today than that I shall always work as my father did.' And so she has.

A point missed by most of the commentariat is that during this Diamond Jubilee tour of the Kingdom and Commonwealth there have been so many church services – culminating in the magnificence of St Paul's Cathedral from where the absence of the Duke of Edinburgh will be felt today. But, even without him at her side the service will be for her a spiritual finale to the hugely successful celebrations.

At the coronation service the Archbishop of Canterbury presented the Queen with the Bible and said: 'We present you with this Book. The most valuable thing that this world affords.' And the Moderator of the Church of Scotland continued: 'Here is Wisdom; this is the Royal Law; these are the lively Oracles of God.'

This is the faith of the Queen as Supreme Governor of the Church of England and as Defender of the Faith.

In a recent speech at Lambeth Palace in front of the leaders of our different faith communities she explained how defending the faith included protecting 'the free practice of all faiths in this country' – a point first made by the Prince of Wales. Both the Queen and the Prince, because of their experience of the Commonwealth, were perhaps among the first to see that the future stability of the world depends on good relationships between the faith communities locally and globally.

Here at home the Church of England acts as the convenor of the faith communities; it also hosts the gathering of the people in tragedy and in joy; and in an atomised world it remains one of the few bonds binding us together. Such is the role of her Established Church in the twenty-first century.

Through her personal example of public prayer the Queen has signalled her own convictions about that most valuable thing that this world affords.

So, when the history of her reign is finally written, there ought to be at least one chapter on how she herself has kept alive the rumour of faith in an age of doubt.

The title of such a chapter? 'The Faithful Queen'.

RABBI LORD JONATHAN SACKS

Margaret Thatcher's funeral

The funeral of Margaret Thatcher was going to require a very sensitive, finely judged script for Thought for the Day. *Her achievements and national importance as our first woman prime minister were indisputable. But so was the bitter resentment in which she was held in many parts of former industrial Britain. It was impossible to know whether her legacy would be as divisive as her political reputation. The Church of England, despite having been once dubbed 'the Tory Party at prayer', had a pretty challenging track record with her. The strength of feeling among her admirers and critics was, in many ways, the only thing that connected them. Striking the right tone on the day of her funeral was going to be tricky for* Thought *as an unchallenged single-voice talk in the middle of a news programme. How could we be impartial and respectful without further inflaming those who had actually rejoiced at her passing?*

In the end, the choice came down to one person. Rabbi Lord Sacks was one of the intellectual giants of his generation, who had always combined speaking from the heart with a theological integrity that appealed just as much to those with no faith as to religious believers. In fact, it was his hallmark. He was the consummate broadcaster and he had had a lengthy relationship with Mrs Thatcher. We spoke about the nature of the day, and the considerations for Thought, *but, as always, he was aware of the pitfalls. The script arrived in good time the day before the funeral, and I didn't need to change a word.*

17 April 2013

As the funeral service for Margaret Thatcher takes place today, I will be thinking not of the public person but of the private one. I knew her when I was a child at school. She was my local MP, and when I had an essay to write about politics, I used to go and see her in her constituency office, to hear what she had to say.

I remember once mentioning the words 'proportional representation' and she glared at me as if I had committed a cardinal sin. 'You're not a liberal, are you?' she said. And I had hurriedly to say that I wasn't advocating it, just writing an essay about it.

Even then, back in 1963, she was being described as a parliamentary Boadicea, brandishing *Hansard* in one hand and a handbag in the other. Yet she was always willing to help a 15-year-old schoolboy whose political affiliation she didn't know and who wouldn't even have a vote for another six years.

In public, her leadership style was more like Moses than Aaron, more conviction and confrontation than compromise and conciliation. But we need both. Aaron was more loved than Moses. The sages said that when Aaron died, everyone mourned, but when Moses died, not everyone did. But without Moses, there would not have been a Jewish people. Sometimes leaders have to be strong at the cost of being divisive, because they see no other way of getting from here to there.

Years later, in 1997, I wrote a book about politics to challenge the statement attributed to her that 'there is no such thing as society'. I thought she'd never speak to me again, but she read it, and commended it to her friends, and stayed as warm as ever.

Which says a lot. She read. She loved ideas. She was intensely considerate to those with whom she worked. And even most of her critics didn't doubt her integrity or courage, or the dignity she showed in her last difficult years. Such values matter in a free society, because politics is about conflict, and without civility it can quickly degenerate into abuse and the war of all against all.

Those who serve their country with dedication and distinction deserve respect in life. How much more so in death. And she did so serve, with all her heart. She loved Britain, and fought for it. She loved responsibility and practised it. She loved freedom and lived for it. She was a fighter all her life. And now in death may her soul find peace.

AKHANDADHI DAS

A historic handshake

Part of the multi-faith journey during the span of Thought for the Day *has been successfully delivered by contributors such as Akhandadhi Das, a Vaishnava teacher and theologian. Originally from Belfast, he was a convert to Hinduism who became Principal of Bhaktivedanta Manor, which was for a long time the best-known Hindu temple in Britain.*

In June 2012 there was a historic moment for the Northern Ireland peace process, when the Queen met and shook hands with Sinn Fein's deputy first minister Martin McGuinness, a former IRA commander. In the knowledge that the Queen had lost a member of her own family during the Troubles, it was described as a 'momentous step forward' as they joined in a gesture that would once have been unthinkable.

Akhandadhi's Thought was written with a personal appreciation of the enormity of the meeting for both of them and he wrote about forgiveness – a subject universally understood. He brought to it both his experience of Northern Ireland plus new stories and fresh insights from the Hindu tradition that broadened our understanding of this extraordinary moment.

27 June 2012

It's an everyday act so habitual we rarely consider its meaning but, today, one brief handshake will carry enormous significance and symbolism. The Queen and Deputy First Minister Martin McGuinness will shake hands at a charity reception in Belfast.

This meeting raises all sorts of conflicting issues and deep emotions for the people of Northern Ireland and beyond. It is precisely because it evokes decades, indeed centuries, of tragic history, of personal and collective hurt and loss, that so many of us are moved by the gesture and hopeful of the future it may contribute to.

The Hindu epic, the *Mahabharata*, recognises the difficult act of balancing justice and forgiveness. Does reconciliation imply condoning past actions? Does it deny consolation to victims by not bringing perpetrators to justice? One sage suggests that there are times for responding with strong action and there are times for forgiveness. Both may be justified in certain circumstances. But, it is knowing which to apply and when that brings peace and progress.

There's a feeling that the meeting of the Queen and Mr McGuinness could not have happened in days gone past. We weren't ready for it perhaps – being still caught up in the politics and the experiences of the Troubles. This is natural, says the *Mahabharata*, because the tendency is to think that forceful response is real action by our leaders; it's only later we see how such an approach may prolong, rather than curtail, continued violence. As it says: if the injured return their injuries, if the defamed return the words spoke against them, or the oppressed become the oppressor, what is the hope for future generations? It's only if people can be as forgiving as Mother Earth that there can be life, peace and prosperity.

Returning regularly to my home town, I have seen how incredibly the province has moved on and this act of reconciliation represents the current mood of the majority. Even so, drawing a line with the past today is a brave and bold step by both the individuals and their communities.

One Hindu saint commented: there's just one fault in those who forgive, and that is that the foolish regard them as weak. But, ignore that – he said – forgiveness is actually a great power. It is the ornament of the strong.

Today's simple handshake may help the people of Northern Ireland make further progress. It will hearten many more who wish peace for the province. It may also stand as an example that, whatever situation we find ourselves in, the time always comes when forgiveness and reconciliation are the all-important keys to a better future. As the *Mahabharata* says: knowledge leads to true satisfaction; kindness gives lasting happiness; and forgiveness brings the greatest peace.

REV. DR ROB MARSHALL

The forgotten army

Rob Marshall is an Anglican priest, originally from the north-east, who has a way of being able to read his Thought *in such a conversational tone that he exudes the feeling he's talking to a single listener. More often than not he has written for Saturday mornings, so although there's often as much news as on a weekday, his natural people-focused approach is a great strength in matching the weekend mood.*

In this script he brings that direct conversational style to bear on the 70th anniversary of VJ Day. The veterans of the war in the Far East had always felt overlooked during the celebrations for Victory in Europe in 1945. But in 2015 they were given a solemn and heartfelt tribute by the prime minister, David Cameron, who spoke of the deaths, appalling injuries and torture they had endured, and thanked them for all they had suffered for our freedoms. In this Thought *Rob Marshall draws on ancient words that offer a glimpse of a shared human experience from many centuries past to illuminate today's wrongs and injustices.*

15 August 2015

Some historians have attributed the title 'the forgotten army' to those who continued to fight in the Far East in 1945 after the war had ended in Europe. Such a description gives added poignancy to today's VJ Day commemorations.

The 2.5 million British and Commonwealth Service Personnel evidently felt even more cut off from their loved ones back home than those who had served in Europe. Communication was difficult and journeys backwards and forwards by sea, often intolerable.

But when it was announced, 70 years ago to this very day, that Japan had surrendered, King George VI prophesied in his speech to the nation that 'we shall feel the inevitable consequences [of this terrible war] long after we have all forgotten our rejoicing today'.

I've been looking at the experiences of some of the veterans and their families who will take part in today's ceremonies across the country.

Alfred Nellis served in the 9th Coast Regiment Royal Artillery. His son Michael says, on the website 'Far Eastern Heroes', that his father was shocked by the pain he went through when he came home. He met the two children he hardly knew. His dad, Michael says, wanted the world to understand what he had been through. But there was some reticence. It was hard to explain. Better not to talk about it. Just leave it there.

This is perhaps where the notion of a forgotten army came in. They were not talked about enough. Three hundred thousand prisoners of war in the Far East, of which one third died in captivity. Perhaps we just couldn't grasp the enormity of it all, with the world in such a state?

Many of us will have experienced, in very different ways of course, what it's like to be forgotten. It's rarely pleasant. But I was surprised, when looking this week, to see how common a complaint it is in the Old Testament ... 'Oh God – why have you forgotten me – why have others not appreciated all that I have done – why am I being ignored?' Such a lament has a rhythm in the psalms – particularly in Psalm 31: 'I am forgotten, as though I were dead. I am like a broken vessel.'

So if being forgotten can be described in terms of a shattered vase or a damaged piece of fragile pottery – it's easy to suggest that the opposite is simply to be recognised and remembered, helping to repair through an act of restitution.

Today Britain will remember the courage and huge sacrifice of those who fought and those who died in the Far East. The 70 years between then and now will not diminish our empathy or gratitude. This is no forgotten army.

FRANCIS CAMPBELL

After the Brexit vote – what now?

Francis Campbell is the softly spoken Northern Irishman who brought to the Thought *rota a world of experience in politics, diplomacy and religion. He had worked with Tony Blair and his team in Number 10, held a historic diplomatic post in Rome – the first British Roman Catholic ambassador to the Pope since the Reformation – before being posted to Karachi in Pakistan, a place not without dangers for a Christian. He later returned to the Foreign Office in London before changing tack completely and entering higher education to set up a new university: St Mary's University at Twickenham in London.*

In the days after the Brexit referendum, it was clear that the pre-vote level of division in the electorate was going to be manifested in great elation or disappointment for each camp after it. England and Wales backed 'Leave' but Scotland and Northern Ireland voted 'Remain' – and the overall vote was very close at 52 to 48 per cent. But whatever a person's view, it was universally agreed this was an important and far-reaching moment politically for the United Kingdom. And Francis Campbell had a heartfelt message, which came from the experience of growing up amid the violence of a divided society during the Troubles.

27 June 2016

The question about our role in the world, and whether we want to be in the EU or not, has thrown up an internal question about the cohesiveness of our own society. The divisions run deep and are quite emotional, compounded by geographic, national, economic, social and cultural differences. Representative democracy also seems pitted against direct democracy. None of these divisions will be resolved easily, or in haste.

Having represented the United Kingdom as a diplomat for nearly 20 years, I have seen similar situations in other countries and reported back to London on crises and upheavals. In my view, when faced with times of tension, uncertainty and unease, diplomacy is always preferable to dogmatic or dictatorial behaviour, even if there is a part of the human mind that craves certainty. Rash judgements or loud voices rarely capture the complexity of the challenge, bring healing or solve the problem.

Our risk in this fast-moving scenario is that we act before we think and find ourselves sleep-walking into an even more divisive society which future generations will struggle to overcome.

So how do we pause amid the pressure of the quick and the instant and a pace of development that seems to change by the hour? A good starting point is the question which the lawyer posed to Jesus: 'Who is my neighbour?'

That question resonates with us particularly today as we ask it within the UK and within our continent and world. Jesus' response to the lawyer was to tell him the parable of the Good Samaritan who helped the stranger while two others simply walked past on the other side. The lawyer acknowledged that the man who showed mercy and compassion to the stranger was the good neighbour. Jesus then instructed him to do the same.

So who are we in this parable? The victim? Those who walked past? Or the one who stopped and helped? The answer is critical because the story shows us how we can overcome divisions and rebuild a cohesive society.

If you think that it's all too difficult, it isn't. Thirty years ago in Northern Ireland, amid a highly divided and violent society, one MP, John Hume, bravely reached out, taking huge risks to speak with those who then believed in pursuing violence to achieve political ends. In doing so, he persuaded them to abandon violence and to embrace democratic means alone. It is one of the best examples of peace-making and bridge-building in our lifetime.

Building community can be done, even when the circumstances seem so divisive and impossible. It just requires Good

Samaritans and more people like John Hume to stop, to think – and then act.

JASVIR SINGH

The morning after Grenfell

On Thought for the Day *all contributors know that if there's an atrocity or disaster, we must do our best to reflect it as soon as possible. It's very rare there's a major story filling the news and the minds of the* Today *audience that we don't say something about. But what that something is, will be very personal to the writer for that day because writing fast, under pressure, you have to draw on what you know and / or can share from your own experience.*

That was certainly the case for Jasvir Singh, the morning after Grenfell Tower caught fire. It was a 24-storey tower block in North Kensington, West London. Soon after midnight a fire broke out in the kitchen of a fourth-floor flat and within minutes the flames raced up the exterior of the building and then spread to all sides. Seventy-two people died on the night. A leading figure within the British Sikh community, Jasvir is a British family law barrister who is vice chair of the Faiths Forum for London. For him the blackened remains of the burned-out tower conjured a memory from his childhood.

15 June 2017

I grew up in west London, and whenever my parents were going to visit our relatives in the East End, we'd drive along the Westway. I remember being amazed by the sights along the way. The BBC Television Centre, a Dairy Crest depot, countless industrial-looking buildings, and a cluster of tower blocks near the roadside. I'd try to imagine who would work or live in those places, and I'd think about the lives that they led, whether I would find them familiar or strange.

One of those blocks I would look at was Grenfell Tower, something I only discovered yesterday in the midst of the news coverage of the devastating fire. The image of the high-rise block engulfed in flames is one which has now firmly lodged itself in our collective conscience.

Some of the people I'd be thinking about 30 years ago will still have been living there until just a few hours ago. Their lives have changed immeasurably, and the survivors now find themselves homeless and without anything to call their own.

Various stories have emerged from the tragedy over the last 24 hours. The desperation of residents jumping from the building in the hope that they'd survive the fall. The courage of firefighters risking their own lives to search for people trapped in the upper floors. The mother who threw her baby out of a tenth-floor window to safety. Families running for their lives with nothing more than the clothes they'd gone to bed in. Each of those accounts are harrowing in themselves, but when brought together, they paint a grim picture of the human cost of the tragedy.

And yet there are also stories once again of selflessness from people of all faiths and none: St Clement's Church, which opened its doors in the middle of the night to become a refuge for residents and which has since become the hub for public donations. Local Sikhs handing out water to survivors and the emergency services. The Muslims who travelled from across the capital to volunteer their help. People transcending the boundaries of faith and culture to help one another, treating each other as family, and more importantly, as fellow Londoners.

We can't imagine the pain that people are going through at the moment, but the instinct that makes us wonder about one another's lives is the very same instinct that shows that we care about each other when incidents like this happen. Those stories make the people familiar to us, and our response can be seen in the outpouring of donations being given to the shelters which have been set up in the local area. They are our neighbours, and we give what we can.

Guru Nanak once said: 'Only the good deeds which you have done shall remain with you, my soul. This opportunity shall not come again.' I'm sure that those words will resonate with many of us.

BISHOP NICK BAINES

A better Brexit

After the Brexit vote of 2016 there were three years of negotiations between the EU and the UK in different phases. The only common denominator throughout that time seemed to be the acrimony and angry voices from all sides. The divorce from the EU meant there was a raft of details to finalise but when this Thought *was written, ten months into the talks, things were not going well. Everything seemed bogged down.*

So it felt very welcome when Nick Baines, Anglican Bishop of Leeds, said that he wanted to know if the negotiations allowed for some bigger-picture thinking in the midst of all the detailed directives. Bishop Nick knows Europe well. He's a fluent German, French and Russian speaker (he worked for four years in GCHQ before becoming ordained) and he is a frequent visitor to the Continent, to Germany in particular. In this Thought *for the* Day *he took a step back and – in that calm forensic way of his – he encouraged everyone to grapple with a bigger question, asking: 'Before we go any further, can we apply some first principles here?' It worked for me.*

31 January 2018

Current debates in Parliament and beyond about the nature of the UK's relationship with Europe go beyond the technical detail of Bills and amendments. Clearly, many people are just fed up with what they see as the trading of insults and misrepresentations that have come to characterise this process, rendering it almost impossible to distinguish what is true and what is fact from what is mere assertion or wishful thinking.

But, underlying all this sound and fury is a much more important question – one that has always been around, but often gets forgotten in the storm of the moment: what is it all for? Or, to put it differently: what sort of a society do we wish to construct and what sort of character do we want our common life to exhibit?

These are not exactly new questions. Even the Ten Commandments form not a string of miserable demands to keep people in their place, but a contour for a mutually respectful, honourable and humble society – one in which people respect each other, care for the poor, honour integrity and work at building relationships of trust and accountability.

I wonder if these existential questions – about what and whom a society is for – too easily get lost when the headlines and the fog of social media just bang away at demonising anyone who dares to differ from one's own position.

I have just read a paper by a Russian military and political analyst who dares to pose a different question. Aleksandr Khramchikhin, deputy director of the Institute for Political and Military Analysis in Moscow, suggests that whereas Russians will still fight and die for the Motherland, their Western equivalents are too soft to die for anything. Harsh? Maybe.

But, I wonder if this is worth pursuing, if not as a model of idealism, then at least as a matter of practical reality. Russians are almost defined by suffering – think of 20 million dead in the Second World War … a million starved or killed in the siege of Stalingrad alone.

It was Martin Luther King who proposed that if we have nothing worth dying for, then we have nothing worth living for.

So, when we have done our trade deals and dealt with the technical and practical challenges of Brexit – however it might turn out in the end – what will we have gained or lost? What is the end to which we aspire? What is the vision of a society for which we will sacrifice anything or everything? What are the moral goods which shape our ambitions and discipline our passions?

These are not vapid questions. The Old Testament prophet was not joking when he wrote that 'without a vision the people perish'. Nor was Jesus when he said there is a danger in gaining the world and losing our soul.

It is a challenge, but, somehow, I need to poke through the fog of debate and not lose sight of the ultimate questions. For what? And for whom?

CANON ANGELA TILBY

The real challenge of tougher A-levels

Every year there are some subjects, like exams, which come around in the calendar and they need to be covered; partly because so many families of those listening will be affected, but also because, more generally, they are the milestones in life that have affected us all at some point. When Michael Gove was secretary of state for education he instituted a wholesale change of A-levels and GCSEs to respond to accusations that exams had become easier with consequent grade inflation. So there was much debate and anxiety around how the tougher exams were going to affect the cohort of 2018.

Canon Angela Tilby had extensive experience in the world of the media, working in television, before being ordained and going to teach theology at Westcott House in Cambridge as a tutor and vice-principal. So she knew the stress for educators and students that public exams bring – but she also knew how demoralising the media hype can be when results are scrutinised each year. Thanks to her instinctive relationship with the audience she knew that if you share something of your own story it invites listeners to care about the individual and the issue – especially when it's as authentic and honest as she is here.

14 August 2018

We are just two days away from the moment of truth for thousands of young people in England, Northern Ireland and Wales – the morning that their A-level results come through. This year's new and tougher exams coincide with a report that the chief inspector of schools intends to challenge teachers not to concentrate too much on exam results. Schools are getting it wrong if they are no more than exam factories. A rich education is more important than rising league tables.

This intervention seems to me to be the latest move in a debate which has been going on as long as I can remember. What do we want from our schools: high grades or rounded personalities? Most of us want both, of course.

I was fortunate to go to a school which valued a rich education. We had our own playing fields, a dedicated art building, there were choirs, orchestras, plays; as well as a rigorous academic programme. And though there were some multi-talented individuals who could rattle off ancient Greek and also captain the hockey team, it was good to discover that most people were really bad at something. My weakest points were maths, art and gym. I had an understanding with a sympathetic gym teacher that I could spend classes looking for the gym shoes I had somehow managed to 'lose' behind a radiator. As for art the most anyone could say about my attempts to paint was that I liked colour. Yet though I was bad at it, a pottery club in a lunch break became the highlight of my week. I never managed to make a pot but I spent the time quite happily moulding bits of clay into shapes that pleased me. I realise now that I was doing something a bit like meditation, switching off the active brain and just being present in the moment.

The writer G.K. Chesterton used to say that if a thing is worth doing, it is worth doing badly. And being bad at pottery was a good balance to the pressure of exams and the nerves and dread that went with them.

I am glad now that I found out at school what I was bad at as well as what I was good at. Testing is a part of life; we all need to strive against ourselves to discover who we are, and exams are like signposts on the way to a greater goal. We used to say a version of the Lord's Prayer which instead of 'Lead us not into temptation' had 'Do not put us to the test'. But the test that Jesus had in mind was the Apocalypse, the final showdown between good and evil. Whatever is revealed on Thursday, it is not the final judgement on our lives, only an indicator of where we are going. For those waiting anxiously for results it is important to realise that failure is not the end, and success is only the beginning.

PROFESSOR ROBERT BECKFORD

The Macpherson Report 20 years on

Robert Beckford is fearless in the subject matter that he believes needs tackling. He was Professor of Black Theology at the Queen's Foundation until 2021, and before that held a chair in Theology and Culture in the African Diaspora at Canterbury Christ Church University. His is an outspoken voice on the way racist ideas and practices currently overshadow any progress being made in trying to ensure Britain's institutions become racially representative of the rest of society.

In 2019 Robert wrote this Thought *based on the shocking admission from the Metropolitan Police force that they were nowhere near reaching their targets on representation. Despite the publication of the landmark* Macpherson Report *20 years earlier – with its direct recommendations to improve the number of ethnic minority officers – the force was still falling way short. Though 43 per cent of the population in its area was from ethnic minorities only 14 per cent of officers were from those communities. Robert's ability to draw on the historical, theological and cultural background to the issue meant he could offer an informed view that trod new territory and cut through the short-term nature of news coverage.*

27 February 2019

Unless there are miraculous advances in medicine to triple life expectancy in humans, I will not be alive to see an ethnically diverse Metropolitan Police force. This is because, according to the Met's HR [Human Resources] department, it will take a century before ethnic parity is achieved between the force and the community it serves.

Diversifying the Met was one of the major recommendations of the *Macpherson Report*, published 20 years ago this week. The report investigated the killing of the black teenager Stephen Lawrence, and the institutional failure which, initially, led to the dropping of charges against two of the suspects. The report made landmark recommendations to promote a zero-tolerance approach to racism in the police, and the wider society.

While there have been significant improvements in policing and combatting racism since the publication, the relentless Islamophobia, rise in anti-Semitism and xenophobia suggest there is still some way to go to reach the zero-tolerance society Macpherson envisaged. But should we have to wait a whole century for the Met to look like its constituency?

Challenging the pace of change for racial justice is played out in one of the great struggles in British–West Indian church history. In the early eighteenth century, Christians clashed over the pace of the abolition of slavery. Almost everyone in civil society agreed that slavery was morally wrong, but there were disagreements on the pace of change. On one side was the Oxford-educated Anglican priest, George Wilson Bridges, and on the other, the Jamaican slave preacher, Sam Sharpe. The Rev. Bridges believed that abolition, if granted at all, should be a gradual process. And he established an organisation in Jamaica to slow down the pace of change. In contrast, the enslaved Sam Sharpe demanded immediate abolition, with no conditions whatsoever. To speed up the march towards freedom, he organised a mass strike of thousands of slaves.

Sharpe won the argument. Within a few years of his protest, emancipation was granted. As a constant reminder that the pace of racial justice is always in the hands of the people, rather than those in power, the history books of the Caribbean speak of the slaves who abolished slavery.

We the people also have a role in speeding up the pace of inclusion in the Met and other institutions which fail to reflect the rich, and diverse, cultural histories of the United Kingdom. Surely, a concerted effort by all of us will make these bodies look very different in less than a hundred years from now.

CHINE MCDONALD

First day out of the EU

In the three years that it had taken to negotiate, finalise and arrive at Britain's actual leaving day from the EU there had been acrimony and highly charged debate. Now the day was here and the UK would never be the same again. It was what the majority had voted for but the nation was still so polarised that something was needed in Thought for the Day *that would speak equally to both sides.*

For our first day out of the EU as a nation Chine McDonald was the person tasked with finding a way of talking to everyone and keeping them with her. Chine had studied theology and religious studies at Cambridge University before moving into journalism and communications. She drew on all those skills elegantly to offer a view that talked about the future in terms of a fundamental element of the Christian faith – hope. What it is, and what it isn't.

1 February 2020

A new day has dawned. Today is the first day in 47 years that the United Kingdom has woken up as separate from the European Union.

For some, this new day marks the start of a great adventure. Prime Minister Boris Johnson said yesterday this is 'the moment when the dawn breaks', describing it as 'the dawn of a new era' – one of national renewal and change.

For others, this new act symbolises not adventure, but a sense of loss – the kind of sadness that comes with saying goodbye, and apprehension about what comes next.

Life is made up of a series of endings and beginnings; transitions from one state to another.

Individuals, institutions and nations are constantly changing, ever-evolving. We continuously find ourselves in the limbo of liminality – that in-between state before crossing the threshold and becoming something else. The transition from child to adult, from bride to wife, from pregnant woman to mother.

Each rite of passage contains within it a moment of the in-between – looking back on what you were and looking ahead to what you are to become – not yet ended and not yet begun.

With this in-between phase might come a certain level of anxiety about what's ahead, held in tension with a sense of excitement at a new beginning.

Whatever our position on Brexit, what is certain is that we are out of the betwixt and between phase – today is that new day.

The next few years will neither be perfect nor will they be wholly bad. Things are never that clear-cut – life isn't black and white, but grey.

As we carve out our way in this new era, each of us should turn our attention away from polarising arguments and instead now work towards ensuring that the United Kingdom is a place where each of us can flourish. This new beginning must not forget the poorest and most marginalised among us.

A theme that runs through the Bible is this idea that every ending is accompanied by the promise of new hope. Ultimately, hope is what Christianity is all about. What I've realised, as I've grown older and seen that life can be painful and hard and heart-breaking at times, is that the Christian hope isn't about blind optimism; it doesn't mean everything will be OK, or promise that the future will be plain sailing. But Christians carry with them a sense of eschatological hope – a hope that at the very, very end, things will be made right.

It is this ultimate hope that C.S. Lewis was talking about when he wrote: 'There are far, far better things ahead than any we leave behind.'

Here's hoping.

BISHOP DAVID WALKER

The Manchester bombing

Since the appalling events at the Manchester Arena in May 2017, when a suicide bomber killed 22 people and injured more than 900 others, Bishop David Walker has found himself speaking on a whole variety of media outlets and platforms on behalf of the families of those who were killed or maimed – and also for the people of Manchester more widely, who were so shocked and affected in different ways. He did the city proud.

As Bishop of Manchester he was used, of course, to being a preacher, an innovative community leader and a spokesman, so it was striking that – three long years later, in the week that the public inquiry into the bombing got underway – he chose to start his Thought for the Day *not by speaking about the city but by speaking about himself, his own feelings and his own struggles with the forgiveness that he believed in. But by a process of*

acknowledging his anger and its proper place, he could foresee how forgive-
ness would be, in the end, part of a greater witness.

11 September 2020

It was a North American TV reporter who put me on the spot.
Two days after the Manchester Arena attack in May 2017, she
asked me outright on camera whether, as a Christian, I was
ready to forgive the man who had killed 22 people, and injured
hundreds of others, 200 yards from my cathedral. 'Not yet,' I
replied. 'Forgiveness, is not a place we can jump to in a short
space of time. For now I'm too angry.'

This week, with the brother of the bomber now serving 55
years or more in prison for his part in the crime, the public
inquiry into the atrocity has opened. Hearing the harrowing
evidence took me back to that interview, and to question myself
on how far I have or haven't moved on, in these last three
years. Unlike 900 others, I bear no scars, mental or physical,
from that dreadful night, nor did I lose anyone close to me.
My faith community was not vilified through association with
the bomber, save by that tiny few who see all religion as guilty
wherever faith is adduced as excuse for a crime. I have no right
to issue any words of forgiveness on behalf of almost a thousand victims, nor in the name of my city. But I am accountable
before God for my own feelings. And I'm still angry.

Angry, but the focus of my anger has changed. It now rests
on the shadowy figures who whisper their words of hatred into
the ears of susceptible young people. Those who spread an
ideology that pretends mass murder will secure a place in paradise; who know that one fanatical convert may wreak havoc
to stun the world. These are far harder to forgive than their
deluded disciples. Their perverse ideology does not blow itself
out with a bomb blast; it cannot be locked in a prison cell, safe
from causing harm.

What Manchester discovered in May 2017 is that hatred will never vanquish hate, only love can do that. We defy the peddlers of hatred, by crossing the boundaries of our differences, drawing ever closer to each other. It's a truth which for me emerges direct from the teaching of St John, that the very essence of God is love. And a righteous anger, to use a biblical term, can be the very fuel by which love conquers hate.

I hope that the Arena public inquiry will produce answers to the questions survivors have carried with them for three long years. Beyond that, I hope that those answers will not assuage appropriate anger, but direct it where it can be most effective: to resist the hate-mongers and to build better lives and communities, in Manchester and beyond.

REV. DR MICHAEL BANNER

Slavery past and present

In response to the Black Lives Matter movement many institutions began to reassess their past, looking for any hidden links they might have to the slave trade in the colonial era. In Bristol in 2020 protestors pulled down a statue of Edward Colston, an early eighteenth-century slave trader, politician and philanthropist. Students at Oxford University campaigned for the removal of a statue of the nineteenth-century imperialist Cecil Rhodes from Oriel College. Several universities launched investigations into their past colonial links, with Glasgow University vowing to pay £20 million in slavery reparations.

This Thought, *by the Anglican priest and ethicist Rev. Dr Michael Banner, was prompted by students at Trinity College Dublin calling for the renaming of their university library. It was named after Bishop Berkeley, the great eighteenth-century Irish philosopher who turned out to have owned a number of slaves when he lived in America. Dr Banner, who is Dean of Trinity College Cambridge – and has recently published a paper subtitled 'Racism, Moral Repair and the Case for Reparations' – brings to* Thought *a very distinctive urbane and wry style and an originality in both his thinking and delivery. Here he asks whether it makes sense to judge the past by the standards of the present.*

9 March 2021

Trinity College Dublin – Ireland's oldest university – has become the latest institution in a long list, including my own university, Cambridge, to launch an inquiry into its links with slavery.

Symbolically, the case of one of Trinity College Dublin's most intellectually distinguished alumni, the philosopher George Berkeley, is rather telling. Berkeley – whose name has been given to Trinity's library, and indeed to a very distinguished university in the United States – was himself briefly a slave owner. Pursuing an ill-fated venture to establish a training college in the colonies, he spent nearly four years in Rhode Island and purchased slaves to work his plantation. He was, to boot, an Anglican clergyman and later a bishop – and as far as we know, his conscience was not in the least troubled by the buying and selling of human chattels.

Discussions about historical links with slavery seem to get quite ill-tempered quite quickly – it is a popular site for a spat in the so-called culture wars. But I wonder whether the generation here of an excess of heat over light has to do with our confusing two different issues – reckoning with the past and reckoning with the present.

Reckoning with the past should surely chiefly mean trying to understand the entanglement of the economies of the last 300 years or more with slavery; but it need entail no 'holier than thou' attitude towards our forebears. George Berkeley's view that a good Christian could own slaves was very widely held and only very rarely challenged until the end of the eighteenth century. Berkeley may have been a phenomenally clever mathematician, but he was a very average moralist – and I am inclined to think that declaring him a goodie or a baddie is a contentious distraction.

Far more important is a moral question we ought to be asking about the present: how should we come to terms with the dependence of the West's affluence on its inheritance of riches generated by slave-produced cotton, tobacco and sugar?

The proposals of Zacchaeus in the New Testament provide one answer to that question. When Zacchaeus, the diminutive chief tax collector, came down from the tree he had climbed to get a better view of Jesus, and had welcomed him to his house, he summarily announces: 'Behold, half of my goods I give to the poor, and if I have defrauded anyone of anything, I will pay it back four times over.'

Of course, any proposal for reparations must finally face some hard practical questions about who owes what to whom. But insofar as we fail to face up to the question of reparations honestly and imaginatively, it is the present and not the past which is morally questionable.

CATHERINE PEPINSTER

Women emerge from the shadows

The vigil at the heart of the story that Catherine Pepinster chose to write about here was held in March 2021. It was a gathering to pay respects to Sarah Everard, a young woman duped and killed by a serving officer of the Metropolitan Police. The increased vulnerability of women in modern life was something Catherine would have been aware of both professionally and personally. Having spent many years as a writer and editor on British newspapers she knew how women in the workplace fared, and also how they were written about.

The fact that Sarah Everard's murderer was a police officer – a man she should have been able to trust – highlighted the vulnerability of any woman who walks alone on our streets. When Catherine left the Independent on Sunday, *where she was executive editor, it was to take up a position as the first female editor in the 176-year history of the Catholic weekly* The Tablet. *Bringing together her personal and journalistic experience with her faith she here reflects on the historical evidence of the price paid by some of the earliest Christian women to stand up for what they believed in.*

1 January 2022

This is the time of year when newspapers and magazines run their most memorable images of the last 12 months, and I was very struck by the number-one choice of a particular collection of 2021 photos.

It was of a young woman prostrate on the floor, surrounded by police, two of them gripping her arms behind her back. She was looking up at the camera, her COVID mask making it seem as if she was not only bound but gagged too. The photo doesn't tell the story as to why this had happened. But it conveyed a vulnerability made all the more poignant because she was held like this at a vigil for brutally murdered Sarah Everard, where she and others were demonstrating at the risks of violence all women face.

However much women have sought and gained equality, their physical strength compared to men's remains a source of inequality and vulnerability. It often makes them targets of those who seek to intimidate and manipulate. But when they courageously bear witness to the violence and abuse done to them, whether by men or even other women, it is all the more powerful. After the Ghislaine Maxwell trial, which focused on the abuse done to young girls by Jeffrey Epstein, one New York prosecuting lawyer this week paid tribute to the women who, as he put it, stepped out of the shadows and into the courtroom to give evidence.

When I turned to my new diary for 2022 I noticed that in the next few weeks, the Catholic Church's calendar of feast days includes five that honour women who also spoke up, even though they faced violence for doing so. Prisca, Agnes, Agatha, Apollonia and Honorine were all young when they became Christians, a choice for which they were victimised and put to death by the rulers of the Roman Empire.

The stories of them all are disturbing, not only for the torture they endured before their martyrdom but also the extent to which their honouring in Christianity is bound up with the extreme violence they endured. Many paintings of these saints also luridly highlight their torture.

At first sight, it might seem that this religion, run for so many generations by men, has a disturbing focus on stories of young women and violence. But these tales can be interpreted in another, different, way.

They also show these young women's commitment, passion and courageous rejection of what their society, including their families, stood for as they chose instead to follow Christ's message of peace and justice. Even 2,000 years ago, these women would not be cowed by violence. They would speak up, and yes, emerge from the shadows.

Chapter Two

International

BISHOP JIM THOMPSON

The morning after 9/11

Out of a clear blue sky, quite literally, on 11 September 2001, two airplanes flew into the Twin Towers of the World Trade Center in New York and altered the course of 21st-century history. Al-Qaeda terrorists had hijacked four commercial US passenger planes. Two were flown into the Twin Towers, causing both to collapse. A third was crashed into the Pentagon. The fourth plane crashed in rural Pennsylvania after the crew and passengers attacked the terrorists on board, preventing it from hitting another target, thought to be the White House. The attacks claimed nearly 3,000 lives and impacted millions more across the globe.

By 2001 Bishop Jim Thompson had moved from Stepney to Bath and Wells. 'Big Jim', as some of the Today *presenters affectionately called him, was one of the longest-serving writers of* Thought for the Day *and had experience of writing on the day after disasters. But 9/11 was beyond anyone's imagining. Bishop Jim intuitively used the word 'war' to describe what he had witnessed on the television, unconsciously foreshadowing what was to follow. His script was widely praised for the way he spoke from the heart that morning. He put into words the sense of shock of a stunned world. Somehow he registered the enormity of an event that was to shape the lives of generations to come.*

12 September 2001

I was sitting late last night in front of a blank piece of paper, my mind numbed by all we had seen, when a fax came in telling me that a daughter of two friends was missing in New York.

The pictures had seemed for a moment like an apocalypse or a brilliantly devised disaster movie, but now this was not myth or virtual reality but life and death.

On a perfect morning in New York, looking impregnable, the vast Twin Towers reduce to dust, and thousands on thousands of people are crushed in the fall. The mayor of New York said the casualties would be more than anyone of us can bear.

So many questions: who did it? How would we all be affected? And rumbling from the ruins, the fear. This volcano didn't come from below but above, raining terror on Manhattan; not a natural disaster but manmade. What just cause could possibly deserve such an evil and unjust response? Will the appetite for retaliation lead to indiscriminate reprisals? Can ever the good in the human mind cope wisely and effectively in the face of such evil?

In this war no attempt was made to avoid civilian targets. Indeed, somewhere people planned – over a long period – this blow precisely against innocent victims. As their bodies are recovered they remind us that buildings can be replaced but lives cannot – they are beloved, and unique to those who love them.

This is manmade, but as a believer in God I still ask: what does God make of it? Perhaps the perpetrators believe in God. Some people even said this was a gift of God. Yet this denies everything that God means to me and I know of no sane faith which would justify it. And I asked God to say something I can say. 'Jesus wept' perhaps, or Christ's own words: 'My heart is ready to break with grief.'

How God must grieve at the way we use the freedom He gives us. I know that even now prayer will be incessant in millions of minds. People waiting for news of a loved one, people already fearing reprisals, people so shocked and scared of what might happen, will turn to God, and maybe use old and familiar words to restore their courage and find confidence for the future: 'God is our hope and strength, a very present help in trouble – Therefore will we not fear though the earth be moved.' The earth has moved. Please God help us.

BISHOP TOM BUTLER

It's war

On 20 September 2001 – barely two weeks after the attacks by al-Qaeda on the Twin Towers in New York – British and US jets bombed surface-to-air missile batteries in southern Iraq. The clock had begun ticking towards the full-blown invasion of Iraq to neutralise Saddam Hussein's 'weapons of mass destruction' – weapons which were never, in the event, found.

Tom Butler, Anglican Bishop of Southwark, was an important voice in the matters of Church and state. A scientist with a PhD in electronics, he had lived in Zambia and served as a bishop in five different dioceses over 30 years. His range of knowledge and experience, together with an ability to communicate simply and directly, made him a national figure. As far back as 1994 he had visited Iraq with David Steel, the leader of the Liberal Democrats, for a humanitarian fact-finding mission to see the effect of sanctions on Iraq's schools and hospitals. They witnessed first-hand the hardship and tensions with which the population lived. Now, in the shadow of 9/11, with rumours of the rekindling of another full-blown Gulf War, Bishop Tom insisted that – with the first blow having been struck by British and American jets – the conflict must be pursued with caution and proportion.

24 September 2001

So it really is war and we have to add images of exploding missiles to the image of the exploding planes and falling towers which are still seared into our minds. There may well be feelings of excitement and patriotism, but these are mixed with feelings of anxiety and dread and a sense that it's always easier to get into a war than to get out, particularly when the enemy are fanatics driven by ideology.

And this is a Monday morning and yesterday as usual I was out preaching the Christian gospel in church and chapel. So how am I to relate that to what's going on in the world today?

Military action must be a last resort – that's what the Christian ethical theory says – when all other ways of persuasion and negotiation have failed. Well, rightly or wrongly we seem to be past the point of no return and military action has started. So next – any such action must be proportionate. Well, what action is proportionate to respond to the murder of around 3,000 unsuspecting people going about their business on a sunny September morning? And it's not just they who have to be borne in mind. What if the worst nightmares are true and on the terrorists' future agenda are plans for germ warfare or briefcase nuclear weapons. Our cities would become cemeteries. The purpose of this war might in some minds be a question of punishment or retribution but it's the prevention of future crimes which should be in the forefront of the minds of those planning the strategies.

So above all, discrimination must drive this war, and not just discrimination between the guilty and the innocent, and God knows too many innocent victims in tower block and refugee camp have already suffered. This must be a war which seeks and eliminates the terrorists without entering into confrontation with whole states. The action must be akin to targeting cancerous cells rather than cutting off whole limbs.

And Christian ethical theory won't let us stop there. Yes, it talks about retribution and punishment and the prevention of future crimes but it also points to justice and reconciliation and healing. And when this messy war is finally over we have all got to continue to share this one precious and vulnerable planet. The aim may be to cut down terrorism root and branch, but by doing that we must not so pollute the soil that nothing good can grow. The present terrorists have grown in the soil of polluted injustice. Perhaps the gospel message is that unless we tend the soil of tomorrow we can't truly win the war of today.

REV. ROY JENKINS

The trial of Saddam Hussein

On 9 April 2003 Baghdad fell to US forces and the Iraqi dictator Saddam Hussein fled into hiding. It was not until December that the once dapper leader was pulled – dishevelled and dirty, disguised by a grizzled beard – from an underground hiding place near his home town of Tikrit. He surrendered without firing a shot.

In March 2004 the French lawyer Jacques Verges announced he had been contacted by Saddam's family to ask if he would represent the former Iraqi leader at the trial where he was to be charged with crimes against humanity. Many were incensed by Verges, who once said he would have defended Hitler. But the Baptist minister Roy Jenkins in this Thought *stepped forward to defend the idea that Saddam deserved a fair trial with a proper defence lawyer. Many listeners wrote to say how much they appreciated the script but others were outraged. One was particularly memorable: 'I regard your views as both treasonable and heretical … intolerable, offensive and unacceptable … I hope to see news of your resignation and of your departure from the UK in next week's* Baptist Times.*'*

29 March 2004

It must be encouraging for any prisoner to hear his newly appointed lawyer coming out fighting, and the man who's just taken on Saddam Hussein has done exactly that.

Jacques Verges suggested yesterday that his client might be killed before he's allowed to face trial. He's also accused the Americans of breaching the Geneva Convention by allowing his dental inspection and the search for nits in his hair to be filmed and shown around the world. They treated him like an animal, he protests.

It's hard to imagine a massive wave of sympathy for Saddam Hussein at the reminder that he might have been subjected to some indignity after being caught in his hole in the ground. We know the horror he inflicted on his people over a generation; we know about the murders and the torture and the fear; we can see that his country is still in pain. If there are tears to be shed, they won't be for the architect of this evil.

So why bother, when our gut instinct tells us that a man who has caused such suffering deserves to suffer himself, and more than some mild indignity? Why should we care at all?

Jacques Verges has made his reputation fighting for people like the Gestapo chief Klaus Barbie and the terrorist Carlos the Jackal, and Slobodan Milošević has also appeared on his case list. I don't know what drives him to want to defend the apparently indefensible. I share the discomfort of many when legal processes are strung out year after year, and tyrants are allowed to mock justice, even if they don't escape it completely.

Yet giving a fair hearing to a man who has denied it to thousands, treating him with the dignity he has stolen from others, is necessary, however unpalatable. The alternative is a triumph for his twisted values.

If we say he has forfeited all rights, then we deal with him exactly as he dealt with his victims: we make him a non-person.

If we approve of torturing him, in the hope that it will persuade him to reveal the hiding places of his missing colleagues or his elusive weapons, we justify his willingness to break minds and bodies.

If we content ourselves with keeping him locked away without proper proceedings, we imperil all the anonymous men and women held untried in prisons across the world – many of them truly innocent.

The biblical injunction to do justice, love mercy and walk humbly with our God is never a soft option. Doing justice properly will always cost us. Loving mercy will always place tiresome restraints on our desire to hit back, and give people exactly what they deserve.

That's why, it seems to me, we do need also to walk humbly with our God, remembering that we, too, depend every day on kindness which we don't deserve. Forget that, and Saddam, and others like him, really have won.

BRIAN DRAPER

School Number One, Beslan

Every parent's nightmare became real for the mothers and fathers of the little Russian town of Beslan in 2004 when their children's school was seized by armed Chechen terrorists. The gunmen held 1,100 people – including 777 children – hostage for three days before Russian security forces stormed the building. Some 333 people died, 186 of them were children – the deadliest school shooting in history.

Brian Draper is a writer, facilitator and retreat guide. A Christian thinker with a contemplative, spiritual approach to the news, he responded to this unthinkable situation by beginning with a scene every parent could identify with – the moment you leave your child at the gates on their first day at school. He has a voice that sounds empathetic and warm and in the retelling of the moment-by-moment account of those waiting outside it was almost as if he wanted, somehow, to allow the listener to be alongside those parents; to share their horror and, standing with them, acknowledge their pain.

4 September 2004

This is a week that many mothers and fathers here in Britain would have been dreading. The new school year brings with it that moment at the school gates when they must learn to let their babies go, when they glimpse the pain of separation and temporary loss, and look forward anxiously to being reunited at the end of the day.

Perhaps we have become desensitised to pictures of children dying, normally slowly through malnutrition in places such as Ethiopia and Sudan. We can't imagine what the parents are thinking, we say, as we struggle to cope with images which, in all honesty, race by beyond our comprehension.

Yet as scenes poured from our screens throughout yesterday, of mothers standing in ghastly impotence, keeping watch at the gates in Beslan, the pictures came into a terrible focus. As fathers tried in vain to push past soldiers and get into the school where their children were held, we sense that we would have tried, with all our might, to do the same.

As people on the periphery jolted at the crash of yet another explosion, taking the emotional impact full on, we almost cowered at home, knowing they'd be thinking in the moments that followed: 'Was that my child?'

Just as it's impossible sometimes to take in a scene of dazzling beauty, so it can be useless to describe rationally how the shadow of evil is cast across the world via satellite and into our own homes.

The celebrated painting *The Scream* is a picture worth more than a thousand words as we inhabit a vortex of confusion, anger, pain and pity and stand alongside mothers, fathers, brothers, sisters, summoning our school-gate fears of loss and separation, and seeking somehow to multiply them.

The natural impulse will be to find someone to pay. At least when a volcano blows, or an earthquake rocks our foundations, if we seek someone to blame then we must seek God. Perhaps in time we may reflect spiritually on the problem of evil, of broken relationships, with God and each other, of guilt and even forgiveness. Christians might look to the innocent teacher from Nazareth slaughtered at the hands of angry men, and thank God that he understands the pain of losing an only son. But, when normal fellow humans take the lives of little children, our symbols of hope, of innocence, of our future as a race, then we're left to wonder despairingly: 'What Were They Thinking?'

It's a question we'd do well, if we can, to dwell upon; in military terms it pays to know your enemy. It might, one day, help us to love even the worst of them too. But for now our thoughts go to Russia, with love.

AKHANDADHI DAS

The tsunami and the selfish gene

On Boxing Day in 2004 a massive earthquake detonated under the Indian Ocean and sent a mighty wall of water, up to 30 metres high, crashing down upon people's homes in 14 countries from Indonesia and Thailand to Sri Lanka and India. A quarter of a million people perished in one of the deadliest natural disasters in recorded history. The world responded with a wave of humanitarian assistance totalling $14 billion to provide food, fresh drinking water, sanitation, and aid to repair the widespread damage to buildings, roads, sewage works and other vital infrastructure.

In Britain the government donated £75 million. But this figure was dwarfed by the response of ordinary members of the public who gave more than £300 million from their own pockets. In this Thought *the philosopher Akhandadhi Das drew on the insights from his Vaishnava Hindu tradition to reflect on the nature of altruism – and why people give.*

11 January 2005

Yesterday, the government increased its pledge of aid to the victims of the tsunami disaster. With the moratorium on debt relief, the total package will reach £200 million. Worldwide, donations are now over £3 billion. It's easy to be cynical that, behind international aid, there may be political or business agendas or too many strings attached. But, I think it's encouraging that recent events have stirred the G8 nations to address the long-term problems of other areas, particularly Africa.

Even more inspiring has been the public response, here and abroad, with many people donating more than was easy for them at this time of year. Seeing such heartfelt generosity, it's worth asking ourselves: 'Why are people being so kind to folk on the other side of the world?' The answer seems obvious – it's what we humans do – we help people. Economists and fund-raisers have analysed the reasons for the success of the tsunami appeals, but I want to delve deeper. Why do people care? What is the philosophical explanation of altruism?

There are basically two different theories. The biological viewpoint is that all human behaviour arises from an evolutionary impulse for survival. This idea might account for selfishness, indifference, even cruelty, but it is baffled by any human activity that doesn't offer personal benefit. It doesn't explain the child emptying its piggy bank into the charity bucket. Can we rationalise that the individual calculates that contributing to the bigger group enhances personal survival? But that's saying that all acts of charity are just selfish and expedient.

Or, is human kindness simply due to our selfish gene being anxious to perpetuate itself? Why, then, are people willing to risk everything for unrelated strangers? Somewhere in this contorted theory, the qualities of compassion, kindness and love have been lost and the question remains: 'Why altruism?'

The alternative explanation is that human behaviour has its roots in our spiritual persona. One of the things that attracted me to Hinduism was the idea that it is the *atma*, the spark of consciousness or soul, which activates the body and brain. What we call human nature is the personality of the soul mixed with the complexities and contradictions generated by our mind and ego.

At the heart of our spiritual psyche is the desire to love and to be loved. Kindness, therefore, comes naturally to us. But, although we are created with this capacity, the issue to love or not is choice. Often, we succumb to selfish motivations. That might bring some immediate pragmatic benefit, but it doesn't fill the yearning in our hearts. But, when we choose to respond unconditionally to the distress of others, whoever they may be, our true nature is revealed. And, that's why we feel the most fulfilling emotions in contributing to the wellbeing and happiness of others.

RHIDIAN BROOK

Live 8 – it was 20 years ago today

Rhidian Brook is a novelist and writer of screenplays. When Rhidian is writing for Thought for the Day, *which he has for 20 years, he always speaks from the heart, and often from personal experience, whatever the subject. He's also a powerhouse of ideas. On occasion he has called ahead of writing a* Thought *to ask if he can try something special to make a mark on a different kind of day.*

The script here created a special buzz. It was written for broadcast on the morning of Live 8 – the follow up to Live Aid – and is constructed entirely with lyrics from songs, many of them by bands who starred in the concerts organised by Bob Geldof and Make Poverty History. The concerts were designed to raise awareness and pressure world leaders to double aid to Africa and wipe away the debts of poor countries. This Thought *says much about Rhidian's creativity and natural feel for the audience, many of whom wrote in to say they loved it. It went down very well in the studio and was picked up in the papers – and reprinted in its entirety in the official Live 8 book* Hello World. *All of which was a most welcome piece of awareness raising for* Thought for the Day *too.*

2 July 2005

Good morning, good morning, good morning.

London Calling, to the far away town …

It was 20 years ago today,

And we've still got something to say

Not talking about London, Paris, New York, Munich.

Talking about my generation

There's a feeling I get when I look to the West. And it makes me wonder.

Where is my beautiful car? Where is my beautiful house?

I want it now; I want it all. I want money.

Get back. I'm all right Jack; keep your hands off my stack.

Money, it's a crime. Share it fairly but don't take a slice of my pie.

I read the news today, oh boy.

Mother, Mother, there's too many of you crying,

Brother, Brother, Brother there's far too many of you dying.

Help! I need somebody

I'm just a poor boy nobody loves me …

Them belly full but them hungry.

You never give me your money, you only give me your funny paper …

Help me get my feet back on the ground – won't you please, please help me

Don't leave me here all alone. Helpless. Helpless. Helpless

Don't walk on by

Ticking away the moments that make up a dull day,

Fritter and waste the hours in an offhand way.

Cos maybe, you're going to be the one that saves me.

There are still many rivers to cross and I still can't find my way over

Sometimes you can't make it on your own.

Don't give up, cos you have friends …

Imagine

Life is bigger; it's bigger than you

Consider this, the hint of the century

The world is full of refugees, a lot like you and a lot like me.

War is not the answer. You don't have to escalate. Only love can conquer hate.

It's easy if you try.

Come on everybody. Mr President. Come on. Come on. Let's go.

Jesus loves you more than you will know.

But it's a hard road to follow and rough tough way to go.

What you going to do about it, what you going to do?

Nothing to do, it's up to you

You can't always get what you want,

But if you try sometimes, you get what you need.

Get up, stand up, stand up for your rights.

With or without you

Give a little bit. Give a little bit of my life for you.

While you see your chance, take it.

Are you such a dreamer, to put the world to rights?

Dry your eyes mate. We can be heroes just for one day.

Today is gonna be the day that they're gonna throw it back to you.

By now you should have found out you realise what you gotta do.

Time to make the change, come on you rock and rollers.

Look at the stars see how they shine for you

With the boys from the Mersey and the Thames and the Tyne …

All the people, so many people, and they all go hand in hand, hand in hand

Nothing to say but what a day

It's going to be a glorious day.

A beautiful day

I can feel it coming in the air tonight, O Lord …

Won't you help to sing these songs of freedom
Redemption songs
Right here right now
You know we've got to find a way
To bring some loving here today.
And in the end, the love you take is equal to the love you make.

REV. JOHN BELL

Guantanamo Bay

Guantanamo Bay detention camp is a United States military prison located in Cuba where Islamic militants and suspected terrorists captured in Afghanistan and Iraq are held, indefinitely, outside of normal laws or judicial oversight. In 2006 the United Nations, after an 18-month investigation, called for the prison to be closed, with the inmates either put on trial or freed. The UN declared that the treatment of prisoners was tantamount to torture – a claim rejected by the US government but endorsed by a British high court judge who declared that America's idea of what constituted torture 'doesn't appear to coincide with that of most civilised countries'.

John Bell is a Church of Scotland minister and a member of the Iona Community. He is much sought after as a speaker, preacher and musician. Primarily concerned with renewing congregational worship at the grassroot, he travels all over the world and often includes the insights gained in his international encounters in his Thought for the Day *scripts. For this* Thought, *he was asked what the Bible had to say on the issue of imprisonment, and, in characteristic style, he was able to say that its opinion was clear.*

16 February 2006

Last weekend I was asked an unusual question by a lady at a conference in Preston: 'Why do we not hear much about the wrath of God today?'

Why indeed? Is it that God has gone soft? Or are Christian preachers trying to make God sound more user-friendly than their Muslim counterparts? Or is there something political behind it ... yes, political.

You see, the popular perception of God's wrath has to do with divine disapproval of personal behaviour, usually to do with sexuality and usually based on a handful of texts pulled from different parts of the Bible.

But read the book itself and you will find that divine wrath is primarily directed at nations and societies regarding the way we communally deal with the marginalised, the economically and socially disadvantaged, the disabled and prisoners.

Yes ... prisoners. Two evenings ago a film was premiered in Berlin. It is based on the personal experiences of three young men from Tipton wrongly imprisoned in Guantanamo Bay. It is, of course, a subjective account but is perhaps as close a depiction of the truth as is possible, given the US government's reticence to disclose much about their offshore detention centre.

A United Nations report published today underscores this suspect secrecy. The UN envoys interviewed ex-detainees, but were not allowed to visit the 500 prisoners presently incarcer-ated. Because they might have yet to be put on trial, no one knows how many might be as innocent as the Tipton Three.

But a clear cause for concern are the allegations made of cultural insensitivity, physical and mental abuse, and forced feeding ... and this happening on an island deliberately chosen because it is outside the jurisdiction of American courts.

The Bible knows quite a lot about imprisonment. Half of St Paul's correspondence was written from that experience, and the Book of Revelation is a coded letter from an exile on an island to people who were being persecuted by their political masters.

But most poignant is Jesus' parable of the Day of Judgement in which it is not individuals who are pilloried for their moral peccadilloes. Rather, nations are gathered before God's throne, and people are sent to heaven or hell depending, among other things, on how prisoners have been treated.

The justice of God cannot be the pawn or possession of political administrations. Where prisoners are wrongfully detained, God is their advocate and the adversary of their captors.

RABBI LIONEL BLUE

A vision for Israel/Palestine

Mention Thought for the Day *to anyone and the first name they'd come up with would be Lionel Blue. He was usually on air on a Monday morning, determined to try to cheer everyone up with his famous signature greeting to the presenters and listeners: 'Good morning, John. Good morning, Sue. And good morning everyone …' He cultivated 'looking on the bright side' because he knew at first hand how hard it was when the black clouds threatened to overwhelm you. He often slipped a line in his scripts about the depression he suffered, particularly in his youth when his life was complicated, and he didn't seem to fit anywhere. But he never left his listeners there, because he believed that God and humanity could make a better world possible. That didn't mean he couldn't see how serious some situations were.*

For 22 days at the start of 2009 the Israel Defence Forces bombarded the Gaza Strip, and then sent in an invading ground force, to put an end to what they called indiscriminate rocket fire by Palestinians into Israel. The Palestinians fired back. At the end of the conflict 1,300 Palestinians and 13 Israelis were dead. A fragile truce was put in place ahead of the Israeli elections but after just two weeks it looked in danger of collapse when Rabbi Lionel Blue wrote this Thought.

2 February 2009

The Holy Land doesn't seem very holy. There's a lot of religion around but a lot isn't top quality, being more concerned with holy places than holy actions, and with building walls not bridges. It's not only stimulated heroism and self-sacrifice but so much sectarianism. Both sides can't see themselves in each other.

I haven't been there for over forty years but the facts haven't changed much. Israel wins wars, but every won war makes another war more likely, and Israel can't afford to lose one – it's too small.

Can any side win a peace? Between the wars there are short opportunities for peace, but if they're not realised by deeds as well as speeches hatred grows. Trust melts away. And the price of peace goes ever higher. One day it will be too high, and it's dangerously near that now.

Forty years ago this joke was popular. The American president says to Golda Meir, prime minister of Israel: 'What aid do you want, Golda?' 'Two of your generals,' she says. 'Which,' he answers, puzzled 'seeing your own generals are real winners?' 'General Motors and General Electric,' she replies.

But now we've become wiser. We know the problem is based on very different concerns, causing fear and hatred, which are spiritual illnesses.

So religion may be more relevant than technology. It's time to ask God, not just to root mindlessly for your own side, but for courage to start to begin to tackle the basic injustices as seen by each side – because they won't disappear into the desert sand, as many hoped. They include: The continuing plight of the Palestinian refugees. The future of Jerusalem. Jewish refugees from Arab countries. No creeping annexation. Equal economic opportunities for all Holy Land inhabitants. And the chance to live in peace and security.

Let's pray for politicians who take responsibility for two peoples not one, with an inclusive vision that wins hearts not territory.

There are some small lights in the gloom. A Jewish, Christian, Muslim village near Jerusalem. Thousands upon thousands of telephone calls between bereaved parents from both sides. A Palestinian–Israeli orchestra and football team. Curious youngsters wanting to meet each other at discos.

Friends of mine have just come back from Israel, attending the birth of a baby. The new father made an impromptu speech. 'A baby isn't born with hate,' he said. 'It's society that puts it in. Which means every baby, every new generation, is an opportunity for wrongs to be righted not repeated.' From his mouth into God's ear!

CANON DR GILES FRASER

Greek financial meltdown

The impact of the global financial crisis of 2007–8 lingered longer in some countries than others. One of the hardest hit was the comparatively poor country of Greece, which underwent a succession of bailouts in which the International Monetary Fund and the EU lent Greece money in return for government promises to save money through public spending cuts and austerity measures. When Giles Fraser wrote this Thought *Greece and its creditors were negotiating the largest debt restructuring in history – and the Greek people were on the streets, fighting with the police.*

Giles, who is a regular panellist on Radio 4's Moral Maze, *is always able to unpack complex situations. In this one, it helped that as Canon Chancellor of St Paul's Cathedral in London he had special responsibility for contemporary ethics and engagement with the City of London as a financial centre. But when in 2011 a group of anti-capitalist protestors occupied land next to the cathedral, and Giles backed their right to protest, he fell out of step with the cathedral authorities and felt obliged to resign. In this* Thought *about the Greek financial crisis Giles, characteristically, once again took the side of the underdog.*

14 February 2012

Riots on the streets. Police using tear gas. Pension cuts total-ling €300 billion and the loss of 150,000 public sector jobs. So who is to blame for the financial meltdown currently trauma-tising Greece?

After the financial crisis broke in the autumn of 2008 it wasn't long before we heard comments that the whole mess could be put down to the greed of bankers and the irresponsi-bility of the finance industry. Politicians, secular commentators and religious leaders all joined in. We need a new and more moral form of capitalism.

So – is this Greek situation something different? And if so, who is to blame for the tragedy that is playing out before our eyes?

It seems clear enough that, like most of us, the Greeks were living well beyond their means even before the financial crisis of 2008. And like us, they bought into the idea that capitalism had become a risk-free enterprise – that it would go on and on delivering ever-increasing prosperity.

The philosophy of 'live now pay later' was endemic. Again and again we were led to believe that bull markets were more natural than bear markets and that the only way was up. In the USA, houses were sold to people that couldn't afford them on the basis that the increasing value of property would eventually meet the cost of the original debt.

And clearly, the Greeks bought into all of this as well – with the added comfort that membership of a shared currency with Germany would more or less guarantee that they couldn't go bust. Thus they started paying themselves considerably more than their economy could afford. But can we really blame indi-vidual Greek citizens for this? For it wasn't just the Greeks that subscribed to the dangerous myth of capitalism's capacity to keep on giving.

And now ordinary Greeks feel they are being unfairly punished, made to pay for the sins of their leaders who, ten years ago, applied to join the euro on the basis of having fiddled the figures.

At the end of last year, the Vatican had a go at tackling the moral issues and – no doubt on the advice of leading economists – called for a redesign of the global financial architecture. But that didn't put food in the mouths of poor Greek children – some of whom are now being handed over to orphanages by parents who cannot feed them any more.

At the weekend a Greek bishop appealed to the Pope to help his country's people through the present catastrophe, pointing out that the heating had been turned off in local hospitals where they were also fast running out of bandages and medicines.

The duty of solidarity and the call to compassion is something we can all respond to – not least on the biblical principle of doing unto others what we would have them do unto us. Maybe what is happening in Greece qualifies as the economic version of a natural disaster, like floods and earthquakes. And if that's the case, perhaps our first move should be to stop blaming the victims.

PROFESSOR MONA SIDDIQUI

Je suis Charlie

Every Thought for the Day *script, written and refined during the course of a day, is never quite 'put to bed' until it goes out on air. Broadcasting into a news programme means we need to respond to the big, breaking news stories and reflect change as the story develops. That sometimes means the whole team starting again.*

At around 11.30am on 7 January 2015 two gunmen forced their way into the Charlie Hedo *offices in Paris, shouting that they had come to avenge the Prophet Muhammad. The satirical magazine had reprinted controversial cartoons of Muhammad in 2006 and five years later provocatively printed an entire edition, which it called* Charia Hebdo *(Sharia Hebdo). The magazine's editor was placed under police protection, but his police guard was shot dead before he could draw his weapon. The gunmen killed 12 people and fled.*

On the day that the killings of the Charlie Hebdo *journalists happened, Mona Siddiqui wasn't scheduled to write but it was obvious to me that we needed a Muslim view of what was unfolding in Paris. We made the switch with that day's writer and watched the news until late afternoon. Mona is a very experienced* Thought *contributor and has proved time and again that she is unafraid to speak bravely and boldly to her own community while opening up a sophisticated understanding of Islam for the general audience. On days like that, the right person can say things that would be difficult for any kind of outsider.*

8 January 2015

'Je suis Charlie' was all over social media yesterday in widespread condemnation of the tragic killing of the *Charlie Hebdo* journalists and policemen in Paris; a show of solidarity with the dead and the injured and an act of defiance against the Islamist perpetrators. This was a cold and carefully planned attack after years of threats against the satirical magazine for its cartoons of the Prophet.

The editor Stéphane Charbonnier, known simply as 'Charb', was one of the victims paying the ultimate price for a magazine which refused to be silenced especially in its portrayal of religions. For some people the magazine was outrageously bold, overstepping the boundaries of decency and taste, while others saw it as clever and inspirational, challenging anything and everything central to the establishment, with its own history and ideals of the French Republic. It's been closed down before, it's run out of money, warned for being too provocative, but it stood resolute, with the editor once saying: 'When activists need a pretext to justify their violence, they always find it.'

And in 2012, he bravely told *Le Monde*: 'I would rather die standing than live on my knees.' For Charb, there was never any intention of giving in to fear, telling the *New Yorker* that mocking Islam must continue 'until Islam is just as banal as Catholicism'. Ridicule against extremism was his weapon, and it angered those who could only confront satire with guns. But in using the Prophet as an excuse to kill, the gunmen chose to ignore the Qur'anic reprimand of Muhammad himself that he had no right to impose his belief on others.

The defence of free speech is again at the forefront and while freedom of expression may never be absolute, let it set its own limits rather than be frightened into submission. I've heard many say that just because you can say something doesn't mean you should and at a purely pragmatic level that may sometimes be true. But it is free speech which gives minorities the right to practise their religion, groups to hold anti-war rallies and journalists to expose the tyrannies and hypocrisies of power. Freedom of expression with all its messy boundaries lies at the very core of liberal societies; if you lose this fundamental and hard-fought privilege, you've lost the very soul of Western freedoms.

These actions will only entrench social tensions about Islam in Europe. The irony of course is that more people will now see the very cartoons these gunmen wanted banned. And they will also see that their actions killed 12 but brought together thousands across the world, waving a pen in their hands, holding vigils and showing that if gunshots try to divide us, the simple act of *being* with one another can still unite us.

REV. DR SAM WELLS

Liberty, equality, fraternity

The day after Mona Siddiqui's Thought, *the gunmen were still at large and coverage of the* Charlie Hebdo *story was still dominating everything else. Police had named the prime suspects who were spotted on the run. Meanwhile a third, similarly dressed gunman shot and killed a police-woman in another Paris suburb. In the evening, the Eiffel Tower briefly went dark in remembrance of the victims.*

How could we return to the story without repeating what Mona had already covered, and with a script that was able to offer a wider perspective? Rev. Dr Sam Wells is the vicar of St Martin-in-the-Fields, one of the best-known churches in London. He has written 22 books, including academic studies on Christian ethics. He also has a way of addressing the news of the moment with a very different eye. He took the founding principles of modern France and examined them in the light of the Charlie Hebdo *story, producing a* Thought *that took the listener to a place that was unexpected and inspired. Two such contrasting scripts on one subject showed the strength of our range of contributors.*

9 January 2015

Four hundred years ago the writer John Donne said: 'No man is an island … every one is a piece of the continent … therefore never send to know for whom the bell tolls; it tolls for thee.' The last two nights in Trafalgar Square, across the road from where I live, crowds gathered in wounded grief and wordless anger. They knew the bell that tolled in Paris, tolled for them. They realised an assault on liberty anywhere is a threat to liberty everywhere. Except France isn't anywhere. It's the place that invented liberty.

Since the French Revolution in 1789 'liberty, equality, fraternity' has been a French national mission statement. These are the virtues France lives by. They don't always sit alongside each other easily: you can tell the story of the last 200 years as a tussle between liberty and equality. When the Third Republic was called 'a people with their heart on the left and their wallet on the right', it meant the French believed in theory in equality but in practice in liberty.

The freedom to publish a satirical cartoon appears to be all about liberty. Hence we get the irony of hundreds of people gathering as a community to support the rights of the individual. But what is a satirical cartoon? A satirical cartoon says: 'Just because you give yourself high-flown religious pretensions or threaten me with violence, you don't get extra respect. Quite the contrary, the more you inflate your self-importance, the more you're asking for your bubble to be burst.' It's actually a conviction about equality.

In the grief and anger that follow this ruthless and bloodthirsty attack, liberty can be elevated to an article of faith – an unquestioned god, all of its own. But virtues aren't like that. Virtues hunt in packs. Truthfulness requires love, and patience requires courage. Liberty and equality aren't gods; they're conditions for making an open and just society. But we've neglected the third word in this venerable motto: fraternity.

We were created in myriad diversity, and we grow up to be people of contrasting convictions and characters. 'Fraternity' is an old-fashioned word. But it names the challenge of our times: what happens when our identities and opinions take us to very different places? Fraternity is the reconciled diversity that Christians call the kingdom of God. Freedom of expression is wonderful, and equality of status is foundational: but they're both in the service of something more important, something glimpsed in the solidarity of strangers gathering to say: 'Je suis Charlie.' The issue isn't straining to uphold liberty: it's working out what to do with people who won't. The real challenge isn't how to live: it's how to live together.

CHIEF RABBI EPHRAIM MIRVIS

Lessons from the Wannsee conference

Holocaust Memorial Day in 2015 was set against the background of an alarming rise in anti-Semitism. In Britain, incidents more than doubled in 2014 and all across Europe – in France, Holland, Italy and Germany – observers recorded a noticeable spike in incidents each time the Israeli–Palestinian conflict flared. 'These are the worst times since the Nazi era,' the president of Germany's Central Council of Jews, Dieter Graumann, said. People were not criticising Israeli politics 'but expressing pure hatred against Jews'.

In this Holocaust Memorial Day Thought, Ephraim Mirvis, the Chief Rabbi of the United Hebrew Congregations of the Commonwealth since 2013, reflects on the sinister beginnings of a devastating genocide and cautions against ignoring rising instances of intolerance in contemporary society, however small. The Nazis had tried three so-called 'solutions' to what they called the 'Jewish question'. They were: impoverishment and forced emigration from Germany; starvation in locked ghettos in Poland; and machine-gunning Jews to death outside their towns and villages in the occupied Soviet Union. Eventually 15 Nazi leaders met in a luxurious country house to formulate a plan to create the gas chambers for 'the Final Solution'. Chief Rabbi Mirvis here issues an impassioned plea for courage in the face of today's renewed hatred and terror.

27 January 2015

I have visited many European sites where millions were murdered during the Holocaust. For me, the site that, more than any other, sends a chill down my spine is the Wannsee Villa in Berlin. It is an elegant country villa on the shore of a beautiful lake. At this picturesque spot, top Nazi officials planned how to wipe out the Jewish people. The official invitation to attend was sent by the deputy head of the SS. It read: 'The Chief of the Reich Main Security Office, Reinhard Heydrich, cordially invites you to a discussion about the Final Solution to the Jewish problem. Breakfast will be served at 9.00am.'

Over a tasty meal, 15 men sat down to determine the fate of the Jews. No one present questioned their mission or its justification. After cognac they began their work to annihilate my people.

Today is the 70th anniversary of the end of the Holocaust. As we remember the fate of 6 million Jews and many other victims, we owe it to those who suffered to ask: have the lessons of the Holocaust been learned?

The first essential lesson is the need for education lest people forget. Our children need to know the truth in order to ensure that the brutality of the Holocaust will not stain the world again. Secondly, we must teach compassion, kindness and selflessness. We must learn to practise loving acceptance of all people created in the Divine image, recognising that everyone has the right to freedom of conscience and expression.

Thirdly, open-mindedness will not suffice. Tolerance without boundaries – in particular tolerance of cruelty, falsehood and intolerance – has proved fatal to liberty. A free society must respond courageously and emphatically when faced by forces of evil that seek to destroy our civilisation.

Since Holocaust Memorial Day last year, anti-Semitic incidents have increased sharply in many parts of the world, including the UK. Recent events have shown the extent to which the civilised world today is threatened by the malign intentions of would-be mass murderers.

Our situation is not nearly as grave as the 1930s, but the lessons learned from then remain true today. Early signs of the breakdown of constructive coexistence must never go undetected. If they are ignored, disregard for human life, lust for power and self-righteous cruelty can simply spin out of control.

On this Holocaust Memorial Day, we must dedicate ourselves to education and develop the courage to protect our society from purveyors of hatred and terror. Let us remember the past for the sake of a peaceful and secure future.

TIM STANLEY

The Pope, Trump and the wall

At the start of 2016 Pope Francis prayed at the border between the United States and Mexico and blessed a makeshift memorial to migrants who had tried to cross into the US. On the other side of the border Donald Trump was campaigning to become American president – and stirring large crowds at his election rallies with populist anti-immigration rhetoric in which he called illegal Mexican immigrants 'criminals, drug dealers, rapists, etc.' and demanded a great wall be built to keep them out. The Pope declared his remarks 'unchristian'. Mr Trump hit back, calling the Pope's comments 'disgraceful'.

This story was right up Tim Stanley's street, on two counts. He is best known for his journalism on the Telegraph *newspaper but he is also a regular panellist on Radio 4's* Moral Maze. *In both places he combines his background as a historian and convert to Catholicism to distinct effect. Donald Trump made a point of grabbing as many headlines as he can but it is very unusual for the Pope to offer what could be regarded as a political comment. Tim is aware that there are divergent views around how best to deal with immigration – an ethical issue that exercises many governments – and in this* Thought *he offers a compromise position.*

23 February 2016

Pope Francis and Donald Trump recently had an argument over a wall, so to speak. Mr Trump wants to build one between Mexico and America to stop illegal immigration. The Pope said: 'A person who thinks only about building walls ... and not building bridges, is not Christian.' Mr Trump initially called the sentiment 'disgraceful'. He and the Vatican have since qualified their remarks and sort of moved on – the row did neither any favours. But me, I'm left thinking about the morality of that 2,000-mile wall that The Donald will construct if he becomes president.

It's certainly true that many walls are a tragic necessity. We live in a fallen world where, historically, people have always had to protect themselves and their resources from thieves or invaders. Supporters of Donald Trump were quick to point out that the Vatican is itself partially surrounded by a wall. In the Bible, God's protection is sometimes depicted as towers, fortresses or ramparts. The strength of Jerusalem as a holy city was reflected in architecture that kept it safe and separate from barbarians. 'May there be peace within your walls,' reads one translation of Psalm 122, 'and security within your citadels.'

But – and this is an important distinction – Pope Francis was not denouncing all wall builders, just those who '*only* think about building walls'. In this regard I'm reminded of the title character in Edward Bond's brilliant play *Lear*, a king obsessed with building a wall in order to keep his enemies out. The wall represents the corroding influence of paranoia and envy – and, while Lear promises that the fortification will bring peace, it actually brings misery to those forced to build it, and seals their ruler off from his own humanity.

So, yes, it's psychologically unhealthy to be fixated on walls. But we still have to be practical. America does have an illegal immigration problem and it does have a right to protect its borders.

Perhaps, then, the Christian duty should not be to tear down every wall in sight but to try to find ways of making them less necessary. If Mexico was richer and more secure, its people wouldn't desire a life elsewhere. We need to beat the drug cartels and enrich the Mexican people. That requires cooperation between rich and poor countries. It means, as the Pope indicated, building bridges.

For centuries popes have been given the honorary title *pontifex maximus*, which literally translates as 'the greatest bridge builder'. I think that's what we need more of in the world today: dialogue and generosity of spirit. A willingness to reach over the wall and to grasp our neighbours by the hand.

MICHAEL SYMMONS ROBERTS

100th anniversary of the Battle of the Somme

If one single battle may be said to symbolise the carnage and futility of the First World War, that battle took place on 1 July 1916 at the Somme. More than a million men on all sides were casualties. On the first day alone 19,240 British soldiers died – the bloodiest day in the history of the British Army. Yet despite this unimaginable cost in human lives, the battle did little to change the strategic outcome of the war. After 141 days of slaughter on an industrial scale the Allies had pushed the Germans back just seven miles.

Michael Symmons Roberts has a fascination with the war poets. Now a professor of poetry at Manchester Metropolitan University he has won several awards for his own poetry – including the Forward Prize, the Costa Book Award for Poetry and the Whitbread Poetry Award. He has written fiction and non-fiction, libretti and much more. He has been described as a 'lyric poet with philosophical and metaphysical concerns' who 'reflects on the world in a way that is informed by a sense of grace, of transcendence'. The centenary of the Somme required something special from Thought *and Michael ensured that is what the audience heard.*

1 July 2016

Paul Fussell in his book *The Great War and Modern Memory* conjures a farmhouse in Picardy hours before the Somme attack, where men from the King's Own Yorkshire Light Infantry stood, with glasses raised. A barrage of shells was reaching its crescendo, so intense it could be heard in England. It was meant to destroy German defences and clear a path for the Somme advance. The commander gave a toast – 'Gentlemen, when the barrage lifts' – and they drained their glasses. Within a day, of that one battalion of 800 men, more than 700 lay dead on the battlefield. The bombardment failed to account for the ingenuity of German defensive tunnels.

'When the barrage lifts' was a toast to courage, but also a prayer. You find yourself wanting to finish the sentence for them – 'When the barrage lifts, may you live to see your families again.' But within a day, that toast falls into self-mockery. 'When the barrage lifts, you will be cut down.' It becomes a prophecy. For decades after, every 1 July an anonymous message was posted in *The Times*' 'In Memoriam' column, saying 'Gentlemen, when the barrage lifts.' An officer's off-the-cuff toast turned from grim prophecy to a memorial, a single-line elegy.

The French Christian mystic Simone Weil tells a story of prisoners in adjoining cells, communicating by knocking on the wall, so the wall is both what separates them *and* is their only means of contact. 'Every separation', she says, 'is a link' between creator and created, between us. Our Somme commemorations will soon be finished, tidied up. Stories like that toast in the Picardy farmhouse will recede into the distance. The separation of history is stark. We are not them. But we *are* like them, and a story, a line from a poem can be a means of contact.

One of the great poets of the Somme – David Jones – describes in his epic poem *In Parenthesis* an injured soldier struggling for cover: 'It's difficult with the weight of the rifle,' he writes. 'Leave it–under the oak. / Leave it for a salvage-bloke, / let it lie bruised for a monument … Leave it for a Cook's tourist to the Devastated Areas'.

Even as battle raged, the poet was imagining people like us, in the future, touring battlefields. Our separation had already begun. How quickly the spark falters, and history falls back into myth. But the poems of Jones, Wilfred Owen, Isaac Rosenberg still hold the voltage to connect us, however briefly, when the barrage lifts.

VISHVAPANI

The Rohingyas and a Buddhist state

Vishvapani has practised Buddhism for 40 years since he was a teenager growing up in south London. He was ordained into the Triratna Buddhist Order in 1992 and has been the primary Buddhist contributor to Thought for the Day *since 2006. His explorations of the relevance of Buddhism and mindfulness to the modern world meant he was the best person to reflect upon the widespread persecutions and killings of Burmese Rohingya Muslims by the army in Buddhist Myanmar – a campaign so grave that more than a million people have been forced to flee to other countries, creating the world's largest refugee camp in Bangladesh.*

This Thought *was prompted by a United Nations report that described Myanmar's action as a 'textbook example' of ethnic cleansing. Others used the word genocide. The report prompted Vishvapani to ask why Burma's Buddhists are committing atrocities against the basic tenants of their religion – but he went further, challenging the very idea of a Buddhist state. Coming from such a highly respected Buddhist, the* Thought *provoked an appreciative response from listeners who applauded his radical thinking on the subject – and also the bravery of his stance.*

12 September 2017

When I hear about the horrific repression that's being inflicted on the Muslim Rohingyas, I share many of the outraged feelings that others are expressing. But I feel something extra as well: shame that these things are being done by my fellow Buddhists for the sake of a Buddhist state and with the support of many Buddhist monks.

How did we get here? I don't want to oversimplify the situation ... or generalise the responses of all Burmese Buddhists. But the question remains: the Buddha said that 'Hatred is never overcome by hatred, but only by love', so how has the faith he founded become associated with such brutality?

It won't do to set a pure, spiritual 'essential Buddhism' against the distorted version that's endorsed by Burmese generals. No doubt, distortion occurs, but our ideals have to be judged by their effects. In practical reality, Buddhism isn't just about spiritual teachings; the domain of Buddhism includes whatever is done in its name or by its adherents. If there's a contradiction between Buddhist teachings and this reality, it's important to understand how it arose.

I would begin by questioning the very idea of a Buddhist nation. Buddhism and the Burmese state have had a long association. The struggle against colonial rule involved Buddhism, Burmese nationalism and the interests of the majority Buddhist ethnic group. The result is that the state and most of the people believe that their interests are also those of their religion. It's a relatively short step for Burmese monks to think the same way, and for some to become cheerleaders for nationalism and racism.

In the process, Buddhist teachings aren't exactly ignored – it's worse than that. Their virtuous ends are used to justify repressive means. Worse still, the association with Buddhist spirituality bathes the state and its violence in a saffron-tinged glow.

I can't do justice here to the complexity of Burmese Buddhism or that of similar Buddhist states. But the qualities Buddhism upholds, such as loving kindness, must extend to everyone, including minorities and political opponents. That implies a democratic and multicultural outlook, rather than one that is exclusive, or even pro-Buddhist. And, as only individuals can manifest those qualities, a state can only ever be Buddhist in a nominal sense.

There can be no special pleading. Buddhists are only as good as their actions, and I fear that some of the actions we're currently seeing are very bad indeed.

PROFESSOR TINA BEATTIE

Zimbabwe and the truth

After four decades in power in Zimbabwe the nation's controversial leader Robert Mugabe was ousted in a confusing coup in 2017. The man who had begun as a liberation hero had slid slowly into corrupt and violent dictatorship. At the age of 93 he appeared to be planning to hand power over to his much younger wife – which proved a step too far for his opponents. But their hesitant moves against him left the country in limbo for several days. In was in this period of uncertainty that Tina Beattie wrote this Thought.

Tina Beattie is a feminist Catholic theologian who was born in neighbouring Zambia and lived there until she was 18. Later she moved to Zimbabwe when black majority rule began there. Her doctoral research – on the theology and symbolism in the Creation story of Eve and the cult of the Virgin Mary – gave her a good grounding in understanding the rewriting and reinterpretation of history. It was a skill she brought to bear in this Thought *on the winners and losers in Zimbabwe.*

16 November 2017

The fate of Zimbabwe hangs in the balance, as that beautiful and troubled country struggles to break free of tyranny.

In December 1980, we went to live in Bulawayo with our young children. Zimbabwe had become independent that year, marking the end of white minority rule. Shortly after we arrived, in February 1981, forces loyal to Joshua Nkomo's opposition party ZAPU attempted a military coup. We were warned to stay indoors, as tanks rolled into the outskirts of Bulawayo.

The uprising was quickly put down. It was a brief interruption in an otherwise happy and peaceful time in my life. Many years later, it was reported that Mugabe's government had launched a vicious purge after the coup attempt, and thousands of Ndebele people had been massacred. That story haunts me. It's a reminder of how fragile and illusory peace can be, when it's built on the silenced stories of the victims.

It's also a reminder of the importance of an independent media, with journalists who have integrity and courage in their pursuit of the facts, especially in these days of alternative news and cyber lies. Yet while facts and evidence are crucial, they're not in themselves sufficient to constitute truth. To discern truth within the raw facts of history is to be caught up in what philosopher Paul Ricœur calls 'the conflict of interpretations'.

I remember visiting a museum in Bulawayo where the captions on the exhibits were being changed. Terrorists were being renamed as freedom fighters, and history was being rewritten before our eyes. The factual evidence – the photos and artefacts – remained the same, but the interpretation was changing. It's a reminder of the saying that history is written by the victors.

Meanwhile, the trauma of Zimbabwean people continues, as the political battles rage on. It's too early to know who the winners will be – who will write the definitive history of these turbulent times. Yet behind every official history, there lurk the hidden victims, the bodies of those whose stories disturb our illusory peace.

When Pontius Pilate asked Jesus, 'What is truth?', Jesus did not respond. For me, that silence is an eloquent affirmation that testifying to truth isn't about abstract propositions and beliefs, nor about factual evidence alone – important though that is.

It's about what we stand for, whom we stand with, and whose stories we seek to tell, in the face of tyranny and despotism.

JULIE SIDDIQI

The Christchurch attack

Julie Siddiqi was driving her son up the M1 to a gymnastics competition when she got the call asking her to write for Thought for the Day *about the overnight attack on Muslims as they prayed in Christchurch in New Zealand. A lone gunman – who turned out to be a hate-filled white supremacist from Australia – had entered two mosques during Friday prayers and launched a meticulously planned assault in which he killed 51 people and injured 40 more. When she first heard the news she could only cry; but writing* Thought, *she said later, helped her process the news and its impact upon her: 'Although New Zealand is so far away, the pain of it felt real and local and personal to me.'*

Julie converted to Islam in 1995 and, after setting up a Muslim charity, did grassroots community work for decades before becoming Executive Director of the Islamic Society of Britain from 2010 to 2014 and a member of the government's National Muslim Women's Advisory Group. But, as becomes clear in this Thought, *she also developed a specific focus on Jewish-Muslim relations. The women she got to know through that were key to her reflection on how society can best combat events such as the Christchurch atrocity. The process of writing this* Thought, *she told me, 'meant a lot on so many levels'.*

15 *March 2019*

Yesterday morning I woke up around 5.30 and for some reason I did what we are all advised *not* to do when we first wake up … I checked my Facebook. The news coming from New Zealand was shocking. Prime Minister Jacinda Ardern brought me to tears as she spoke with firm conviction but in a sincere and compassionate way. She said of the victims: 'They are us. The person who has perpetuated this violence against us, is not. They have no place in New Zealand.'

The most shocking aspect was the blatant way the main attacker carried out his evil act. He broadcast it live online in a chillingly calm and calculated way.

I remembered my children; once again I had to tell them about another atrocity, feeling so close to home although on the other side of the world. How will they process this in their teenage world with their multiple identities?

My Jewish friend called me from her car on the school run. She listened to my anger and frustration in a way that only friends do. At the end she said three words. I love you.

And a London rabbi who used to live in New Zealand sent me the prayer he wrote for today's Shabbat service.

Community and faith leaders attended vigils, to reach out a hand of friendship, to show support and love. Archbishop of Canterbury Justin Welby tweeted, encouraging Christians to visit their local mosque for Friday prayers. Government officials issued firm statements of the kind I have never seen before, words that were strong in condemnation and giving a show of support and encouragement of resilience.

On social media Muslims are asking difficult and raw questions, 'What will these vigils do?'; 'What use are they, no one really cares.'

The pain is understandable, I know where those questions are coming from. It feels so overwhelming, so personal, beyond comprehension.

At least two of our most popular newspapers had to turn off their online comment facility because people were saying things like 'the Muslims should never have been allowed in a place called Christchurch anyway' or 'they deserved it'.

These men are part of a growing group online and offline around the world. They were allowed to operate in a way that was under the radar. We cannot be complacent, more needs to be done.

It's not always the case but yesterday my mobile phone was my friend. I welcomed the constant buzzing of messages of love and support, reminding me that there is more good than bad in the world, that together we are stronger.

They are not empty words, they are the fuel that will motivate me as I pick myself up, join together, not allow these acts to divide us further.

And yes, as Prophet Muhammad taught us, our mosques *will* remain open as places of hospitality, with a warm welcome.

HANNAH MALCOLM

A brother's killer

In recent years, stories from the United States of police violence against black people have appeared more frequently and the situations are increasingly shocking. When a white policewoman was convicted of the murder of her black neighbour, Botham Jean, in Dallas in 2019, two of the dead man's relatives offered strikingly contrasting responses. His father announced that he forgave the police officer but wanted a stiffer sentence. But Botham's brother, after saying that he forgave the officer, then asked the judge's permission to cross the floor of the court so that he could give the murderer a hug.

The Thought *on this subject is by Hannah Malcolm who is training to be a priest in the Church of England. A graduate of Yale Divinity School, she regularly writes and speaks on subjects at the intersection of Christianity and ecology. But here she focuses on what it means to forgive – and on the relationship between forgiveness, repentance and justice.*

5 October 2019

On 6 September 2018, off-duty Dallas police officer Amber Guyger shot and killed Botham Jean in his own apartment. This week she was found guilty of murder and sentenced to ten years in prison. While this case might easily have been passed over as one more statistic in a history of violence against black men at the hands of white police officers, it captured public imagination due to the response of Botham's 18-year-old brother Brandt – who announced that his Christian faith had led him to forgive policewoman Guyger, getting up to hug her after she was sentenced.

Brandt's response was gracious, unnecessary and misunderstood. Public discussion of his words reveals our tendency to treat forgiveness as an easy salve for a wound that will heal. Forgiveness – like repentance – is not the work of one-off hugs and tears. Brandt will grieve his brother for the rest of his life, and, if he chooses, will also carry the lifetime weight of seeking to forgive.

In the Lord's Prayer, Christians ask that God will 'forgive us our sins as we forgive those who sin against us' – they forgive because they have been forgiven, not because their forgiveness removes the need for repentance from those who have harmed them. We do a disservice to Brandt's forgiveness if we treat it as an alternative to justice – they are not mutually exclusive options. Instead, one should flow out of the other. In his letter to the Romans, the apostle Paul writes: 'shall we go on sinning so that grace may increase? By no means!' Or, to paraphrase Paul, shall we go on killing black men so that we can be inspired by forgiveness from a traumatised teenager? By no means.

The court proceedings are also a painful reminder of our warped distribution of sympathy. A society that more easily identifies the image of God in a white police officer, than in the black man she killed, is not ready to understand the grace Paul describes, either for the perpetrator or the victim's family.

As Botham Jean's mother Allison made clear, Brandt's forgiveness belongs between him and God. She said: 'What Brandt did this afternoon was to heal himself, to free himself from what has been wrapped up within him for the last year … I don't want forgiveness to be mistaken for a total relinquishing of responsibility.'

This does not absolve Guyger of the associated sins of racism and corruption, but it is an offer that Guyger may or may not choose to accept. Should she choose to accept it, she will encounter the kind of grace that leads to a lifetime of repentance and service – a much longer commitment than the reduced jail sentence she will serve.

BISHOP GULI FRANCIS-DEHQANI

An alternative view of Iran

In 2020 Iran's most powerful military commander, General Qasem Soleimani, was killed by a US drone at Baghdad International Airport while he was on his way to meet the Iraqi prime minister. The strike had been ordered by US President Donald Trump. The world looked on with trepidation. Soleimani was the second most powerful person in Iran, after Ayatollah Khamenei. What would his assassination unleash?

The extraordinary life of Bishop Guli Francis-Dehqani made her the best-placed Thought *contributor to address this issue. At the age of 13 she had arrived in Britain as a refugee fleeing with her family from Iran after an assassination attempt on her father, who was the Anglican bishop in Iran. Her mother had been injured and her brother had been murdered. Bishop Guli, who is now Anglican Bishop of Chelmsford, was anxious to alert listeners to a greater complexity about Iran than was usually portrayed in UK newspaper headlines. The escalation in tensions between Washington and Tehran were a fearful sign. Yet, she suggested, two paths now opened up.*

7 January 2020

A couple of weeks ago I stumbled across a new short movie by Iranian filmmaker Mohammadreza Kheradmandan. *Thursday Appointment* lasts around two minutes and it's about a man visiting his wife's grave. Stopping at traffic lights he sees a young couple having a fierce argument in the car next to him. Spurred by tender memories of his wife and the love poetry of Hafez he gives away the flowers he was taking to his wife's grave in a gentle gesture to encourage the young couple's reconciliation. The film is a poignant portrayal of a side of Iranian culture we're not so used to seeing in the media.

I'm an Iranian myself, and arrived in England as a refugee in 1980. I'm acutely aware of the best and worst that my country of birth has to offer. I'm not going to justify or defend the politics of Iran nor of anywhere else. But as the world holds its breath to see what happens as a result of the assassination of Qasem Soleimani, I want to offer two simple thoughts. First, there is more to Iran than meets the eye. Long before the rise of Western civilisations, Iran was contributing on a global scale to advances in medicine, architecture, literature, poetry, philosophy and the sciences. The impact of these achievements goes deep and lives on in the conscience and experiences of Iranians today. Secondly, memory is a powerful thing which can be utilised for good, or for ill.

In planning the path ahead, President Trump is choosing to remember the kidnap of American hostages during the Iranian Revolution 41 years ago. American weapons are now poised, we're told, across 52 targets, one for each hostage. But in this season of Epiphany there is another memory too we might choose to recall, of wise men believed to be from Persia travelling to a stable in Bethlehem to worship a newborn baby.

Nations today, whether at war or negotiating peace, do so under the banner of flags. The magi had no flags but journeyed instead under the light of a star. The stars are great levellers for they shine in the same skies above us all, wherever we live and whoever we are.

My hope and prayer is that ongoing responses in Iran and the West to the death of General Soleimani will draw, not on traditions of violence and revenge, but on the best traditions of East and West. For me as an Iranian and a Christian these are reflected in Iran's poetry, its rich culture and in the worship of the magi at the feet of the Christ child.

REV. DR JANE LEACH

Quarantine in Wuhan

Twelve days before Dr Jane Leach wrote this Thought for the Day *the authorities in China announced that no one was allowed to enter or leave Wuhan, a city of 11 million people, where a new coronavirus had infected 291 people. Six of them had died. Few of us in Britain noticed. We were preoccupied with Brexit. The United Kingdom had withdrawn from the European Union on 1 February.*

In this prescient Thought *the Methodist minister and academic, Jane Leach, was way ahead of the news agenda in bringing all this together. Among the concerns she touched on before other commentators were virus incubation, vaccine development, disease control strategy and the history of quarantine, which had its origin in the Venetian word* quarantena *meaning 'forty days'. Jane, who is Principal of Wesley House, the Methodist theological college in Cambridge, was also one of the first to highlight that the virus would hit the world's poor hardest. I remember this brilliant script with great pride.*

3 February 2020

Over the weekend, as our focus has been on other things – not least our leaving the European Union – coronavirus has been quietly spreading at a frightening pace. There are now more than 14,000 confirmed cases in 18 countries, and 46 million people are subject to restrictions to try to contain the disease.

'Take back control' has been one of the soundbites of the Brexit campaign, but this virus is a terrifying reminder of the things we cannot control. New diseases in a new host are often most dangerous. Incubation periods are not understood, new vaccines need developing and new problems are posed. Never before has anyone tried to contain a new virus in a city, like Wuhan, of 11 million people.

Quarantine is an ancient strategy. The term originated with bubonic plague and dates back to 1377, when the seaport of Ragusa officially issued a 40-day isolation period. But isolating those with diseases goes back much further than that. The Bible, for example, gives ample illustration in its instructions for dealing with contagious skin conditions. While the choice to isolate the few is designed to protect the lives of the many, the horror of being trapped inside a cordon, cut off from loved ones or fearing for loved ones, can hardly be imagined. Often it has been compounded with religious ideas of uncleanness that project the cause of the disease on to those already suffering. Ideas that Jesus challenged as he invited his followers to think again about what it means to 'choose life'.

While containment may still be an important disease control strategy, according to Professor Tim Benton of Chatham House we need to see coronavirus as a part of a pattern of diseases that are bridging the animal–human gap. While this has always happened, urbanisation and the intensive human interventions that are disrupting ecosystems are making us all more vulnerable.

Of course, some will always be more vulnerable than others. Poorer city-dwellers are more likely to be cleaners and sanitation workers, elevating their chances of encountering disease. They may also have weaker immune systems because of poor nutrition or lack of access to healthcare. In some cultures, people also use urban wildlife for food.

Caring for the poorest, ensuring that people at the margins have access to good sanitation, food and healthcare – these are values often repeated (not least on *Thought for the Day*) as part of a vision for 'choosing life' – and as often dismissed as soft, or compromised in the name of profit, or pushed to the bottom of the agenda because 'charity begins at home', and yet it is literally true that in the case of a virus like this, the world's population is only as strong as its weakest link.

It's in all our interests, whether decisions that govern our lives are made in Brussels or in London, urgently to cooperate across the globe in making radical changes to the living and working conditions of the poorest and to the ways in which we interact with the environment. Not because it's nice to be nice. But because, as research helps us understand better how the world is interconnected, so we understand better what it means to inhabit the ancient religious invitation to 'choose life'.

PÁDRAIG Ó TUAMA

100 years of a partitioned Ireland

This script from Pádraig Ó Tuama was written long after the worst times of the Troubles in Northern Ireland – and by an Irishman to boot – but it starts with a line that resonated strongly from my own work on Thought *during that turbulent time. The BBC was sensitive, and rightly so, to generalisations and wrong assumptions being broadcast by writers and contributors on this side of the Irish Sea. Compliance rules tightened significantly over the years and we had to ask Rev. Dr Bert Tosh, former Head of Religious Broadcasting for BBC Northern Ireland – who generously took our calls at all hours – to look over scripts about Northern Ireland for any sensitivities.*

Pádraig Ó Tuama is a poet and theologian whose work brings together interests in language, violence and religion. On the centenary of the partition of Ireland he was the obvious choice to explain the historical background and to reflect on the Good Friday peace agreement. For five years, until 2019, Pádraig led the Corrymeela Community, Ireland's oldest peace and reconciliation organisation, and his burgeoning profile as a writer and public performer grows apace.

5 March 2021

A few years ago at a festival in England I got into conversation with a fella while queueing for a burger. We chatted about this and that, then he said to me, 'I'm embarrassed to ask, but Northern Ireland or Southern Ireland; which one do we own?' Ironically, people here –whether nationalist or unionist – do find a certain unity in being frustrated when questions like this come. The guy in the queue was nice. I liked him, but his question was problematic, mostly because of the verb 'own'.

Trying to find religious wisdom when religion has so much blood on its hands in British-Irish history is problematic. So I turn to the Gospel of Thomas – one of the apocryphal gospels, not part of the Christian canon – to find something that hasn't been colonised for sectarian use.

In that gospel, someone comes up to Jesus and says: 'Tell my brothers to divide my father's possessions with me.' Jesus turns to him and says: 'Oh man. Who has made me a divider?'

Divide – border making, partitioning, language laws, penal laws, pain, terror … we know so much about dividing here. And Jesus – whether he likes it or not – has been made a divider. History is long here, and the past isn't always in the past.

In 1800 the Act of Union was signed making the United Kingdom of Great Britain and Ireland. And then in 1921, the UK changed again, with Ireland being partitioned and a new United Kingdom of Great Britain and Northern Ireland was formed.

The constitution from the emerging Irish Free State included a territorial claim on the newly partitioned jurisdiction of the north. But change came again: 80 years later, in the Good Friday Agreement, the governments of Westminster and Dublin renounced constitutional claims to the territory of Northern Ireland.

In effect, the governments declared that – given centuries of conflict – no government possesses the jurisdictions of the north; the people do. And the people can decide. And whatever the outcome of any change of formal government, everyone here will always be able to identify as British or Irish or Both. 'Who has made me a divider?' Jesus asks the man in that apocryphal gospel.

Governments – with long pride and pain and territorial and constitutional claims – sought to say to a divided people: find peace … we'll possess and protect that. Too many people have suffered in our long history for territory to be decided by a government.

The peace agreement here grants parity and esteem to people who wish to campaign for us to be in the UK or not. But, more importantly for me, the peace agreement says that whatever jurisdictional arrangement Ireland has, now or in the future, the governments of Ireland and Britain will always be involved, in order to ensure the safety of all who live here. That commitment must not be denied, or divided.

BISHOP NICK BAINES

Refugees lost in the Channel

The flow of migrants crossing the English Channel in dangerous inflatable dinghies increased significantly in 2018. But Nick Baines, the Anglican Bishop of Leeds, had been concerned about the problem for some years and had previously suggested we should focus on what was causing refugees to flee their homes in the first place. In 2021 more than 25,000 migrants made the perilous journey across the Channel. Then, late one night in November, came the news that a dinghy carrying 30 people had capsized, drowning 27 of its occupants. It was the deadliest incident in the Channel since the collecting of data began in 2014.

Nick Baines, who had already written a Thought for the Day *script on an entirely different subject for the next morning, heard the news and wrote again, finishing at 1am. No names had been given for the victims – men from Iraqi Kurdistan, Afghanistan, Ethiopia and Iran, and the group also included four women and two children. So Bishop Nick's* Thought *reflected on what God knew of each of them. His script was so powerful when it was broadcast that it was chosen by presenter Clive Myrie to feature on Radio 4's* Pick of the Year.

25 November 2021

I was on a train back from London to Leeds last night when I caught up with the news that some people had drowned in the Channel while trying to reach England from France. By the time I got home the number had risen to over 20 and a song of lament was going around inside my head.

Some years ago the Canadian songwriter Bruce Cockburn was in Afghanistan. He happened to be at Kandahar Airport as the coffins of fallen soldiers were taken on board an airplane for repatriation – that is, the return of the bodies to those who loved them back home. He wrote: 'Each one lost is everyone's loss, you see; each one lost is a vital part of you and me.' It is a hauntingly simple and beautiful elegy in the face of human mortality. It's full of empathy for those whose world would now have changed for ever and whose grief would be unbearable.

But the point he makes is that if we don't have our basic humanity in common, what is then left? This reflects the famous John Donne assertion that 'No man is an island entire of itself; every man is a piece of the continent, a part of the main. If a clod be washed away by the sea, Europe is the less …'

It seems that both Cockburn and Donne were able to penetrate through the dominant politics and positioning of their day and find the truth at the heart of it all – that whenever people die, a hole is left into which pour the tears of the bereaved. The difference between the fallen Westerners in Afghanistan and the drowned Easterners at Calais is that we label the latter, question their choices, and forget their identity.

The French president, Emmanuel Macron, put it well when, recognising human solidarity, he offered first his sympathy to the families of those who drowned. This isn't just a time for politics; rather, it is a time for digging deeper emotionally and being touched by tragedy. I don't know the names or circumstances of those who have died, but their death changes the world.

This goes to the heart of Christian faith when faced with tragedy and loss. The Judeo-Christian tradition begins with people being 'made in the image of God' and, therefore, being of infinite value – a value that goes beyond their economic or utilitarian function. Every person matters absolutely – not just those we deem acceptable.

Naive sentiment? Maybe. But, it also happens to go to the heart of what Christian faith refuses to negotiate.

Each one lost in the Channel had a name, a history and people who loved them. God knows their name even if I don't.

REV. LUCY WINKETT

The women of Ukraine

It can be hard, with events which come round year after year in the calendar, to know whether, or how, to mark them. But Lucy Winkett here makes something special out of a Thought *for International Women's Day.*

Lucy was ordained in 1995, one of the Church of England's first women priests, and she was the first woman to join the clergy of St Paul's Cathedral. Since 2010 she has been Rector of St James's Piccadilly, a church with a distinctive tradition whose previous rectors since 1685 – four of whom became Archbishop of Canterbury – have had the reputation of bringing something exceptional to the Church.

In this Thought *Lucy considers the idea of women in the West feeling solidarity with the women of Ukraine as they struggle to maintain some semblance of normality in their lives under the devastating assaults of Vladimir Putin's armies. She concludes that solidarity is not enough.*

8 March 2022

Today, International Women's Day, was founded by the German activist Clara Zetkin, a day when the situation of women, especially the inequalities they experience receive some focus and attention. But the reason it's this day, 8 March, is because of the women of St Petersburg in Russia. In 1917, women went on strike and took to the streets on this day demanding 'Peace and Bread'. If the women of Ukraine were able to leave the underground shelters they are in today, they might demand the same.

Today Russian and Ukrainian women find themselves on opposite sides of a brutal war. Any war polarises, separates, brutalises. It makes liars of truth tellers, killers of pacifists: teachers, journalists, scientists become simply refugees. Women across the world in Iraq, Myanmar/Burma, the Central African Republic, and many more places, know what it is to be shelled, assaulted, to be left, to have said goodbye for the last time.

Christian spiritual practice has a way of demanding I pay attention to this suffering by encouraging deep connection with it. It's not about trying to assume some kind of false solidarity – that I as a woman somehow know what every other woman experiences – that would be foolish.

Of course, the experience of Ukrainian women today is in some ways unimaginable. But Christian tradition says this in itself isn't good enough; declaring another woman's experience just 'unimaginable' produces more separation, more assumptions of irreconcilable difference. But reconciliation is the core of Christian living. And so, as one Russian Orthodox monk teaches, part of a Christian commitment is to 'keep your mind in hell and despair not'. Both of these halves are important. Don't look away. Go to that hell in your imagination. At the same time, do not despair.

And so, alongside the practical donations and solidarity events, I commit to listen, to imagine, to pray. To insist to the woman of Ukraine that she remains a mysterious, precious soul, not a statistic, whose distress I have witnessed, whose voice I have heard. And that I will remain forever stricken, complicit in the knowledge that this cruelty is part of our shared humanity.

To the women of Ukraine, holding unfamiliar weapons, queuing at the border, shepherding your children and your elderly parents, bracing yourselves for the next siren, for the next shell: I am you. You are me.

There is no Them. There is only Us.

REV. DR ROB MARSHALL

A psalm for Eurovision

Rob Marshall is a Church of England priest with a deft touch in marshalling popular culture to illuminate his theological points – as he demonstrates in this Thought *written on the eve of the 2022 Eurovision Song Contest. It was set against the background of a week of intense fighting in Ukraine, as Russia continued to launch airstrikes and artillery attacks in the Donetsk region and Ukrainian fighters were still holding off the Russians in Mariupol.*

Rob is currently Rector of Digswell in Welwyn Garden City but he has had a wide background in communications throughout his ministry and his PhD was written on the future of faith in a digital age. In this Thought *he reflects on the song which was the Ukraine Eurovision entry and draws out parallels between it and those psalms of the Hebrew Bible which gave people a voice in times of great adversity.*

14 May 2022

I'm going to make two confident predictions about tonight's Eurovision Song Contest. First, the UK's ritual humiliation will not be as bad tonight; we have Sam Ryder singing a good song. And also that Ukraine's entry will be there or thereabouts when the final results are counted.

If any song is a unique combination of lyrics, music and the manner in which it is performed, Ukraine's offering 'Stefania' – sung in Ukrainian by the Kalush Orchestra – is guaranteed to get the goosebumps going and to lift your spirit.

Written before the Russian invasion the song, from the start, has a prophetic aura to it. It's a hymn of love to a mother called Stefania, with the refrain 'the field blooms and it turns grey' – celebrating the mother's innate wisdom and proclaiming that she probably knows even more than Solomon. Because of the bond between mother and child, the young one always does everything to make sure they are able to return home 'even if the roads are broken'. I challenge anyone not to be moved.

Many of the Hebrew psalms are, of course, songs: performers, instruments, singing and clapping all feature frequently within them. This week, at a church service, I read Psalm 135 – 'Praise the Lord for the Lord is good; make music for it is lovely'. The Temple songs gave hope to the faithful. However grim and terrible the situation was, the songs bear witness that there was nothing that faith in God, and in each other, cannot overcome.

Performed in the midst of a shocking and tragic conflict, tonight's Eurovision song from Ukraine is for me a modern psalm of hope against adversity. And if you do watch or listen to the song later this evening – be mindful of the young performers' exuberant confidence and faith in the future.

Temporarily removed from the frontline in their homeland they exude brave positivity. They are provided with a stage, for a few minutes, to communicate the antithesis of everything the current conflict is about. And they do it with energy and courage.

If then, the biblical psalms all have elements of life story, personal experience, an appeal to some aspect of spiritual truth and hope for the future, Ukraine's Eurovision song is certainly brimming with all those things. Especially a desire to finally make it home despite the broken roads. 'Stefania' is my feel-good Eurovision Psalm of the Moment.

Chapter Three

Culture and Society

REV. DR COLIN MORRIS

The price of power

Rev. Dr Colin Morris brought a huge life experience – from Methodist minister to African missionary, presidential adviser and senior BBC executive – to bear on his contributions to Thought for the Day. *He once said: 'There is a transient topicality about broadcasting which rarely survives the cold light of tomorrow's dawn.' Yet many of his* Thoughts, *which were sparked off by the events of a given moment, dealt with perennial aspects of the human situation. So that, as Colin put it: 'What is said about Iraq one year is relevant to Bosnia another year and then to Kosovo …' and on and on.*

This script is a case in point. The detail of the events he mentions in his opening sentence have, for many of us, been lost in the mists of the past. Yet out of them Colin, one of the most astute and often profound thinkers of his generation, draws some universal lessons about the high price that power always exacts for its services.

6 March 1999

It's been an extraordinary week. In the skies over Iraq, British aircraft have been bombing military installations in order to protect the Kurdish people; in the House of Lords, the plight of the tortured and disappeared of Chile was the subject of a judgement; and now we have taken up arms with the intention of ending the massacre of Kosovans.

It all adds up to a comprehensive answer to the old biblical question; who is my neighbour? We preachers tend to utter pious clichés about the God-given unity of humanity and our duty towards the oppressed and downtrodden; now our rhetoric may have to be paid for with human life, and without any heavenly voice or blinding light around to assure us we are doing the right thing.

'What is the alternative?' – how often have we heard that this week? In complex international affairs, we are rarely given a choice between the obviously right and the clearly wrong, which is why we acknowledge prayerfully the awful responsibility that rests on our leaders, who've had to explore what alternatives there are, and then make an agonising choice.

Jesus tells a story of wheat and weeds, good and evil, growing in a field together, and it is impossible to separate them until the harvest. What he's saying is that even the very best actions of which we are capable will have both good and evil consequences, and we must act on the balance of probabilities. We recognise with penitence that we are bound to do harm and hurt some people as we struggle to liberate and protect others.

This issue is about power as well as morality, and the Bible has a lot to say about the use and abuse of power. A reporter standing on the deck of a US aircraft carrier the other day said: 'This is a great armada led by the most powerful nation on earth!' The Old Testament prophets warned again and again that God distrusts great concentrations of power. 'He has torn down the mighty from their thrones and exalted those of low estate,' says the Magnificat. Power always exacts a high price for its services; it is intoxicating; it easily becomes self-justifying, though those with experience of war are more sceptical about what it can achieve.

In any conflict Christians pray not for the victory of our side but the victory of God's righteous will – such prayers release into human affairs a creative factory capable of spanning unbridgeable gulfs and breaking apparent deadlocks. Call it the grace of God. In recent memory, South Africa and Northern Ireland were written off as intractable problems, but inexplicable changes of mind and heart took place and the unthinkable happened. No region, not even Kosovo, is beyond the range of that grace.

Opinion polls and integrity

Part of the multi-faith journey during the 50 years of Thought for the Day *has been successfully embodied by contributors such as Akhandadhi Das, Vaishnava teacher and theologian. Hinduism was much less well-known in the UK in the early days, so he had to start from a place of limited knowledge for a large proportion of the audience, to explain elements of this tradition, practised in countries on the Indian subcontinent. Akhandadhi had lived in the community of Bhaktivedanta Manor, then the best-known Hindu temple in Britain. When he broadcast on* Thought, *pegged to the current affairs of the day, his soft Irish accent and storytelling ability helped open up a new understanding of that faith.*

This one used the political opinion polls as a peg off the back of the 2003 Labour Party conference. Having to avoid any party-political bias, he then unpacked a more interesting area altogether; the implicit expectation that politicians should be better people that the rest of us. And when Akhandadhi talked about the way leadership and representation worked within Hindu communities, many people will have been hearing that perspective from a practising Hindu for the first time.

29 September 2003

This week the Labour Party enjoys its annual get-together by the seaside. Probably, a major topic of discussion among the delegates will be the latest opinion polls. Never before has our society's views been so canvassed and analysed. But, this is a double-edged sword for politicians. Yes, they may be able to tailor policies and manifesto promises to suit our interests. But perhaps the fact that we know that they know what we want has increased our expectations of what our leaders could and should be doing for us.

It's fair to say that the world's religious traditions are not big on democracy and universal suffrage. Hinduism, for instance, commends the idea of voting for a person to represent the views of a group – but is wary of choosing someone to govern the group. It sees a clear difference between electing representation and electing government. That's because there is the sense that a representative just has to be one of us, but government has to be better than us. It may seem old-fashioned, but those in political power do have a role as moral authorities. One could argue that modern governments are solely concerned with the priorities of allocating resources. But, the choices we make in caring for others – whether they be poor, old, young or sick – are ultimately moral judgements.

Politicians, therefore, need to be less selfish and more caring than the rest of us – they need to be better people.

There is a story of Rama, a king of ancient India, who would regularly go out among his subjects in disguise to hear their concerns. On one occasion, he noted that the main cause of complaint was a question about his own integrity. He took this criticism to heart, because he recognised that, in failing to meet the moral expectations of his people, he might erode their ethical and moral commitment and, thus, he would be responsible for diminishing rather than improving the quality of their lives.

I believe that our sense of happiness is not just dependent on material circumstances, but in living a balanced life and being true to our soul. When the feelgood factor is down and things aren't meeting our expectations, it's easy to blame the government of the day. But, the cause may not simply be whether or not the social services have improved, trains are running on time or there is more money in our pockets. I think, more often, a sense of dissatisfaction is linked to how we perceive our leaders are performing as moral authorities over us. Is their level of personal probity and integrity enriching or impoverishing our own sense of moral values? Because, that issue, perhaps unconsciously, is at the heart of our expectations.

Thought for the Day

VISHVAPANI

What Buddha tells us all about our biases

By the start of the new millennium Thought *had been working to include contributors from each of the world's major faith traditions. Vishvapani was to become our regular Buddhist voice. He is a respected Buddhist teacher and mindfulness expert – a practice that has gained a lot of attention in Western countries including Britain where long working hours and the pressures of modern life are creating mental health problems.*

This kind of script from 2007 brought to the slot a different approach to the inner spiritual life. And as Buddhism was enjoying a wave of interest and Western adaptation, Vishvapani's contributions were even more welcome. The examples in this Thought *on metaphors, in life and politics, located him in the central areas of concern of the* Today *programme, but he had to tackle them without revealing a personal party political allegiance. It also had to work in combination with other* Thought *scripts in that week or month to maintain a sense of balance.*

2 June 2007

When I first heard as a child that Europe was divided by an Iron Curtain I imagined a huge wall of steel behind which everything was in shadow – and also freezing cold, which was why people said there was a Cold War. And when I heard the terms left and right wing, I imagined all the politicians standing in a long line according to their views, and shuffling about when someone switched policies.

These metaphors simplified the truth into an image, and when Tony Blair argued this week that the terms 'left' and 'right' are outmoded, he was suggesting that the image no longer matches reality. Rather, he said, we need pragmatic solutions that may cut across 'tribal' party lines, and be guided not by ideology but by underlying values.

There's nothing wrong with metaphors, but it helps to notice how they mould our thinking. When we speak of 'progress', we imagine humanity moving in space. When we speak of moral 'sickness', we think of the mind as if it were a body. But we easily forget that these are images, not realities, and the ideas that develop around them can be a trap. Some historians argue that American policy in Vietnam was governed by the image of falling dominoes. If one falls they all will, they thought, forgetting that dominoes and countries work in different ways.

Religion, especially, often understands life through images. There are ideas as well, but these are usually embedded in stories and myths. The question for the Buddha was how we respond to them. They may point us towards the truth, but if we're driven by a need for certainty we'll fix them into dogmas and religious institutions that become ends in themselves. He described his own teaching as a raft. It's useful – in fact essential – for crossing a stream on the journey to wisdom; but once you reach the other shore and know the truth for yourself, the raft can be left behind. Words, ideas and images are not reality.

Tribal politics is another kind of dogmatism that tells you where to line up on the left–right spectrum. But you can't get away from metaphors. Tony Blair proposed a new distinction between those open to global economic change and those closed to it. That's another image that implies other assumptions and value judgements. To get at the truth for ourselves we need to see past political and religious rhetoric, and then do something much harder: look honestly at the biases underpinning our own beliefs.

BISHOP JAMES JONES

What are prisons for?

On 2 September 2008 the Today *programme came live and direct from one of Britain's jails. In 'Life on the Inside at HMP Liverpool', one of the programme's presenters, Evan Davis, interviewed the prison governor, Alan Brown, and Michael Spurr, the operational head of HM Prison Service. In addition to getting a taste of life inside, Evan learned that 1,386 prisoners were being housed in the prison at an average cost of £23,871 per prisoner per year. Around 10 per cent of the inmates were estimated to have a serious mental illness, Michael Spurr revealed.*

It was Bishop James who was left to put flesh and blood on the bare bones of such statistics. He delivered Thought *live from inside the prison in the city in which he had won the hearts of the local people as Bishop of Liverpool for 15 years – not least for finally exposing the truth surrounding the deaths of 97 Liverpool football fans who died in the Hillsborough tragedy. His script was so well-received that he was invited back on to the* Today *programme the next day to discuss it. Bishop James was Bishop to Her Majesty's Prisons from 2006 to 2013, he presented a Radio 4 series* The Bishop and the Prisoner, *and as a member of the House of Lords spoke on criminal and restorative justice. In this* Thought *he confronted listeners with the humanity and vulnerability of men often dismissed as irredeemable.*

2 September 2008

In my time I've been in about ten different prisons. Getting in is always the same – the forbidding high wall, the secure doors, the passport for ID, the handing over of your mobile phone – these symbols of freedom surrendered. Very few of us ever get to go inside a prison, yet most of us have an opinion about who should be there.

Over the last ten years I've been to this prison a number of times. It's the first place I've ever been given a round of applause

at the end of a sermon! I like coming and I like meeting prisoners. I confess that something happens to me as I come from the
outside to the inside. On the other side of the walls whenever I
hear of yet another crime I feel all the anger that should rise up
in us all for yet another innocent victim. But once on the inside,
and face-to-face with a prisoner in his cell, the mood can change
as you shake the hand of flesh and blood. There's no denying the
severity, or even the barbarity, of their crime. But often beneath
the banter there's this pang of loneliness, this flicker of honesty,
this sigh of sorrow that calls out from behind the eyes.

Of course, some may dismiss this as romantic and sentimen-
tal. But I remember on my first visit here one burly, tattooed
prisoner butting his head close to mine. And in a low voice
saying: 'Father, don't think there are any men here who don't
cry in their cells at night.' Prison chaplains will tell you they
have many conversations with prisoners about God. They echo
the poem of R.S. Thomas:

> We ransack the heavens,
> the distance between
> stars; the last place we look
> is in prison, his hideout
> in flesh and bone.

The fundamental question facing our society is whether we see
prisons as warehouses to store the incorrigible or greenhouses
to restore the redeemable. The way we answer that question
will determine the sort of prisons we build. Especially today
when we hear that charities such as NACRO and Turning Point
are joining the list of those bidding to run new prisons.

In his famous parable the 'Prodigal Son', Jesus tells of the
father begging the reluctant elder son to come into the party to
celebrate the return of his penitent younger brother. Jesus told

this story to shame self-righteous people who were outraged by the low life that he was gathering into God's kingdom.

The sight of the father pleading with the elder son to accept the repentance and redemption of his errant brother is a parable for our own times. Although there's clearly a small number of criminals who are never safe to release back into the community, the challenge for us is to create prisons that believe in the possibility of redemption for the 80,000 people in our prisons today.

REV. JOHN BELL

Unfair to a lady

All over the world women are paid less than men for doing the same job. In the UK the gender pay gap remains, despite the 1970 Equal Pay Act. John Bell of the Iona Community – an international ecumenical Christian movement working for justice and peace, the rebuilding of community and the renewal of worship – was prompted to this Thought *following a survey by the Equality and Human Rights Commission. It showed that a wide gender disparity remained – despite improved access to education for girls, and higher rates of participation of women in the labour market. John is well known for speaking up for those who don't get a fair hearing.*

Various explanations are routinely put forward for the pay gap: gender stereotypes, social norms, women's 'role' as unpaid carers and domestic workers, discriminatory practices in the workplace and the 'motherhood penalty' since the disparity increases with the number of children a woman has. But John Bell, always a strong advocate of self-scrutiny, in this Thought *turns his critical gaze on another problem – the Christian Church.*

8 September 2008

'Why can't a woman be more like a man?' That's a rhetorical question from a revered West End musical. But if answers were an option, someone in the audience might shout: 'Because it would cost too much!'

That would certainly be the case if the fair lady in question were to be one of the gilded few who, having presided before and during the credit crisis, continue to shake hands with themselves and receive massive bonuses in the process. Stephen Hester, the new chief executive of the Royal Bank of Scotland, was reported at the weekend as being the beneficiary of £9.7 million from an institution in which the British taxpayer has no small interest and a great deal of capital. No wonder that last year one in five Oxford graduates ended up in the City. But how many of them were women?

Ah, there's the rub, as we discovered yesterday when it was revealed that bonuses and sweeteners in the City are prone to gender bias. The findings of a survey by the Equality and Human Rights Commission, which has a substantial project involving almost a quarter of finance-sector workers, revealed that female employees earn on average 39 per cent less basic pay than their male counterparts. And when it comes to bonuses, they get around 20 per cent of what might be called masculine supplements. What is it with women? Are they financially naive? Are they busy multitasking when they should be single-mindedly increasing their personal portfolios?

Or is it because the financial industry is still a boys' club?

The industry I represent, if one could call it that, is not innocent of mistreating or even degrading women. The Christian Church has a long history of failing to recognise or encourage female giftedness. Hence most traditional church buildings are rectangular with people sitting in rows facing the man at the front.

As in architecture, so in liturgy. Until very recently, when a woman had a miscarriage or delivered a stillborn child, there were few prayers to represent these particular losses which even yet affect one in four women. Men, who were mostly in charge, didn't make provision for what they couldn't understand.

And this in blatant contradiction to Jesus whose most loyal followers were women, whose prime examples of faith, generosity and love were women, whose first evangelist was a woman, and who even used female illustrations in his talks.

That's partly why they wanted to get rid of him. He was a threat then, as now, to a male hegemony. To heed him is to take all people seriously. It's much easier in the boys' club.

RABBI LIONEL BLUE

21st-century worries

For many people, reading this script will evoke in their mind's ear the sound of the inimitable voice of Rabbi Lionel Blue. A rabbi in the Reform tradition, he was a Monday-morning treat for millions. Lionel spoke very directly to people. His insights may have sounded homespun but they contained a wealth of knowledge, theological learning and incisive thinking, shot through with the fruits of his own rather harsh life experience.

We knew about his family – namely his mum and his auntie – his upbringing, the war years, his love of food and cooking, his relationship with God, his depression and his sexuality. The latter two were linked; as a gay man and a religious professional he had a tough time 'finding himself'. Most of all he understood at a profound level what made people tick – as with this script and its message about worry and anxiety. He cared deeply about people. He wanted to soothe and uplift them; and they could tell.

But what also made Lionel so loved was the way he put vignettes and jokes in every script. Very Jewish and very tuned into a popular psychology, he not only endeared himself but he kept everyone with him. If the joke hadn't come listeners would have thought he was ill! There was some very good religion in there as well, but sometimes you had to listen hard to get it. It was his favourite kind.

5 December 2011

Dear Listeners, we've had a shock. The 21st century is becoming another century of worry and the fault's in us not our technology. In Europe it isn't difficult to see what happened. We spent more than we earned and mortgaged the future to bridge the gap. Well, the future became the present, as it always does and now we can't pay the bill. Banks and pensions ceased to be secure in the frenzy to make a fast buck. We were only economical with the truth.

In the crises of the last century people panicked and sought scapegoats to avoid their own responsibility. That's when Hitlers happened. Well, we haven't reached that point yet, but we could.

That sense of shared responsibility is important. It's why the talk is currently about people in all sectors needing to feel they're in it together. It worked in the past. I remember as a kid, when slumps made life even tougher than now in the poor parts of London, in some ways life was more decent. Front doors were rarely locked – the key dangled on a string behind the letterbox, available to all. Electronic home fortifications suitable for suburbia and Alcatraz were unknown.

Here's some personal tips to cheer you up because worry sharpens anxiety, which makes problems worse:

Remember a lot of worries cancel each other out.

Also list all the things you ever worried about and tick the ones that actually happened. Not many I suspect. It was the things you didn't worry about which happened, but that's a thought for another day.

If I can't get to sleep from worry, I think up some Jewish light-bulb jokes which help; it's better than counting sheep.

'How many Jews does it take to change a light bulb?' Two – one to change the bulb and another to tell him how to do it better.

'How many psychoanalysts does it take to change a light bulb?' One – provided the light bulb really wants to change.

How many Jewish mothers does it take to change a light bulb? None – 'Don't worry about me. I'll sit alone in the dark.'

And a word about prayer. The sincerest and shortest prayer I know is 'Help'. Don't ask for miracles but courage. Perhaps a simpler lifestyle could be a comfort not a tragedy and some of the best things in life really are free, like friendship, kindness, compliments and kisses. This isn't schmaltz but personally tested – so Don't Panic!

CANON DR ALAN BILLINGS

Being British and multi-faith

The eyes of the world were to be turned on Britain in 2012, said Alan Billings, thinking ahead to the London Olympic Games and the Queen's Diamond Jubilee. But visitors should look deeper, he says in this Thought. *One of the lessons Britain has to offer the world is the way that, as a society, we have learned to value the differences between religions – rather than fearing them as is so often the case elsewhere in the world.* Thought for the Day, *I hope, has been very much part of that process.*

Alan Billings has learned this through personal experience. Born in one of Britain's most multicultural cities, Leicester, he went on to study theology and philosophy at Emmanuel College, Cambridge, before being ordained as a priest in the Church of England. He then served for years as a parish priest in inner-city Sheffield, and was active as a member of the group that produced the Faith in the City *report, which brought the Church into conflict with the government of Margaret Thatcher. He later held senior academic posts in Oxford, Birmingham and Lancaster where, as Director of the Centre for Ethics and Religion, he researched inter-faith activities in the north-west mill towns, asking whether religion was a help or hindrance in building community cohesion. This* Thought *gives his answer to that question.*

9 January 2012

Politicians and commentators are at one in saying that 2012 offers Great Britain a unique opportunity to tell its story to the world. The Royal Jubilee and the Olympic Games will command global interest. News media will come here from every country. They'll not only report the great events, but will also turn their attention to the country itself. What is modern Britain like?

I hope they'll notice something about us that is, if not unique, at any rate rare in the world today, and of real importance. It's the way the different religious groups that make up modern Britain have, in the main, learned to value and not fear religious pluralism.

Our acceptance of religious pluralism means that we have rejected one way of reading the world and its conflicts. This is the idea put forward by Samuel Huntington some years ago that a clash of civilisations – the Christian West and the Islamic East – is inevitable.

The journey we have made to being relatively at ease with pluralism is instructive. When I was first a priest in the inner city, the presence of different faiths was noticeable. It was here that inter-faith work had to start. One unintended consequence of those early conversations was that it led us to become more aware of our differences as we became more self-conscious about our respective faiths.

Over time, dialogue turned into friendship, and we have come to see that while our different faiths are important to us, they are not the only ways in which we think about ourselves. I might not share my friend's Islamic faith, but that is not all that defines her. She is also a parent, a school governor, an opera lover, a research scientist. In these and other areas which are just as critical to her sense of who she is, we have much in common. In some of these areas we find ourselves in the same group. Yet no one group of the many we belong to defines absolutely who we are.

Eventually, this sent us back to our scriptures to find and value those passages that speak of our unity as human beings, not our differences.

In many other parts of the world religious difference continues to be separated out from the multiple identities that all people have and made the one factor that must determine identity. The deadly truth of that is being played out now, rather obviously in Nigeria and Kenya, but also in those places where the Arab Spring is happening. In these emerging Arab democracies, religious difference is already being used to foment anger for political advantage.

The lesson we are learning here, therefore – that we must do everything we can not to define ourselves by one factor alone, and to see ourselves as having not one significant identity but many – will be something worth reporting globally.

REV. ROY JENKINS

Food banks – giving and receiving

Food banks that give out food to families at risk of hunger were virtually unknown in Britain before the financial crisis of 2007–8. Since then their use has steadily grown because of a combination of recession, inflation and government austerity cuts. When Roy Jenkins wrote this Thought *in 2012 more were opening every week and Church Action on Poverty estimated around half a million Britons had used them. The media was full of powerful pieces to camera that brought home the desperation of penury. The audience reacted with a mix of empathy and fear.*

But for a Thought for the Day *writer it can present a problem. All the world's major religions expect their followers to help the hungry and those in need. But it's also the kind of subject where theological reflection can sound like a political comment, which is outside the* Thought *brief. Rev. Roy Jenkins is a long-standing contributor, a down-to-earth Welsh non-conformist pastor whose views have been shaped not only by his theology but also by his long experience of listening to people as they share their troubles. In this* Thought, *he takes a canny sidestep to avoid the politics and instead reflects not only on what it means to give but also why it is good to receive.*

14 March 2012

More than a hundred thousand people needed the services of Britain's food banks last year. As this programme reported yesterday, that number has nearly doubled in 12 months; and we can find the very existence of this provision unsettling. We're familiar with queues for basic foodstuffs in refugee camps, in regions suffering famines or hit by earthquake or flood. But in this country? It can be something of a shock to the system to learn about individuals and families who might go hungry without a parcel of groceries to tide them over.

I spent a couple of hours in a food bank a few weeks ago. It was an impressive community enterprise, sponsored and staffed by local churches, but drawing on the goodwill of schools, traders and shoppers who'd buy an extra item at a supermarket and pop it in a collecting bin. Between the shelves of pasta and tinned tomatoes, the baked beans and the breakfast cereals – six tons of it, apparently – I heard the stories of some desperate people: benefits had been stopped, they'd lost their job, health had broken down, a family rift had left them homeless ... a litany of sudden destitution. It was the speed with which normal life had been plunged into crisis which caused some the greatest shock, and with it the embarrassment of needing such help, the sense of personal failure and the fear that other people would find out.

At a time when all welfare provision is under scrutiny, there's much rhetoric about 'scroungers and cheats' abusing the system, rather less cleverly, of course, than those able to pay experts to hide away their millions. It's worth remembering the people who'll walk past a food bank a dozen times before plucking up the courage to step inside. That swallowing of pride takes real guts, and it was good to see the sensitivity of the helpers who were clearly concerned to remove as much of the discomfort as possible.

Few of us want to appear dependent: witness the rugged determination of many older people to resist support to which they're entitled; and the intense frustration of some who've spent a lifetime caring for others who now find it painfully difficult to accept that they're the ones who must be cared for.

The Christian faith, like others, commends the good life as one spent in loving service of God and of other people. But it makes clear that the willingness to receive is just as much a part of what it means to be truly human. We enter the world totally dependent, and however confident and self-contained we might become, we do so only in relationship with other human beings and with gifts which are exactly that – abilities, skills, which are first given. And we never outgrow our need to receive love – human and divine. But it can take both humility and courage to recognise it.

RHIDIAN BROOK

The limits of my kindness

Rhidian Brook has a thing about homelessness. In fact, it's a subject that he has written about on Thought for the Day *more than any other. And it's a good subject because while lots of us get stuck at the stage of arguing about whether to give money to a beggar on the street, he's already a step ahead of us. He exposes truths and absurdities everyone can recognise but writes with a style that takes you to new places.*

In this Thought, *as always, he reaches for sacred writings in his everyday situations and often quotes the psalms or New Testament. Here he uses the Letter of St James to get inspiration for his own actions. All the time he's thinking out loud, unembarrassed to admit to feeling less than charitable at various points. He owns his faith and speaks from the heart but most of all he sounds like himself – which is sometimes harder to do than you might think. His conclusion comes slightly out of the blue at first, but it's his realisation that he's been on the wrong track all along.*

12 March 2013

Here's a saying I think few would disagree with: 'Suppose a brother or sister is without clothes and food and one of you says to him, "I wish you well; keep warm and well-fed," but does nothing about his physical needs, what good is that?' While the moral logic of this passage from [the Letter of] James is perhaps easy to accept, as I discovered this week, practising it can prove much harder.

On Sunday evening I was walking home from a dinner with my wife. The cold snap had started and with the windchill it was about minus five degrees; we were almost home when we saw a man sleeping in the doorway of a shop. We asked if he was OK, and he said he was. I was ready to leave him there when my wife asked him if he'd like a bed for the night. He said yes and, seconds later, I found myself carrying his bag back to our house wondering what we were letting ourselves in for.

I'll happily buy a homeless man a cup of tea, a meal, even a sleeping bag but, for all sorts of sensible reasons, offering a bed feels like a line you probably shouldn't cross. As we reached the front door, we told him that we had children and that this was not common practice for us, but we were going to trust him. He said he respected this and so we crossed the threshold.

With our guest tucked up in the spare room, I must confess that I lay in bed wondering if I should lock the kids' doors or go and hide some of the valuables. I was convinced we'd pay for our naive, impulsive gesture. The next morning I found everything in its right place. Our guest was asleep on the sofa, and after letting him have a bath (an offer somehow more challenging than offering him a bed) he began to tell us how he'd ended up on the street.

His story was a mix of poor choices and bad luck, regret and self-pity. He was grateful for people's help but was critical of the system. As I listened it confirmed that he needed more than a one-off kindness. Our action would make little difference in the long run. For some reason, the more I found out about him the less sympathetic I felt. My impatience to get on with my life was more powerful than any desire to help him further and, perhaps unfortunately for both of us, I had found the limits of my kindness.

The rest of that passage from James goes on to say that faith, if not accompanied by action, is dead. Yet it also states that we should do the good we know we ought to do, as the opportunities present themselves. Maybe in the end, it's not our goodness that's the issue; it's our willingness to take a risk. As someone once said, faith is spelt R.I.S.K.; it's just not always the kind of risk that can be calculated.

MARTIN WROE

Eulogy v. résumé virtues

I first encountered Martin Wroe's work via his journalism. He had got into it while studying theology and ended up on the staff of the Independent *and later the* Observer. *He is now associate vicar of St Luke's Church in Islington and a freelance writer. His slightly left-field take on life and faith felt perfect for our Saturday slot. At the weekend the news doesn't stop, but finding a slightly different tone to events – even, as here, when he needs to be mindful that it's only a couple of days since a fatal air crash – Martin is able to ease in a more relaxed feel.*

Martin suggests that how we live is more important than what we believe. Religion, he has written, has an image problem, unlike spirituality. Religion is hard, where spirituality is soft. We are shy of certainty, and suspicious of authority. Yet we retain the longing for some deeper, richer narrative by which to navigate our days. In this Thought *he does just that by exploring the writing of American author David Brooks, in the context of a seminal moment in a school career. Everyone has a memory of the feeling of moving up from primary to the 'big school', be it for ourselves or our children.*

19 July 2014

'We recently started a family.' 'This week one of the kids graduated from university.' Where do the years go?

Many schools broke up for summer yesterday – young people are waiting for results or looking for work. You remember when that was you, you notice how quickly the days pass, how soon your time will be up.

And you look at the news this past few days and realise that nothing is certain. You suppress a feeling of dread at how fragile everything is, how ordinary lives can be torn apart by catastrophe.

So a letter from headteacher Rachel Tomlinson, to children leaving her Lancashire primary school this week, was inspiring. She praised her Year 6 pupils for their results but reminded them that academic tests measure only a part of who they are.

The people who mark those tests, she wrote, don't know that 'your friends count on you to be there for them'. Or that 'sometimes you take care of your little brother or sister after school'. Or 'that you can be trustworthy, kind or thoughtful'. There are many ways of being smart, she concluded.

Or, to put it another way – there are many ways of living a good life.

The American author David Brooks makes a distinction between résumé virtues and eulogy virtues. Résumé virtues, he says, are how you did in those tests, the evidence of your skill-base, what you bring to work as a grown up. But eulogy virtues – these are different. This is what people will say about you when your life is over.

At your funeral no one will mention your exam results. The hours you spent at work – your title or salary. People will remember a different edition of your life: 'He loved playing with his kids ...' 'She'd always stand up for others ...'

Maybe they'll say: 'She was generous and patient ...' 'He was loyal and brave ...' 'She always listened and was so discreet ...'

Eulogy virtues are hard to measure, but easier to witness. They're not about your qualifications in life but the quality of your life. They are a glue that holds families and friendships together – that helps us negotiate life's toughest tests.

A good eulogy paints a picture of someone who recognised their human flaws – and tried to face them down.

Are we mean, or consumed with envy? Do we hold grudges? Do we ever shut up and let others speak? Can we forgive?

As families mourn those they've lost on Flight MH17, one image stood out. A memory of a brilliant pioneer in AIDS research. His friend recalled how 'often times he was cooking for his five girls while on conference calls discussing HIV'.

A snapshot of a good life. 'Teach us to number our days,' says the psalmist, 'That we may apply our hearts to wisdom.'

In a time when world leaders struggle to wage peace and foster friendship, our hope lies in young people with the courage, compassion and character to do it in theirs.

RABBI LORD JONATHAN SACKS

Orwell and free speech

When Rabbi Jonathan Sacks won the prestigious Templeton Prize in 2016 in recognition of his work in affirming life's spiritual dimension, he was described as 'one of the world's great voices for moral, spiritual and historical awareness and for global peace'. Such voices come along rarely and it was a great good fortune for Thought for the Day *that he was such an unstinting supporter of the slot.*

Rabbi Lord Sacks knew the importance of reminding the audience of the values and lessons of history that require daily nurture and thought. But this wasn't an academic exercise for him. He loved doing it. He also understood how to talk to the whole audience and at the same time be utterly authentic in expressing his Jewish faith. In fact, he relished the opportunity to speak to those of different faiths to his own and those who held no faith. He was a brilliant communicator, broadcaster and human being.

The subject of being able to disagree, as a crucial way of understanding each other better, was central to his philosophy. It was what he called 'the Dignity of Difference'. The increase in 'cancel culture' and 'no platforming' in recent years was a cultural shift that troubled him greatly.

10 November 2017

Coming into Broadcasting House this morning I saw for the first time the statue, unveiled this week, of George Orwell, with its inscription on the wall behind: 'If liberty means anything at all, it means the right to tell people what they do not want to hear.' How badly we need that truth today.

I've been deeply troubled by what seems to me to be the assault on free speech taking place in British universities in the name of 'safe space', 'trigger warnings' and 'micro-aggressions', meaning any remark that someone might find offensive even if no offence is meant. So far has this gone that a month ago,

students at an Oxford college banned the presence of a representative of the Christian Union on the grounds that some might
find their presence alienating and offensive. Luckily the protest
that followed led to the ban being swiftly overturned.

But still I'm sure this entire movement has been undertaken for the highest of motives, to protect the feelings of the
vulnerable, which I applaud, but you don't achieve that by
silencing dissenting views. A safe space is the exact opposite:
a place where you give a respectful hearing to views opposed
to your own, knowing that your views too will be listened to
respectfully. That's academic freedom and it's essential to a
free society.

And it's what I learned at university. My doctoral supervisor,
the late Sir Bernard Williams, was an atheist. I was a passionate religious believer. But he always listened respectfully to my
views, which gave me the confidence to face those who disagree
with everything I stand for. That's safety in an unsafe world.

And it's at the very heart of my faith, because Judaism
is a tradition all of whose canonical texts are anthologies of
arguments. In the Bible, Abraham, Moses, Jeremiah and Job
argue with God. The rabbinic literature is an almost endless
series of Rabbi X says this and Rabbi Y says that, and when
one rabbi had the chance of asking God who was right, God
replied, they're both right. 'How can they both be right?' asked
the rabbi, to which God's apocryphal reply was: 'You're also
right.' The rabbis called this 'argument for the sake of heaven'.

Why does it matter? Because truth emerges from disagreement and debate. Because tolerance means making space for
difference. Because justice involves *audi alteram partem*, listening
to the other side. And because, in Orwell's words, liberty means
'the right to tell people what they do not want to hear'.

RABBI DANIEL GREENBERG

Reclining seats

Rabbi Daniel Greenberg is a barrister specialising in legislation with many years' experience in the private and public sectors as a parliamentary counsel. Now an officer in the House of Commons, he was appointed a Companion of the Order of the Bath (CB) in the New Year Honours list in 2020 for services to Parliament. He is also a contributing consultant editor to the Oxford English Dictionary. *So he has a broad spectrum of knowledge across legislative and other areas.*

A relatively new contributor to Thought for the Day, *he has brought his training in ethics, the law and religion into a variety of subjects. This one – on the different ways passengers recline their seats in aircraft – was his debut for* Thought *in August 2018. It shows how apparently trivial decisions can unconsciously reveal important social attitudes. What is revealing here, as Daniel shows, is that even small daily dilemmas can uncover the mindsets that drive people to behave in ways that promote self-interest over the good of the community.*

17 August 2018

Flying back from holiday this week I saw three kinds of behaviour when the seatbelt light went out after take-off. Some people pushed their seat back immediately with an air of entitlement. Some sat bolt upright throughout the journey. And some appeared to wait until they wanted to sleep, and then they looked over the back of their seat, and sometimes spoke to the person behind, before deciding what to do.

The aircraft cabin is a microcosm, a sealed community brought together for a few hours. In a world that concentrates increasingly on rights, I can concentrate on enforcing mine: I can push my seat back because I have a right to do so; if it cramps you, then pass on the pain and push your seat back into the person behind.

This reminded me of the rabbinic writing – *Ethics of the Fathers* – where the rabbis disagree about how to describe a person whose attitude to life is: 'I'll keep what's mine and you keep what's yours' (or 'I'll look after myself and you look after yourself'). Most rabbis describe this as neutral behaviour; but some describe it as the worst behaviour imaginable. Why such a fundamental disagreement?

One answer involves a variant reading of the Ethic. If one person says: 'I'll keep what's mine and you keep what's yours', that's neutral; but if lots of people say it, and it becomes the defining attitude of a community, then it becomes the worst behaviour imaginable in religious terms, simply because it makes the entire community pointless, or spiritually sterile. In rabbinic terms, God didn't create a world with lots of people only for us to ignore each other, or to focus only on enforcing our own individual rights.

The tiny ephemeral microcosm community of an aircraft can be a spiritually or morally neutral experience; or it can become a small but significant opportunity to think about each other's needs as well as our own, and to create a community that radiates spirituality or, if you prefer, creates a useful social contract.

We all have different ideas about how and why we came to share this world. But perhaps we can all agree that if we see other human beings as an opportunity, and not simply as an obstacle to the full exercise of our own rights, our relationship with others can be the starting point for our own spiritual, ethical or simply human development.

REV. PROFESSOR DAVID WILKINSON

Artificial intelligence and being human

Will robots ever take your job? When the term artificial intelligence (AI) was coined in the 1950s it felt like something from the realm of science fiction. But today robots work alongside humans in factories, driverless cars are being test-driven on the roads, and algorithms run everything from online shopping to stock exchanges. There have been suggestions that over the next two decades, 35 per cent of British jobs are at risk of automation. But is risk the right word?

Rev. Professor David Wilkinson is a Methodist minister who is Principal of St John's College at Durham University. He's also a professor in systematic theology and before that was a theoretical astrophysicist. His current work involves the relationship of Christian theology to contemporary culture. In this Thought *he considers not just the technology and ethics of AI but also the idea that machines may one day be intelligent, creative and self-aware. But will they ever have the capacity to love? David Wilkinson poses questions about what makes us truly human – and ends in a place beyond the current thinking of most of us.*

4 February 2019

Some decades ago my mother was replaced by a computer. Her job was pressing buttons on an electromechanical adding machine to work out electricity bills. In my generation I am faced with just how far this growth of technology will go in replacing not just jobs but more fundamental aspects of being human.

This evening *Panorama* begins Intelligent Machines Week on the BBC, looking at the future of work. A Deloitte report published today suggests that 60 per cent of jobs here in the north-east are at medium to high risk of being replaced by robots and artificial intelligence. Yet the implications are complex. Brynjolfsson and McAfee in *The Second Machine*

Age argue that while some jobs will disappear, others will be created and some existing jobs will become more valuable. This scenario is extremely important for education, training and financial sustainability.

But are there wider implications for spirituality? Will these intelligent machines become conscious and what might this mean for our self-understanding of what it means to be human? Here we need to be careful in navigating the complex relationship of science and science fiction. The Channel 4 series *Humans* and Alex Garland's *Ex Machina* present an almost inevitable emergence of human-like consciousness in artificial intelligence. Yet the science is still uncertain about this possibility, even if the fiction poses useful questions. Equally, those who categorically rule it out by asserting that human beings will always be unique because of a mysterious dualistic soul need to take the rate of scientific advance seriously.

There are, of course, no intelligent machines in the Bible but it does have a lot to say on what it means to be human and created in the image of God. In the Genesis narratives human beings are created for community, and within that given the gifts of intimate relationship with God, responsibility and creativity – which for me includes the gift of science. In the New Testament the image of God is seen supremely in Jesus, showing that at the heart of being human is love.

My mother found more fulfilment with children as a school dinner lady rather than typing rows of figures. I welcome intelligent machines taking away drudgery in work, but also want to engage in the discussion of how we structure our world so that all can experience what it means to be fully human. And if the intelligent machines which come from our God-given creativity eventually emerge as self-aware and with a capacity to love, then why should they not be loved by God?

CANON ANGELA TILBY

The yob within

Canon Angela Tilby had broadcasting in her bones long before she became an Anglican priest. She joined the BBC and worked mostly as a television producer, but also produced and presented radio. After a 22-year career she left to become ordained in 1997. The wonderfulness of Angela is that she's a thinker who is able to come up with really unusual ways of looking at things. She always manages to combine her experience as a writer and journalist, a tutor, a scientist, a theologian and someone fascinated in people to take listeners to territory they hadn't thought of until they hear her Thought.

Take this one for instance. The increase in crime and anti-social behaviour was getting loads of newspaper coverage. It was treated as a threat to the wellbeing of ordinary people because it was out there, and it was everywhere. The problem was invariably presented as an 'Us and Them' dilemma, which is perhaps understandable as a place to start on that kind of societal issue, but Angela here suggests it's more complicated than that.

24 October 2003

Graffiti, casual theft, foul language, car crime, sick in the streets. The recent shop-a-yob campaign sponsored by the *Sun* is one symptom of a growing revolt against anti-social behaviour. There's a weighty Bill steamrollering through the House of Lords designed to crack down on the 60,000 recorded acts of anti-social behaviour which occur every day. The proposed legislation means that the police can be called in if two or three people believe that something unpleasant is going on – which could be which 'looks', note, *looks*, intimidating or aggressive.

The Bill seems designed to arouse the law-abiding majority to hit back. Nip bad behaviour in the bud. Suspicion is ground enough to get you shopped. It's the revenge of the privet hedge. But it worries me because, just like the bad behaviour it's meant to prevent, it depends on feelings and fears.

It's part of the shallow emotionalism that runs through our whole society. We've gone along too easily with the pop psychology which tells us that *any* expression of feeling is justified as long as it is sincere. So when people get angry, or feel frustrated, they feel it's all right to swear or threaten obscenely. In fact, it's almost shameful not to. You've got to keep your self-respect after all. And if you don't respect yourself no one else will.

So we are being wound up to be more suspicious of one another, more fearful, more ready to take offence. We've forgotten the lesson of the nursery that giving expression to rage can make everyone hate you; once you start taking offence, the whole world seems to be insulting you.

I'm not suggesting we don't have a problem, but we're in danger of making it worse. A civilised society trains people to understand emotion, rather than simply to emote. Religion helps us to see our behaviour as though through the eyes of God. We are accountable. We will be judged.

After the Reformation it became fashionable for parish churches to have the Ten Commandments inscribed on their east walls so that the worshippers had to look at them as they prayed. The Commandments used to be recited by the priest at the beginning of every communion service. I once thought this awful and legalistic and opposed to the Christian ethic of love.

But as society has reduced love to mere sentimentality, I find I've changed my mind. Dry, laconic, boring; the famous 'Thou shalt nots' could never have been described as exciting but they do prohibit us from wrecking other people's lives. No one can get emotional about the Ten Commandments, and that's exactly why they're useful. They remind us of the need for restraint over our emotions: because murder, theft, adultery, defamation and covetousness all begin with emotions which then get out of control. It's one thing to shop yobs, but it might be much better to confront the yob within.

BISHOP PHILIP NORTH

Superforecasters v. prophets

In the aftermath of the Iraq War – when it had become horribly clear that all the secret service predictions about Saddam Hussein having 'weapons of mass destruction' were incorrect – a US intelligence agency decided to study the science of predictions to find out what had gone wrong. It organised an online tournament in which hundreds of participants were asked to predict the answers to hundreds of questions about future events. It was won, hands down, by a team led by a political scientist named Philip Tetlock who went on to publish a book explaining his techniques. He called it Superforecasting: The Art and Science of Prediction.

Philip North, the Anglican Bishop of Burnley, read it and discovered that Tetlock's 'superforecasters' were intelligent but more importantly open-minded, deeply curious, and adept at sidestepping their own cognitive biases. Bishop Philip has served in a range of church placements – from impoverished inner-city parishes to the great Catholic pilgrimage shrine of Our Lady of Walsingham – so he has developed the ability to discern the needs of people in a wide variety of circumstances. How, the bishop wondered in this Thought, *were superforecasters different from the prophets of the Old Testament? He suggests that it depends on whether we see the future as fixed – or capable of being changed by human interactions.*

21 February 2020

Superforecasting. It's a great word and it is something many people learned about for the first time this week. The term was coined by Philip Tetlock who noticed that some people just seemed to have a gift for predicting the future in almost any subject area, regardless of their level of expertise.

Superforecasters pride themselves on being dispassionate. They leave behind them personal emotions or opinions and focus on pure science; analysing data and the forecasts of others in order to come to objective predictions of where the world is going. Very handy for businesses and politicians. As long as they get it right, that is.

Well, of course, there is nothing new under the sun, and one could easily argue that the pages of the Bible are brim full of superforecasters, it's just that they used the rather simpler name 'prophet'.

The prophets of the Hebrew scriptures also prided themselves on leaving out private opinion. They claimed to be reading the mind of God as they forecast judgement on their nation, foretold conquest and invasion, denounced hypocrisy and warned of bad times to come.

However, there is one big difference between the two. Superforecasters predict the future, but they do so in a way that can seem fatalistic, even disempowering. Here's what's going to happen so you'd better get real and get used to it, they seem to say. The future is a given. We may be able to plan for it but we cannot determine it.

The prophets by contrast offered individual people a choice. It was this. If you love God, stand up for justice and care for the poor then the future can be good. If, however, you continue to live in your own selfish ways and disregard the needy, then judgement is on its way. It is over to you to decide. For the prophets the future is negotiable. It is determined by our words and actions. It is something for which everyone bears some responsibility.

So let me finish by doing some superforecasting of my own. I forecast a future in which men and women learn to live in harmony with creation, not despoiling it or plundering it for their own selfish ends but cherishing it as stewards. I forecast a future in which every single child is loved and has access to good education and rich opportunity. I forecast a world in which disputes are settled by conversation and mutual understanding rather than by destructive conflict. I forecast a world in which poverty is eradicated and all have enough. Now that may seem to some impossibly naive. But that's the future I'd love to see, so that's the one I'm going to work for.

PROFESSOR ANNA ROWLANDS

Animal Farm

Anna Rowlands is a respected political theologian who is the holder of the St Hilda Chair in Catholic Social Thought and Practice in the Theology Department at Durham University. Anna's first background was in politics but after three years of studying the subject at Cambridge she decided all political questions were actually theological ones. This 'co-belonging', as she terms it, is now the lifeblood of her academic work. As a practising Catholic as well as an academic theologian she is concerned with faith in action – what communities are doing in the real world for its transformation. She hopes that Catholic social teaching can be made accessible more broadly, not just to Catholics but to all people of goodwill.

This script about Animal Farm *plays to all Anna's strengths: her depth of understanding of people, society, classic writers, and how their ideas speak to us on different planes – not least the registering of important milestones in the cultural life of the nation.*

17 August 2020

Today is the 75th anniversary of the publication of George Orwell's *Animal Farm*. Published in 1945, the book famously satirises Stalin's Russia. The animals of Manor Farm, led by their pig compatriots, rise up against the neglectful Farmer Jones. The new seven commandments of the farm teach: 'All animals are equal.' But the pig leaders betray this vision, and the commandments are amended: 'All animals are equal, but some animals are more equal than others.' Thus, Orwell exposes all politics turned into self-serving narcissism.

During lockdown I've returned to a group of mid-century writers, to which Orwell belongs. Copies of Albert Camus's *The Plague*, also written in the mid 1940s, have flown off the online shelves. Using the allegory of a virus to explore the experience of fascism, Camus shows how viruses come in many social forms. As Camus and Orwell were writing, W.H. Auden was composing *The Age of Anxiety*. Four characters sit in a New York bar, discussing the 'frightened lands' they inhabit.

At the heart of this fiction is a common set of questions: how do we get as deeply into the world as possible, look at it without illusion, understand the suffering we create, but also finding the courage to resist and to hope? These writers trouble us with these questions.

Orwell, Camus and Auden all wrestled with Christianity. They were as critical of religious institutions as of secular ones. But the politics of the 1930s and 1940s brought Auden, at least, back to his Christianity. He believed that the command to 'love one's neighbour' was *the* teaching that could enable resistance to power gone awry.

For Auden neighbour-love meant seeing the unique value of every human being. Being able to see the infinite worth of an imperfect other is, for Auden, an insight that comes to us from outside ourselves, but is the kind of insight you have to choose to really own for yourself, again and again. For it means being willing to revolt in the face of every system that decides some human beings are worth more than others.

The great miracle for Auden is the moment when you choose to 'love your crooked neighbour with your crooked heart'. When we do we image God, who, Auden says, numbers each particle, knows each thing by its Proper Name. God is the very opposite of indifference. God is not like an algorithm.

Great poetry and literature, Auden wrote, 'makes nothing happen'. But it does extend our knowledge of both suffering and love, and by doing so, makes all the more urgent the choice that lies before us: to actively choose to inhabit a more genuinely human world.

PROFESSOR ROBERT BECKFORD

Star Trek goes trans

Professor Robert Beckford is a tour de force. He is passionate about ideas and their place in the world. He is now Director of the Institute of Climate and Social Justice at the University of Winchester but I can remember the first time I met him well over 20 years ago when he had become the first tutor in Black Theology at the Queen's Foundation theological college in Birmingham. From the outset his was clearly going to be an important voice.

Robert's career in academia has constantly opened up new platforms for his message. He has now written a dozen books, made a BAFTA award-winning documentary and more than 20 television and radio programmes, and has engaged in innovative work on gospel and black music. All these genres are used to the same end: to confront injustice in African mainland and diaspora communities. This Thought, *which deals with ethnic diversity, same-sex relationships, non-binary and trans characters, dovetailed with themes of love, salvation and resurrection – all seen through the lens of popular culture – is a Beckford classic.*

5 *September 2020*

Star Trek: Discovery, the latest incarnation of the *Star Trek* franchise, is to break new ground in science-fiction television by introducing the first-ever non-binary and trans characters later this year. The actor, Ian Alexander, will play the trans character, 'Gray', and similarly, the actor Blu del Barrio will play the non-binary character, 'Adira'.

It is not the first time *Star Trek* has gone where no programmes have gone before. In the show's 50-year history, the writers have consistently confronted cultural barriers by portraying characters or depicting scenes that resist the mores and values of the time.

The first TV series back in the late sixties, for instance, pioneered ethnic diversity in casting and subject matter. The crew of the USS *Enterprise* was made up of a dynamic array of nationalities, ethnicities – and an alien too! The writers did not stop there. Recently, the series has featured same-sex relationships and leading roles for women of African and Asian American heritage.

Religious themes of love, salvation and resurrection have also peppered the programme's storytelling. However, for some fans, the appeal of the franchise is its equal commitment to subverting religion: some of the TV episodes and action movies actively seek to debunk the beliefs of crew members or those of a people in a far-flung alien planet.

Less controversial is the literary idea that science-fiction programmes are metaphors; they help us reimagine new ways of existing, unfettered by the inhibiting social constrictions of contemporary society.

Science fiction as metaphor has much in common with apocalyptic or extreme images and visions in the New Testament. At the end of the Bible, the Book of Revelation portrays a titanic struggle between good and evil. The outcome is a world free of pain, injustice, inequality and racial strife. All people are free to exist as intended, and in harmony with each other and the environment. The architect of this new world order is the Lamb of God – who is the symbol of universal peace and justice.

But the Book of Revelation's dramatic image of a hopeful future is not a fleeting illusion or just for the end of time. There is more to the genre than meets the eye, because, as apocalyptic literature, the writers of this drama want their readers to see the imaginary future as a present reality. And the Book's revelation of the Lamb of God is the model we must follow to confront and transform the dangerous and discriminatory world in which we currently live.

In the Bible's version of science fiction, acceptance of difference is possible in real life, in the real world today, and not just on some distant planet or galaxy far away.

PROFESSOR TOM MCLEISH

Music

Tom McLeish is professor of natural philosophy in the Department of Physics at the University of York. A theoretical physicist he is renowned for his work on increasing our understanding of the properties of soft matter. He has also spent many years illuminating the relationship between science and religion.

But this Thought *on the value of music is the one that has earned one of the biggest reactions in his time on the slot so far. Among them was a flood of responses from grateful musicians who had felt marginalised and let down during the COVID pandemic, in spite of what they have contributed. They variously described his* Thought *as 'brilliant' and as 'spot on regarding education'. One listener talked about a project being run in the north-east that had shown 'making music together can have a huge impact on the self-esteem, confidence and behaviour of primary school pupils'. For* Thought for the Day *the connection with our audience is very important*

– both the praise, as here, and the brickbats, on other occasions, help inform our editorial choices and remind us of the breadth of people listening.

26 February 2021

'Ah, music,' reflects Professor Albus Dumbledore, in J.K. Rowling's *Harry Potter and the Philosopher's Stone*. 'A magic beyond all we do here!' I think the wizard would understand the frisson of excitement around the tentative announcements this week that the Reading and Leeds music festivals plan to go ahead this August.

Music has indeed proved to be a sort of magic during these difficult months. I am not the only listener who would always have said that music was important to me, but have learned over the pandemic just how important. Listening to favourite pieces, to music radio stations, singing or playing a bit if we can – we have even discovered how much live music matters – even if it is streamed. I'm so grateful for the ingenuity and perseverance of musicians, from professional orchestras to student music societies, who have found imaginative online ways of passing on to us this wonderful gift.

Robert Schumann, I confess my favourite composer, and no stranger himself to darkness and depression, said of his vocation: 'To send light into the darkness of people's hearts – such is the duty of the artist.'

But music does more than cheer; it also resonates with our need to create – Paul McCartney, who announced his forthcoming memoirs this week, said that one of his biggest thrills still is 'sitting down with a guitar or a piano and just out of nowhere trying to make a song happen'. Music expresses important things that words cannot.

Music is a force for change. 'I will sing and make music with all my soul,' begins the hymn of praise to God that is Psalm 108, but reading on reveals that it is actually sung from a dark place of captivity and oppression. Its music isn't a decoration; it's the beginning of a liberation. And the Bible's starkest warning, to a nation that oppresses the poor while gorging on luxury, is to say: 'The music of harpists and musicians, flute players and trumpeters, will never be heard in you again.'

Do we value music enough? In the light of its power to heal, express and transform, doesn't it belong closer to the core of education than we currently place it? And have we done enough to help the musicians who have given so much over the last year, but who face growing uncertainties, and now suffer additional difficulties in touring in our neighbouring countries? They have given us much reason to hope; can we give some hope back? As that psalmist sang: 'Awake harp and lyre – I will awaken the dawn'.

PROFESSOR TINA BEATTIE

And the wee donkey

Tina Beattie was, for many years, Professor of Catholic Studies at the University of Roehampton in London. More recently she has written fiction and she still comments on issues of Catholicism, gender, art, theology and psychoanalysis, as well as women's sexual and reproductive health and rights. She also has a finger on the pulse of contemporary culture. In one of her Thoughts, *for instance, Tina suggested the BBC include a same-sex couple on* Strictly Come Dancing, *quite some time before it actually happened. She said it would cheer everyone up – and it did!*

In this Thought, *she talks about two drama series that were among the most popular on television at the time – and certainly the most talked about in the media.* Call the Midwife *was brilliantly adept at catching the atmosphere and people stories of different eras in 20th-century Britain. The anti-corruption police drama* Line of Duty *had enjoyed huge audiences for years, but much was now being made of reports that this was its very last series.*

4 May 2021

Two recent BBC television series have provided compelling Sunday-night viewing for many of us – *Call the Midwife*, followed by *Line of Duty*. I'll avoid any spoilers for those who haven't watched this week's final episode.

The faith of *Line of Duty*'s Superintendent Ted Hastings (played by Adrian Dunbar) has been a matter of widespread speculation. He even made the cover of the Catholic weekly *The Tablet*. His Catholic mutterings could be taken as mild expletives or prayers, maybe both. His words 'Jesus, Mary and Joseph and the wee donkey' have gone viral on social media.

Hastings is a compromised character and all the more credible for being so. His mistakes weigh heavily upon him, but he also has a passion for justice. His set pieces are all about the need for integrity, accountability and truth in public life. In the final episode, he speaks of atonement, and he says: 'Who's going to judge what I did? Her, the law, my colleagues, God?' Hastings's sense of justice flows from his faith in a just God to whom he is ultimately accountable beyond all corrupted human laws and institutions.

In different ways, *Line of Duty* and *Call the Midwife* illustrate two key biblical themes: justice and mercy. The characters and storylines might easily invite reflection on the prophet Zechariah's words: 'This is what the Lord Almighty said: "Administer true justice; show mercy and compassion to one another. Do not oppress the widow or the fatherless, the foreigner or the poor. Do not plot evil against each other."'

True justice is merciful and compassionate. It has a concern for the vulnerable, and it can accommodate our regrets and remorse, for we share with Hastings the less than perfect realities of the human condition.

Mercy shines through the vocations of the religious sisters in *Call the Midwife*. For me, the closing lines of Sunday night's episode segued seamlessly into the final episode of *Line of Duty*. The narrator, read by Vanessa Redgrave, reflects on how together in mutual support 'we listen, we witness, we learn, and we love.' She observes that 'being human is not always easy, but it can be so very beautiful.'

I see that wounded beauty shining through some of the flawed central characters in *Line of Duty*, with their pursuit of justice through all those tangled labyrinths of loyalty and betrayal, compromise and corruption, loss, sorrow and love.

BISHOP LORD RICHARD HARRIES

Truth in public life

At the time of this Thought, *the war in Ukraine was filling the news bulletins with new horrors on a daily basis. The women and children fleeing for their lives, the men who stayed behind to fight for their land, and the Russian soldiers duped into a military invasion they weren't expecting or trained for. At home the headlines had all been about investigations into whether rules were broken and Parliament misled. The Metropolitan Police had finished their investigation into the scandal dubbed 'Partygate' by the media, and the long-awaited Sue Gray report was still to come.*

Bishop Richard Harries has a vast experience of writing for Thought *through every era and eventuality: political turbulence, international crises or national issues. He has written into the moment on many occasions when the important thing was to speak to a situation that was exercising the audience and commentators alike, while staying within the slot's parameters for avoiding party politics. When that happens he often draws on his extensive personal experience and knowledge of places and people. His particular signature is to use literature, poetry or examples of great art to make his point with wisdom and elegance.*

18 March 2022

On top of the bombs and having to flee their homes what is really upsetting Ukrainians is that when they ring their friends in Russia they find that Ukraine is being blamed for the war. They have been fed a very different story. So we have two totally different narratives. What makes us think that our narrative is the true one? (After all, every state has its own perspective, and we share the same flawed humanity as Russians.) One simple fact: in our society, lies can in the end be exposed.

During the Cold War, I paid a number of visits to the old Soviet Union, and then again, after the Wall came down, when I talked to someone who had been a senior civil servant in the old regime. I asked him what he thought could prevent such a totalitarian state arising again. He thought for a little and replied: 'The memory of what went wrong.'

My instinctive reaction at the time was that this was a very flimsy basis to prevent another despotism, and so sadly it has proved. The only secure bulwark against authoritarian rule is really strong public institutions, the rule of law backed by an independent judiciary, a free press, and a government accountable to a parliament that has been genuinely freely elected. These safeguard the possibility of truth in public life and that truth desperately matters.

Truth is fundamental to all life. The worst crime in the scientific community is falsifying the results of an experiment. The worst crime in journalism is making up a story that never happened. The worst crime in democratic politics is lying to parliament. Truth is essential to any kind of civilised life – more than that, there could be no possibility of any human relationship without the assumption that most people, most of the time, are speaking the truth – and without that assumption there could be no rational life and therefore no *Homo sapiens* at all. The remarkable French intellectual Simone Weil wrote: 'Christ likes us to prefer truth to him because, before being Christ, he is Truth. If one turns aside from him to go towards the truth, one will not go far before falling into his arms.'

No wonder Plato and Neo-Platonists down the ages have thought that Truth, along with Beauty and Goodness, have a kind of life of their own, however difficult this is philosophically to make sense of. But whatever we make of the metaphysics, one thing is certain. The importance of truth in both private and public life cannot be underestimated.

BISHOP DAVID WALKER

Privilege and entitlement

Dr David Walker, after studying at King's College Cambridge, was ordained as a priest in the Church of England and he followed a conventional path as a curate and vicar before being consecrated as a bishop in 2000. But there is nothing conventional about Bishop David in his ministry.

Now bishop of his native Manchester he is a member of the Third Order of the Society of Saint Francis whose members make a binding promise to follow a simple Franciscan rule. He is also a prominent figure in the Affirming Catholicism movement, a liberal strand of Anglo-Catholicism that embraces the ordination of women. In addition he chairs the Church of England's main endowment fund, which invests over £8 billion globally to support the work of the Church, including in its poorest communities. And he is heavily involved in the Ethical Investment movement and in supporting monastic communities.

The breadth of his spirituality, churchmanship and wide interests is reflected in this Thought. *It touches on the Queen's Platinum Jubilee, the war in Ukraine and lawbreaking by Prime Minister Boris Johnson (following Sue Gray's report into partying in Downing Street) to explore the relationship between privilege and entitlement. More than that, he turns the spotlight on himself, and on us.*

30 May 2022

I live a pretty privileged life. In fact, when I rated myself against 15 dimensions of privilege, as part of a recent safeguarding course, I ticked every box – bar youth and beauty. In itself, I see privilege as morally neutral, a mere matter of fact. It's what I do with it that matters. Do I open or shut doors for others? Do I help the voiceless be heard, or shout them down? Do I use my influence in the cause of justice, or against it? In this Jubilee week, many of us will wish to celebrate how our Queen has used the particular privileges of her position in the service of nation, Church and Commonwealth.

But privilege can prove hard to prise from its evil twin, entitlement.

The Bible tells how, long ago, God forged a close relationship with one specific people. That privileged status gave them a unique place in his plan. But it brought with it the call to be a blessing for all peoples, to exemplify hospitality to the stranger, and to work to redress disparities of wealth and status. Jesus chides those, especially the leaders of his day, who think and act as if mere ancestry and position entitle them to divine support.

Entitlement poisons our relationship to the world around us; affording exemption from applying to ourselves the same rules that we expect others to follow, while infecting us with a sense of impunity. It creates a culture which justifies the president who invades a neighbouring country, claiming its territory as his due, and the private soldier who sees looting and rape as part of his spoils of war. Less dramatically, it legitimates the man who perennially interrupts female colleagues, and the boss who touches junior co-workers inappropriately. Fail to set the right culture and otherwise high-achieving, intelligent people can be led to indulge in the very behaviours they had crafted laws to ban, as Sue Gray reminded us last week. Frustrated entitlement, that sense of being deprived of our rightful superior place, fuels the fires of racism and twists some to terror.

The poison of entitlement has, I believe, one known antidote: humility. Never to be confused with the humbling that follows embarrassing revelations, freely chosen humility forms an abiding attitude to life. Jesus embodied it; St Francis of Assisi exemplified it. Holy women and men of many faiths seek it. From rulers to rough sleepers, anyone – privileged or unprivileged – can, if they choose, possess it.

Chapter Four

Sex, Race and Social Change

ANNE ATKINS

Homosexuality

Anne Atkins's debut on Thought for the Day *caused a furore. The press picked up on it immediately and overnight her name was everywhere: in the newspapers, on radio and television. Not far behind was the audience reaction; it prompted over 1,000 letters and calls but, far from the general media expectation that she would incite the wrath of the public, the majority of correspondents were supportive of her stance. The steady stream of letters demonstrated a perception that many listeners were pleased that the liberals who ran the BBC had allowed an evangelical Christian to say what many listeners thought for once – expressing a traditional Christian view.*

Suffice to say within a month she was given her own Agony Aunt column on the Daily Telegraph. *But despite her best efforts to denounce homophobia early on in this* Thought, *the accusations against her stuck. In addition, the disputes over her view that ordination numbers in the Church of England were going down was robustly challenged by the Church and Richard Kirker of the Lesbian and Gay Christian Movement, though she had quite a civilised debate with the latter on* Today *the next morning. There was no doubt Anne Atkins was very firmly on the map.*

10 October 1996

An all-day celebration has been planned in Southwark Cathedral to mark the 20th anniversary of the Lesbian and Gay Christian Movement. Various churches have expressed concern but the celebration will go ahead.

I want to make one thing clear. Homophobia is reprehensible. Discriminating against people on the grounds of their sexual orientation, which they may or may not have chosen, is indefensible. It is shocking that the armed forces can dismiss an employee, not just because of what he has done, but what he might do; not because of his behaviour, but his feelings. This is like court martialling a man, not for desertion, but for being frightened before battle.

But what we do with our feelings is another matter. Nobody is condemning the Bishop of Argyll for his feelings.* He didn't break his vows when he fell in love. It was what he did afterwards that caused the rumpus. One's sexual desire and one's practice have always to stay separate.

We don't have, on record, any conversation between Jesus and a sexually active homosexual. But we know what he said to the woman caught in adultery, so we can imagine a similar scene: a group of rather self-righteous, macho people bring a gay man to our Lord. He should be stoned, they say. He was caught having sex with another man. Jesus looks at the pious mob. Fair enough, he replies: anyone who's never committed a sin can throw the first stone. They shuffle their feet, look embarrassed, move off. Now, Jesus says to the accused: go and sin no more.

One of the truest clichés of all time is that God loves the sinner but hates the sin. It's the Church's duty to love and welcome everybody, because Jesus' message is for everyone. But it's also the Church's duty to condemn sin. It's this that we're failing to do. Soon, no doubt, we'll have an Adulterer's Christian Fellowship or a Sex Before Marriage Christian Fellowship. I see no reason why the list should ever end, unless and until the Church comes back to God's standards of morality. Not that we reject those who don't keep them. But that we know, and say, what they are.

Yesterday, a report was publicised called 'Numbers in Ministry', which said that candidates for ordination in the Church of England are steadily going down. Surprise, surprise. In an age in which bishops are supporting a cathedral event celebrating 20 years of gay sex, we should hardly expect anything else. If the trumpet sounds an uncertain note, who will prepare

---

* The Roman Catholic Bishop Roddy Wright had caused a media storm earlier that year when he eloped with a divorced mother-of-three.

for battle? Sadly, the note from the Church of England today is so uncertain you'd think it was a cracked penny whistle.

REV. JOHN BELL

The love that dare not …

John Bell is a member of the Iona Community but he is also an ordained minister in the Church of Scotland. In 2008, when this script was written, all of the mainstream Christian denominations were struggling with how to cope with the divisions opening up over the traditional theological understanding of issues of sexuality: sex before marriage, cohabiting and, most divisive of all, same-sex relationships. Campaigners were beginning to force the Church to respond to calls for inclusion and fairness for all. But, for church leaders, the dilemma as they saw it of reinterpreting the New Testament remained.

John has always been a popular preacher. Driven by a heart that demands 'justice for all' he is unafraid of speaking his mind, even deliberately challenging. But he does it in a way that takes the very scriptures that seem to be the bar to change and revisits the passages. He is knowledgeable and measured in the way he writes and often surprising and arresting in his final Thought. What made this so different was that the listeners knew that a directive had been issued by the Church of Scotland forbidding its ministers to speak publicly about homosexuality until a Special Commission set up by the Church's General Assembly had had its findings discussed. John found an ingenious way to get round that. In truth, the ban was almost a gift.

18 July 2008

'Night after night on my bed, I have sought my true love.' This is not so much a personal testimony as a quotation from the Bible. It came to mind a few years ago when I was visiting a church in New Zealand where the congregation was exercised because a sex shop had opened up across the street. It had a large noticeboard which advertised items you wouldn't normally find at a Tupperware party.

In discussing this predicament with the minister, I suggested that, since the church also had a large noticeboard, it might offer alternative inducements. Hence I proposed he might put up a poster saying:

> NIGHT AFTER NIGHT ON MY BED,
> I HAVE SOUGHT MY TRUE LOVE.
> WANT TO FIND OUT MORE?
> COME TO SAINT JOHN'S AT 6:30 ON SUNDAY.

The Song of Songs, from which that quotation comes, is not a book frequently read, although it says a lot about healthy erotic sex. It is attributed to King Solomon, who certainly knew quite a bit about the subject, having entertained 700 wives and 300 concubines. Curiously, though a direct ancestor of Jesus, he is never taken as a model of good practice.

Nor is Isaac ... the son of Abraham and one of a number of biblical patriarchs with unusual dating practices. It is his father who sends a servant to find a wife for the boy. Subsequently, the servant brings back a girl called Rebecca to meet a man whom she has never seen. No sooner has Isaac met her than he takes her into his tent and beds her in consolation for the death of his mother.

I don't think I've ever been at a wedding ceremony yet where the vicar asks the groom: 'Do you come here earnestly seeking marriage to this woman because you are missing your mum?'

Nor, come to think of it, have I ever heard a minister ask a couple: 'Do you come here seeking holy matrimony because that is preferable to burning with desire?' ... yet that perspective on marriage is offered by St Paul.

It is interesting how, in matters of human sexuality, Christians feel free to pick and choose the bits that suit them. We elevate to the status of a litmus test of piety one aspect of sexuality about which the Bible is comparatively silent. (I'm sure you'll know the issue to which I'm alluding without my having to be explicit.) And yet more positive expressions, we leave alone – like seeking my true love on my bed night after night.

Ditto for the Ethiopian eunuch. He never gets much of a mention in hymns, prayers or preaching. Is it perhaps because only Scots can easily pronounce his 'condition'? At any rate, he is the first adult whose baptism is explicitly recorded in the New Testament. Even though, as a eunuch, he would have been spurned and victimised by some communities because of his 'irregular sexuality', he was embraced and totally accepted by the fragile, fledgling Church.

I wonder if that story has any bearing on the current divisive issue, the name of which I will not mention.

CLIFFORD LONGLEY

Living in sin?

In the run-up to the 2010 general election the leader of the opposition, David Cameron, promised to change the tax system so that it favoured married couples. Almost one-in-four unmarried couples break up before their child's fifth birthday, he claimed, compared to less than one-in-twelve married couples. The Liberal Democrats attacked the policy as 'patronising drivel that belongs in the Edwardian age'. Meanwhile the Labour government pointed out that the Conservatives' figures on the tax breaks didn't add up at all. David Cameron admitted he 'messed up' and reversed his promise within hours.

Thought for the Day regular Clifford Longley, a national newspaper journalist of long standing, used the affair to poke fun at the politicians. But, using his distinctive forensic skills, he identified an elephant in the room. Drawing on his decades as religious affairs editor at The Times, *and as author of a number of major reports on the relationship between church teaching and contemporary political values, he asked why the churches were so curiously silent in the debate. In this* Thought *he probes more deeply beneath the politics.*

25 January 2010

Government and opposition are currently having a bit of a marital disagreement about marriage and cohabitation – whether it's just a lifestyle choice that's nobody else's business, or whether marriage is good for you and especially for the kids, and so ought to be encouraged.

There is one surprising voice missing from this debate, and one astonishing piece of information that may explain that silence. I'm talking about the major churches, still big players in the marriage business. The issue of couples living together outside wedlock takes them a long way from their comfort zone. And the startling fact? Well, it's that four out of five people who are living together do eventually want to get married. They are not anti-marriage. It still enjoys overwhelming popular support. And the vast majority of couples arranging a wedding with their registrar or church give the same address.

Living together has become the major gateway into marriage in modern Britain. It's not an alternative so much as a rite of passage. Not long ago it used to be called 'living in sin'. The problem for the churches is that if they can't call it that any more, what can they usefully say instead? They point to the fact that marriages are statistically more stable than cohabitations. But is that a cause, or just a correlation? If living together is the more tentative arrangement, you would expect it to be, well, more tenuous. So the relative stability of marriage may just be a self-fulfilling prophecy or even a tautology, not cause and effect.

The churches still conduct about a fifth of all weddings, but it's a declining figure. Is there any connection? Probably.

If a couple expect the priest or vicar to tut-tut at their living arrangements, aren't they more likely to avoid the embarrassment by choosing a registry office or wherever they fancy – but without benefit of clergy?

The Church of England had a report some years ago which inched towards accepting pre-marital sex and cohabitation, but was roundly denounced for doing so. The Catholic Church is more open-minded than you might think, at least at parish level, but technically sex outside marriage is still a sin. Nevertheless there is a tendency to talk about common law marriage as if it still existed – it was abolished in 1754 – or to say that a couple is 'married in all but name', 'married in the sight of God' and so on.

It was only a few hundred years ago that marriage in church was made obligatory. Before that, the line between cohabitation and marriage was deliberately kept blurred. Returning to that situation might be the only way out of this impasse. If marriages are made in heaven, maybe only God knows for certain who is and who isn't. But that wouldn't give politicians their soundbites.

RABBI LIONEL BLUE

My gay life

Rabbi Lionel Blue was a very special person for all kinds of reasons but this Thought *encapsulates the kind of courage, self-giving and honesty that made his contribution to* Thought for the Day *so important. This one was a landmark moment. He had talked to the listeners about his depression before; his struggles to be comfortable with himself in his younger years; and the difficulty of coping with the fear of going to prison for his sexuality before homosexuality was decriminalised in 1967.*

But this Thought *was the first time he had talked on air about his life with his partner. In it he relishes the new openness that changed social attitudes had made possible, even when the old fears re-emerged from the shadows. And he talks about what God had taught him and his partner about spiritual love and sharing. As ever, Lionel spoke without self-pity, and with his signature humour and masses of charm. His* Thought *opened the gates for a flood of support from listeners.*

21 April 2010

Jewish jokes about gay people have become so much kinder in my lifetime. Two women meet. 'How's your son?' said the first. 'Fine,' replied the other. 'He's a specialist with rooms in Harley Street.' 'And how's your son?' 'He's a homosexual,' said the second. 'So where's his office?' replied the first.

I appreciate the new openness because I've been a gay religious bureaucrat for 40 years and it hasn't been easy. My partner and I have lived together faithfully for over 25 years and it mostly don't seem a decade too much. This morning I just want to add some overlooked aspects of our lives.

For example, there's been much discussion about straight children adopted by gay parents. There may be different views on this, but at least such things are talked about in the open now. My situation wasn't exactly comparable being the gay youngster of straight parents but it was in an overwhelmingly straight society when aspects of homosexuality were still illegal. I still remember the burden of furtiveness, the fear of blackmail that destroyed steady relationships. Many young people had breakdowns. Some tried suicide. I tried myself. One cleric threw me out. Another told me to go abroad. But young people now, thank God, get a better reception, though in some countries life imprisonment and execution might be returning as in grim Hitler–Stalin days.

So why bother about religion? Because though religion has a lot to learn about sex and gender, it taught me a lot about spiritual love and that sex isn't the purpose of our life on earth. Also gay people have their own spiritual needs. I needed a lot of

God to transform friends into a family and a house into a home. Also same-sex relationships were a more complex fit socially and psychologically, and spirituality and laughter helped.

Other problems come with age. Which care homes would accept our derby-and-derby situation? Is there room for us at the inn? Would civil partnership be easier for the survivor? We don't want to be excluded from each other's funerals, as often happened.

The first step forward is simple but needs God-given courage. The sharing of each other's life experience and truth, whether gay or straight, in the presence of God without dismissive putdowns or passing the buck.

Humour would help a lot. Two ancients sit in their car, holding hands and gazing sleepily at the sea. 'We ought to get civilly partnered you know,' said one slowly. 'But who would want us now?' moaned the other despairingly. God would! He enjoys his oddballs and their healing laughter.

CATHERINE PEPINSTER

Sex abuse and silence

In 2001 the Dean of the Vatican's Congregation for the Doctrine of the Faith wrote two letters in Latin – one instructing that both be kept secret – to every Catholic bishop in the world instructing them to send him all their files on allegations of child sex abuse in their area. The Dean was Cardinal Joseph Ratzinger, who later became Pope Benedict XVI. Behind the scenes he began zealously trying to clean up what he privately called 'the filth'. But in public the Catholic Church worldwide maintained an unforgiveable silence on the subject.

Catherine Pepinster is one of Britain's leading Catholic journalists. The sex-abuse scandal gravely disturbed her throughout her 12 years as editor of the Catholic weekly, The Tablet *– for which she continues still* *to write about the abuse topic. Not long before she wrote this* Thought, *Pope Benedict had castigated the bishops in Ireland for 'grave errors of judgement' in their handling of the paedophilia scandal. But his words were immediately undermined by the refusal of the Pope's ambassador in Ireland to appear before a parliamentary inquiry into the issue. Catherine in this* Thought *articulated the response of many ordinary Catholics in the pew.*

26 July 2010

Earlier this week I was fortunate to be able to visit St Walburge's, one of the most magnificent Catholic churches in the country. These days St Walburge's is open infrequently for most of the houses that once surrounded it have been demolished and the population has moved elsewhere. But as I looked around this stunning Grade I listed church in Preston, I was aware of what I can only describe as its prayerful silence and the thousands upon thousands of ordinary people who'd prayed there over the years. It's a quiet that offers a balance and a wellbeing that you only get when, as Cardinal John Henry Newman put it, the busy world is hushed and the fever of life is cast aside.

Many people find such peacefulness incredibly appealing. The maker of a new film about the nuns of Tyburn Convent, for instance, says that he has incorporated into his day an hour's quiet after he saw how the sisters lived with silence forming such a large part of their time.

But there is another kind of silence that has also existed in the Catholic Church – a deeply damaging silence – which meant that sex abuse of children by priests was kept hidden away. When courageous victims tried to speak out, they were ignored or even punished. Claim after claim tells of bishops responsible for abusive priests moving them around and doing little to help the victims.

Accusation upon accusation has led to an unprecedented apology from Pope Benedict to the people of Ireland in which he expressed shame and remorse for what has happened. But for many it was still not enough.

Tomorrow Catholics attending Mass on Palm Sunday will hear Luke's gospel story of Jesus' entry into Jerusalem on a donkey. As the crowd shouts in acclaim, the Pharisees tell him to silence his followers. But Christ says: 'I tell you, if these keep silence the very stones will cry out.'

Now it seems as if the very stones are crying out about child abuse. The damaging silence has been swept aside; the truth must be spoken.

Next week is the most solemn week of the Christian calendar as people recall the crucifixion of Christ, and the harm done by this kind of silence will be on many Catholics' minds.

We know that many of the child-abuse cases date from years ago and changes, especially in Britain, have successfully been made to improve child protection in the Church, work with the police and keep clearer records.

Yet ordinary Catholics like me are still angry, still ashamed, and still broken-hearted. In that other silence, the prayerful time of Mass, we will be wondering what can be done to heal the victims, and yes, heal our Church too.

BISHOP LORD RICHARD HARRIES

Civil partnerships inside church

The first civil partnership between a same-sex couple took place in 2005. Lawmakers had deliberately avoided calling it a marriage because of a long history of opposition from many religious groups intent on preserving a traditional heterosexual view of marriage. Legislators also ruled that civil partnerships could not take place on religious premises. But then, in 2011, the government announced the intention to lift this ban. Religious conservatives mounted a new rearguard action to prevent it – as did the Catholic Church, the Church of England and the Evangelical Alliance.

As Bishop of Oxford, Richard Harries had long been one of the more liberal voices on the bench of bishops. After he retired in 2006 he was made a life peer and as Lord Harries of Pentregarth spoke often in the House of Lords where his voice was frequently raised on issues of fairness and social justice. When conservative Christians tried – unsuccessfully – to block the government's decision to lift the ban on same-sex partnerships in churches, Bishop Richard spoke out clearly on the side of equality in this Thought *the following morning.*

16 December 2011

I once paid a pastoral visit to some almshouses, in one of which a retired clergyman was living. I didn't know anything about him, so when I knocked on the door to say hello, I was reluctant to say: 'Are you married or on your own?' so slightly tongue in the cheek I said: 'Do you have a partner?' 'Oh, Bishop', he replied, 'has it come to this?'

In fact, partner is rather a good word. It implies a close, collaborative and mutually supportive relationship, and it is good that people are now able to register them as civil partnerships if this is what they want. Yesterday the House of Lords was packed for a long debate on new regulations which allow such civil partnerships to be registered on religious premises if, but only if, the church in question has chosen to allow them.

The idea of people of the same sex in a deep relationship for which they feel grateful to God is not such a new idea as people think. There is a memorial in the chapel of Gonville and Caius College in Cambridge, erected for a Thomas Legge in the seventeenth century by his friend John Gostlin, which shows a heart of flames held aloft by two hands and the words below 'Love joined them in living. So may the earth join them in their burial. O Legge, Gostlin's heart you have still with you.' That is just one of a number of such memorials that show such sentiments.

The great Cardinal Newman, for example insisted on being buried in the same grave as his great friend Ambrose St John. He described this as 'My last, my imperative will. This I confirm and insist on.'

It is of course a mistake to understand Newman's relationship and others in twentieth-century terms – for through twenty-first-century eyes everything is likely to be seen as saturated with sex. What is not in doubt is that [until the fourteenth century] there used to be an elaborate church ceremony for what the Greeks called *adelphopoiesis*, which literally means 'making brothers' but which some have chosen to translate as 'same-sex unions'.

This is of course a very divisive issue for the churches, and yesterday the focus of the debate was whether there is enough protection for those churches which have theological objections to allowing their premises to be used to register civil partnerships. The clear mood of the House was that there was such protection.

So those churches and synagogues that do want to hold such ceremonies will be allowed to, and those who don't want to won't be forced to. Everyone can act according to their conscience within the law. And even more, for those who want to commit themselves to one another before God, there will be gratitude that this is now possible.

CARDINAL VINCENT NICHOLS

Human trafficking

One of the most hidden yet burgeoning crimes against human beings is trafficking. The desperate plight of men, women and children traded across the world is growing in the public consciousness. The issue had been put in the spotlight in spring 2014 when Cardinal Vincent Nichols, the Catholic Archbishop of Westminster, organised and chaired a two-day modern slavery conference in the Vatican. It showcased a joint initiative between the police and the Church that had begun in London three years earlier.

The conference had the support of Pope Francis, which was of vital importance in promoting similar schemes across the world. The gathering was attended by the then home secretary, Theresa May, and the commissioner of the Metropolitan Police, who heard the Pope describe trafficking as 'a crime against humanity'. The profile of the work, and the enormity of the damage done to real lives, made it an excellent subject for a Good Friday Thought for the Day *by Cardinal Nichols.*

18 April 2014

Today Christians throughout the world will come together to venerate the cross of Jesus Christ. The figure of the crucified Jesus will be held aloft, carried in procession, touched and kissed with loving devotion. Today we have eyes for the suffering he bore, the wounds inflicted on his body.

As I prepare for the church services of this Good Friday, the words of two popes spring to mind. Standing just outside St George's Cathedral Southwark in 1982, Pope John Paul II said that the cross of Jesus represented the suffering of all humanity, 'from the first Adam to today'. In contemplating the suffering of Christ, then, I open my heart to the suffering of every person today.

Last week Pope Francis spoke with equal candour at a conference against human trafficking in the Vatican. Organised by the Bishops' Conference of England and Wales, the conference brought together police chiefs from across the world, including our own commissioner of the Metropolitan Police Sir Bernard Hogan-Howe and also the home secretary, Theresa May.

They came together to work out what practical steps could be taken towards the eradication of human trafficking throughout the world. The model which was on offer to the conference was an initiative in London in which the police and the Church have been working together for the past three years.

We heard the harrowing stories of victims from different countries. Women described in moving testimony their cruel treatment and the fear with which they lived. Delegates from the law enforcement agencies and the Church listened – in order to understand how best to build an active network to combat trafficking by working collaboratively.

Pope Francis spoke of the crime of human trafficking – slavery in modern dress – as a terrible 'wound in the body of Christ'. He appealed in the strongest terms that this trade in which children, women and men are bought and sold as if they were no more than commercial goods, be halted. 'Enough!' he cried.

Then he said these words: 'Humanity still hasn't learnt how to cry, how to lament. We need many tears in order to understand the dimension of this drama.' He was asking us to cry!

Good Friday, today, is the day on which Christians learn again to shed tears of compassion, tears for our crucified saviour, tears for every victim of abuse, tears for the destitution of so many in the world today, tears of shame and anger at the slavery that disfigures our modern world. They are tears which should be shed as, together, we all resolve each to play our part in the healing of our wounded world.

TIM STANLEY

Pope Francis, condoms and AIDS

On the eve of World AIDS Day in 2015 Pope Francis was asked if the Catholic Church would drop its opposition to the use of condoms in the fight against AIDS. The Pope had just visited an AIDS hospital in Uganda where he had kissed the HIV-infected children. Reporters were probably hoping that Francis would go further than his predecessor Benedict XVI, who said that using a condom can represent a step in the right direction where it shows concern for the other person. Instead, Francis told them they were asking the wrong question.

In his Thoughts, *Tim Stanley regularly talks with passion about the importance to him of his own faith journey. He has written of being raised as 'a good Baptist boy', before becoming an Anglican and then converting to Catholicism. He has been open to change in his politics too. After being chair of Cambridge University Labour Club he voted Conservative for the first time in 2017 and became a strong supporter of Brexit. In this* Thought, *Tim agrees that journalists were indeed asking the Pope the wrong question. What they should have been asking was why Francis kept talking about mercy – and the importance of the Pope's shift away from command towards compassion.*

3 December 2015

Pope Francis is in trouble again. Flying back from his tour of Africa he was asked by a journalist about the role of contraception in tackling AIDS. The Church, of course, condemns the use of condoms. His Holiness appeared to dodge the question – talking instead about poverty and war. The translators of papal equivocation pounced. Conservative Catholics said he'd practically endorsed condom use; liberals described his vagueness as 'shameful'.

In the midst of this controversy it was forgotten that the Catholic Church is the largest private provider of care to HIV patients in the world. Now you might think: 'What good is that? It is Church teaching that discourages contraception and if the Pope really wants to help he should change it.'

But the Pope isn't going to do that because, well, he can't: he does not have the power to rewrite dogma. Nor does he probably want to – because Francis has different priorities from those of his critics; priorities tied to mercy. Francis made a point of visiting HIV-infected children in hospital while he was in Uganda, and kissing each one of them. He tries to embody the spirit of St

Francis: a friar who put himself down among the poor and the sick, to let them know that their agony is shared. The change that this Pope is bringing to the Church is therefore a shift in rhetorical emphasis – from commandment to compassion.

To that effect, he's designated the coming year as a Year of Mercy. What do Catholics mean by 'mercy'? Well, one aspect is telling someone if they're making a mistake. But there's little point endlessly condemning people for their sins: shame rarely saves anyone. It is better – and more merciful – to show people that there is a road back. And that they won't make the journey alone.

I speak from personal experience. I converted to Catholicism ten years ago and one of its most appealing qualities was the practical, tangible nature of its forgiveness. I sinned, so I went to confession, admitted what I'd done and honestly tried to atone. Some compare the feeling to having brushed one's teeth clean. Certainly it is a necessary, human thing to unburden oneself of guilt – and faith offers a solution like no other on the market. Tell your troubles to a priest and he'll tell you that you are loved.

Finally, there is the kind of mercy that puts food in bellies and offers refuge from the storm – no questions asked, no strings attached. That's the mercy of the Good Samaritan, who stopped to help an unfortunate soul from a different tribe. That's the compassion this hands-on Pope wants us to show the poor around the world in this difficult time. As Francis has said, they are in need of our mercy now more than ever.

CANON DR GILES FRASER

Puritanism and *The Handmaid's Tale*

When the Anglican priest Giles Fraser joined the Thought for the Day *rota he cut through from the outset. That is in large part because his style is upfront, warm and unashamedly honest. He was Vicar of Putney when he started, then moved to St Paul's Cathedral as Canon Chancellor but after a difference of opinion – over the handling of the Occupy movement's encampment on the steps of St Paul's – he resigned and took over as priest-in-charge, St Mary Newington, for the next ten years. He recently moved to St Anne's in the parish of Kew.*

He has therefore served some of the most advantaged and the most disadvantaged congregations across London. It gives him rare insights into many worldviews and when you add to that his background in philosophy, his innovative theological mind and his combative journalism, it's not hard to see why Giles can take a small part of something happening in the news and add layer upon layer of thought-provoking ideas to it. This Thought *was prompted by a heavily advertised start to the new dystopian drama,* The Handmaid's Tale, *that, even in the trailer, looked as intriguing as it did unnerving.*

29 May 2017

You don't have to look very hard to find some pretty disturbing stories in the Bible. Take this one from the Book of Genesis.

Rachel cannot conceive, so she invites her husband Jacob to have sex with her handmaid Bilhah instead, in order that they might have a child through her. Bilhah falls pregnant and gives birth to a son – and then is forced to hand the baby over to Rachel and Jacob, for them to bring him up as their own. The Bible does not record what Bilhah thought of this arrangement. But 30 years ago, the novelist Margaret Atwood did. And her bestselling book *The Handmaid's Tale* began its serialisation on Channel 4 last night.

And powerful stuff it was too. *The Handmaid's Tale* describes a fundamentalist Puritan sect called the Sons of Jacob taking control of the United States of America and forcing women into reproductive slavery. In this Republic of Gilead – a reference to the hill country where Jacob once camped – women are forced to wear modest Puritan-style clothing, and take the blame for inviting any unwanted sexual attention. And the sexual violence inflicted on the Handmaid, imagined within the context of a religious ceremony, includes one of the most disturbing scenes that I have ever seen on television. This is clearly how Atwood imagines what happened to Bilhah in the Book of Genesis.

The Handmaid's Tale makes for uncomfortable watching, not least because, as a number of commentators have pointed out, these days it doesn't feel as much like fiction as one would hope.

But however much I think it important for Christians and Jews to witness dystopian versions of their own scriptures – and to acknowledge the bigotry and fanaticism that has been inspired by them – I nonetheless take issue with Atwood's familiar portrayal of Puritanism. And here I'd like to bring in another novelist of Atwood's generation, the excellent Marilynne Robinson, who has long sought to rescue Puritanism from its association with life-denying moralism, not least in her remarkable novel, also called *Gilead*. For Robinson, the point about the central Puritan claim that we are all sinners is not that it writes off human beings as worthless and disgusting, but quite the opposite – that it gives us grounds to treat each other with forgiveness and understanding. That's why the idea that all human beings are sinners 'is kindlier than any expectation that we might be saints', she insists.

Robinson also reminds us of the considerable role that Puritans had in the formation of American democracy. Having fled a totalitarian regime in England, it was the Puritans of New England that first formulated the proto-democratic political principles that became the United States of America. This is why I'm not entirely convinced by Atwood's warning that Puritans could become a threat to the values of the United States. Because Puritans were largely responsible for those values in the first place.

REV. DR SAM WELLS

Taking the knee

'Taking the knee' exploded in the public consciousness when the blatant racism on the streets of America prompted a prominent athlete to use his fame to draw attention to the injustices affecting black people. There was indignation and criticism, alongside praise and support. But whatever the range of views, it provoked a movement. However, in all the news coverage no one made the point about the religious significance of the gesture – mostly because in a secular news culture there's not necessarily the expertise to unpack it.

Sam Wells, vicar of St Martin-in-the-Fields, is used to preaching from one of the most famous pulpits in London but he also has a strong reputation in America where he worked in South Carolina for seven years before he and his family returned to Britain in 2012. In this script – a big story with wall-to-wall coverage – he did brilliantly what the slot does at its best. He offered a profound and powerful theological and social/ethical view to make a point you wouldn't have heard elsewhere. And that feels added value for the Today *audience.*

25 September 2017

Before a pre-season American football game a year ago, the San Francisco 49ers quarterback Colin Kaepernick refused to stand for the national anthem. He said, 'I'm not going to stand up to show pride in a flag for a country that oppresses black people and people of colour.' The gesture brought the Black Lives Matter movement into the hallowed presence of the national anthem and flag. This last weekend over a hundred black and white elite players knelt in protest when the Stars and Stripes were raised and 'The Star-Spangled Banner' rang out.

'Taking the knee' highlights many racial ironies in America. Colin Kaepernick, before he was frozen out of the sport, was highly paid; but historically sports, the military and the church have tended to be the only routes to prominence for African Americans, since, in Kaepernick's words, 'America invests more in its prison system than its education system'. The founding story of America is that people fled persecution in Europe to find freedom in the New World. But the black story is the opposite: people were deprived of their freedom in Africa to be dragged to slavery in the Land of the Free. It's also ironic that taking the knee is being portrayed as insulting to US troops, since African American soldiers have long died in disproportionate numbers to defend a country that gave them so little.

Kaepernick was baptised Methodist, confirmed Lutheran, and attends a Baptist church. When he knelt in complaint, he was taking the devotional practice of private prayer and making it a public statement of political protest. He was saying Christianity isn't simply about personal piety and individual salvation: it's about portraying a new society and organising communities to advance that vision.

Colin Kaepernick didn't invent the iconic politico-religious gesture. On the first Palm Sunday Jesus rode into Jerusalem, imitating the triumphal march of the Roman conquerors but mocking it by choosing a donkey for his steed. 'Who could be threatened by a man on a donkey?' you'd think. But they were. Taking the knee is a gesture of genius, because how could kneeling before flag and anthem be anything other than respectful of the values on which America believes itself to be founded? It's the fact that kneeling in submission is exactly what African Americans had to do as slaves for 300 years that makes the gesture prophetic and poignant.

Taking the knee is a breath-taking gesture because it says, 'You've made us subservient despite the higher values you say our country is founded on. Now let's see those higher values.' Wouldn't it be wonderful if whenever we want to express hurt, protest and nonviolent witness, it became conventional to take the knee?

DR CHETNA KANG

Sexual and spiritual intimacy

When Dr Chetna Kang joined Thought *for the Day she was a very welcome addition to the contributor rota as she is both a practising psychiatrist and our first Hindu woman. She is a priest in the bhakti yoga tradition who wrote: 'If you ask three Hindus what Hinduism is, you will get three completely different answers.' In fact, she explained, it's a shorthand for followers of the body of books called the Vedas, which were written around 5,000 years ago by Vedavyas, who was said to be an incarnation of God. Within modern Hinduism, bhakti yoga is one of the main paths towards spiritual fulfilment, combining all types of yoga, processes of inner development and external practices such as pilgrimage.*

Chetna's professional life also offered Thought *a new dimension. As a psychiatrist she has for over 20 years been diagnosing and treating mental health problems. She is passionate about raising awareness around mental health and working to reduce stigma. Dr Kang is on the executive committee of the Spirituality and Psychiatry Special Interest Group of the Royal College of Psychiatrists. In this* Thought *she looks at the oversexualisation of our society and explains why Hinduism values an intimacy that can be just as important as sex.*

22 September 2018

I was interested to read a recent BBC news article about three couples in long-term relationships who were not sexually intimate. Their reasons were varied, and entirely reasonable. It made me think how often the media is saturated with imagery and articles focused on stimulating our sexual appetite, but this article raised the very real question of how can we connect with our partners more deeply.

Within Hinduism it is commonly known that yogis, priests and monks practise celibacy as a stepping stone to spiritual enlightenment. The aim is that by controlling your senses you are giving yourselves a greater opportunity to focus on the inner self rather than connecting with the parts of ourselves that the world sees. What's less commonly known is that, although the Vedas don't discourage physical intimacy, it should not be seen as the primary way to connect with your spouse. Being able to connect in a way where you view yourselves as partners on a spiritual journey can be just as spiritually fulfilling as being a celibate monk.

Hindu saint Rupa Goswami speaks about the science of relationships in general and he gives a formula of six loving exchanges. Two out of the six deal with revealing your mind in confidence and listening respectfully and attentively to the other. While the topic of conversation may vary, the purpose is what he is more instructive about. He guides his followers to have an attitude whereby, whether they are talking about household chores, their fears and desires or even deep devotional topics, the aim is to be of service to the other, to create more love within themselves, between each other and with God. These may seem like very simple tools but, for Goswami, they are a timeless and effective way of bringing life back into our relationships.

If we can make more time to connect with each other through this type of dialogue, I believe we can become less reliant on what often feels like a purely physical need but is one of the many ways our inner core is crying out for connection. And I think that being in a romantic relationship with someone doesn't just have to be about a physical and psychological union, but can also be a catalyst for moral and spiritual growth.

RABBI LAURA JANNER-KLAUSNER

My transgender child

As the former senior rabbi to Reform Judaism, Laura Janner-Klausner was very used to teaching and preaching to her congregations in London and speaking to different groups, including women's organisations, outside of her own faith community. Her multi-faith work with Muslim women is well known.

In this brave and very personal Thought, *Laura chose to enter into a subject that has become almost toxic in the hothouse atmosphere of social media particularly, but the wider media more generally. The subject of transgender had become so sensitive and febrile that it was hard to express a view, make a comment or even ask a question to learn more about the issue. Individuals such as J.K. Rowling were publicly vilified and even organisations, such as Stonewall, with a track record in campaigning for LGBTQ+ rights, came in for criticism.*

Laura Janner-Klausner wanted to inject some balm into the situation by taking the bold step of talking about her own family situation – and her own non-binary child, Tal, now 27. Laura hides nothing of the turmoil for herself along the way, but she is open, explanatory and encouraging of us all to reach out and seek the information that will help with understanding. That's surely why so many people made contact after the broadcast to praise her courage. It felt a seminal moment for Thought for the Day.

9 October 2018

When I was just 14 weeks pregnant, the ultrasound sonographer concluded that our eldest child was a girl. At birth, we gave her an Israeli girl's name, Tali. Tali's body indicated that she was a girl but her mind, heart and soul were not female, and are not.

Now, as a 27-year-old, her pronoun is not 'she' or 'he' but 'they'. Tali is now Tal – a unisex Israeli name and they do not identify either as a woman nor as a man but as a person whose gender is non-binary.

As I responded this week to the public consultation on the Gender Recognition Act for England and Wales, I was tearful. My tears were tears of protection, loss but also pride. This consultation closes next week and it revisits the 2004 Act which enabled basic rights for trans people. It considers how to make the process of gender recognition less bureaucratic and invasive, and how to include broader definitions of gender.

Our views of gender are influenced by deep-rooted cultural and religious assumptions. Jews tend to read the Creation story through a gender-binary prism – God made a man and then a woman. But my colleague, student rabbi Lev Taylor, points to rabbinic interpretations that overturn these assumptions. It's unclear that Adam was the first man – as the Hebrew word 'Adam' acts as a noun, not a name. It's from *adamah*, meaning earth. Adam was an 'earthling'. Another interpretation of the Hebrew text suggests that the original human being had one body with two sets of genitalia and two faces, a type of 'primordial androgyne'.

We do not live in a sterile paradise, in the Garden of Eden. We live in a delightfully messy reality in which our curiosity is the real Tree of Knowledge. However, this curiosity has become risky as some of the public discussion on the Gender Recognition Act is so fierce that many people are too scared to debate it for fear of a fiery backlash.

Asking questions does not mean you are transphobic but that you may not understand definitions and experiences that are totally new to you. While the anger and fear felt by trans and gender non-binary people is understandable due to years of persecution and exclusion, it's legitimate to be curious, uncertain, ambivalent or disagree with this legislation.

When Tali, now Tal, was born they were so beautiful that as I wheeled them down the hospital corridor, people looked at us and asked: 'Is she really yours'? Yes, she was beautiful and they're still beautiful and handsome and they're still mine.

We're so blessed by having a trans child.

REV. LUCY WINKETT

25 years of women priests

Lucy Winkett was one of the first generation of women to be ordained a priest in the Church of England and she was the first woman to be Canon Precentor of St Paul's Cathedral. She is a trailblazer without a doubt. In person, she is also welcoming, calm and thought-through. She listens better than most and is full of ideas, which is perfect for the days when there is no obvious subject for the next day's Thought for the Day.

This one was an anniversary, so the subject was a given for that day, but it was also a special landmark for Lucy personally. It was about marking the journey for the women who became priests that day, but it was also honouring all those who had walked with them through the long years of waiting.

Over the last 25 years there have been obstacles and negative attitudes to deal with, but after 20 of those years the first female bishop was announced following a historic change to canon law. Little by little women clergy began to receive the praise and profile they deserve. But there is more to do and Lucy is co-founder of 'Leading Women', a national development programme for women clergy. Yet, typically, the overriding mix Lucy achieves on this day is joy, gratitude and excitement about the future. Bring it on.

12 March 2019

Twenty-five years ago today, the first women were ordained priests in the Church of England. After decades of waiting, hoping, pressing for women to be able to follow their calling, and looking for ways to address the concerns of those who disagreed, it happened.

Not long after my ordination, I was standing at the altar, celebrating communion under the dome at St Paul's Cathedral in London, in the middle of the day with hundreds of people in the building. A man stood looking at me intently for some time before he asked one of the cathedral staff: 'Why is that priest speaking in a woman's voice?' For him, it was simply not possible to have a person who was both a priest and a woman. Something didn't compute. Wasn't imaginable.

In the Gospel of John, Jesus says to one of his closest disciples, Mary Magdalene: 'Go and tell my brothers that you have seen me.' He asks her to be the sole bearer of life-changing resurrection news as a witness directly to his male followers. In contrast, elsewhere in the New Testament, St Paul wrote in a letter: 'I do not permit a woman to teach a man.' My answer to Paul has always been respectfully – well, Jesus did. This isn't just about ordaining women in a society where the majority of people live their lives without reference to church. It's about the possibilities of women being bearers of new truth in society too, learning to be courageous speakers even – to a predominantly male establishment when they think they won't be believed.

And so I say: what an immense blessing to be alive in this generation. But I also want to say Yes to the spirit of adventure that such a fundamental change can release.

For me, this creative future will mean being an ever-more compassionate Church served by many more priests from minority ethnic backgrounds; served by many more priests who are free to express their love for their beloved, whoever they are. Many more priests, women and men – energetic and curious, willing, like Mary Magdalene, to hear new truth, ready to speak up and be counted as she was. And that this sacrificial priesthood is offered as a gift to a society increasingly unfamiliar with the Christian story.

And so on this anniversary, remembering the creativity and courage that it represents, I want to say in solidarity: Me Too. And with high expectation: what's next?

JAYNE OZANNE

The living hell of 'conversion therapy'

In 2003 the Today *programme started what has become a yearly ritual of inviting guest editors to make the editorial decisions for one of the programmes between Christmas and New Year. On occasions an editor would ask for a* Thought for the Day *from a particular person from the rota, or for a different voice altogether. In 2019 Grayson Perry was guest editor for Boxing Day so I asked Jayne Ozanne to do* Thought. *Jayne is an evangelical Anglican who had set up the Ozanne Foundation in 2017 to actively promote the full inclusion of LGBTI people in the Church. It aims to eliminate discrimination based on sexuality or gender – and embrace and celebrate the equality and diversity of all.*

Having herself suffered the horrendous experience of being put through 'conversion therapy', Jayne then founded the Ban Conversion Therapy Coalition – to work to safeguard LGBT+ people from abuse. Conversion therapy has now been condemned around the world and banned already in seven countries. In July 2017 she persuaded the Church of England to call on the UK government to ban it, and in 2019 she presented Pope Francis with the evidence of the harm caused by conversion therapy. A passionate campaigner for her cause, her Thought *was neither hectoring nor tub-thumping, but personal, honest, and rooted in the love that her faith tells her is at the core of everything.*

26 December 2019

How good was your Christmas cracker joke this year? Mine normally just leaves me groaning, even if they're written by friends, such as this year's: 'How many vicars does it take to change a lightbulb?' To which the answer of course is: 'Change?!!' You see, we all find change difficult.

When I was a management consultant, I used to explain that the two main drivers of change are always 'passion' and 'pain'. People change either because they have no option to, as the pain they are enduring is just too great, or because their desire (or passion) for something better is so strong.

Passion and pain. Passion is always preferable, although sadly it is usually pain that ultimately spurs us into action.

I know this to be true in my own case – where the mental anguish of trying to square the impossible circle of wanting to love and be loved by another woman, which I thought was totally unacceptable in the eyes of God, nearly cost me my life.

My story of the pain I endured is echoed by so many others who have found themselves trapped between their religious beliefs and their intrinsic human desire to love and be loved. Indeed, this 'living hell' originally drove me to seek out conversion therapy, involving yet more pain and trauma – and resulting, of course, in no change, save to my ever-diminishing levels of hope.

Finally, faced I felt with no other option, I took what has to be one of the most difficult decisions in my life – I dared to believe that whoever I chose to love, God would continue to love me – for that is the meaning of unconditional love. Love with no caveats or exception clauses. I allowed myself to love and be loved, and the impact of that love was transformational.

While I acknowledge that people have different theological positions on this, I know from experience that changing one's religious view is possible and is usually due to a revelation made through love.

One person who has spoken powerfully about changing her views is Megan Phelps-Roper, who was once part of an American Church that condemns homosexuals.

In explaining what helped her most, Megan shares that it was the kind and patient interactions of the people that she met on social media. Surprising as this may seem, Megan says: 'They did not abandon their principles, just their scorn' – proof, if we ever needed it, that the best way to help someone change is always through loving engagement rather than angry or painful exchanges.

For love changes everything.

JULIE SIDDIQI

Things some people would rather I didn't say

The debut album of the Welsh singer Duffy was the bestselling album in the United Kingdom in 2008. Rockferry, *and the hit single 'Mercy', won her a Grammy, three Brit Awards and brought her worldwide attention. But in 2011 she virtually vanished from the music scene. Nine years later she explained why. She had been drugged at a restaurant on her birthday, taken to a foreign country on a plane, and was then held captive in a hotel room and raped.*

Her story was made public just as a group of Muslim, Christian and Jewish women were about to launch a Faith and Violence Against Women Coalition. The two events came together for Julie Siddiqi, an insightful critic of society's tendency to minimise the voices of women – something the coalition was seeking to address by focusing on the experience of survivors of abuse inside Britain's religious communities. After her stint as Executive Director of the Islamic Society of Britain, Julie set up a group called Together We Thrive, which brings together Muslim women from all backgrounds to build resilience and change. Here she bravely speaks out on an issue about which many Muslim men would prefer she remained silent.

27 February 2020

The pop singer, Duffy, chose to speak out this week about an ordeal that she says kept her from being in the public eye in recent years. She shared how important it was that a journalist listened to her last summer, as she told her story for the first time.

Listening to women, hearing their stories, being there for them – these are crucial and so needed.

As someone who does a lot of work with different faith communities, particularly with women, I have realised the power and benefit of standing together. It is also important to work with men – allies who can walk with us, support the work and call things out where necessary.

Speaking up, speaking out about sensitive and challenging issues, is hard. Faith communities struggle to hear truths that can shatter illusions of all being OK and in order. When I say, for example, that one third of mosques in Britain don't have a space for women to pray, some people would rather I didn't say it.

I do understand the concern of those in Muslim communities who worry about stereotypes and myths that these truths may reinforce. But I also know that unless we speak out, unless we are willing to confront these difficult realities, things will never change, and I am convinced that we can gain more respect, not less, when we tell the truth and are more upfront. We must not let our worry for what others might think always stop us from challenging the status quo. There are some helpful and collaborative conversations happening with Muslim men in parts of the community too and that is encouraging to see.

In the Quran, Muslims are taught that we must be 'steadfast upholders of justice, witnesses to the truth for the sake of God, even if is against ourselves, our parents or our relatives'. And when I speak to women in different faith communities, there are many stories to tell – of domestic and spiritual abuse; lack of women in leadership positions; misuse of scripture to reconfirm patriarchal norms; and powerful and brave women in our history written out or marginalised. Conversations between women from the various faith communities quickly start to uncover these similarities.

Next week a conference is taking place in London to launch a new Faith and Violence Against Women Coalition – initiatives like these are positive and necessary and will bring about change. I've found that my friendships and connections with women of other faiths are a source of encouragement and give me great strength to speak up.

It's hard, if not impossible, for anyone to do that as an isolated voice. Together we really are stronger and together we can thrive.

PROFESSOR ROBERT BECKFORD

My mum, my dad and the metalwork teacher

Robert Beckford was born to Jamaican parents in Northampton and raised in a Black Pentecostal church. But it was his white middle-class RE teacher, he says, who sowed the seeds in him to think about religion and culture. And his maths teacher, who was an ardent communist, introduced him to politics and the work of the black empowerment leader Malcolm X. But the young Robert was not so fortunate in his metalwork teacher, as he relates in this Thought.

Four decades on from those schooldays the intersection between religion, race, culture and politics still provides the central focus for his career. As an activist scholar he works across disciplines – as an academic theologian, filmmaker and musical innovator. The titles of a few of his works – Jesus is Dread, God and the Gangs, Jesus Dub, Is God a White Racist? *and* God Is Black *– give a clear indication that his metalwork teacher did not have the final word.*

9 June 2021

A school teacher racially abused me in the first year of secondary school. My parents' response to the incident taught me a great deal about how Christians respond to discrimination.

It was 1976. In my first metalwork class, my schoolmates and I, barely out of primary school, were introduced to our first project. I struggled with the design phase and so, like any enquiring school-boy, raised my hand to signal that I needed help. My teacher responded with a startling comment. He said: 'If you don't get this right, I will put you on a banana boat back to Jamaica.'

I was shocked. Some of my classmates were equally stunned, but others laughed out of a sense of pre-pubescent embarrass-ment. After school, at home, I rehearsed the incident for my parents. They were dismayed but had contrasting responses to my predicament.

My mother, a deeply spiritual woman of prayer, declared she was going 'to talk to Jesus'. This turn of phrase was code for intercessory prayer. Like the German theologian Dorothee Sölle, my mother understood prayer to be an act of protest to God against injustice. In contrast, my father was more of a liberation theologian, and therefore visible direct action in the earthly realm preceded any form of spiritual reflection. He told me he was going to 'talk' to my metalwork teacher.

The recent booing of the England football team by some of their fans – for their anti-racism gesture of taking the knee – along with the reporting of the England and Wales Cricket Board's investigation into players' historic racist and sexist tweets – took me back to the events of 1976, and the question of how to respond to racism.

Should we protest in private or public, in prayer or direct action? Much depends on how we view racism. Is it a personal difficulty to overcome or a human catastrophe visited for far too long on black and brown people? For my father, it was the latter: racism was a great human suffering which he had to confront unequivocally.

Now, I don't know what my father said to the teacher, but I can say that my classmates and I never experienced any form of verbal discrimination again. I am not saying my mother's prayers didn't count in some way, but in the young minds of my schoolmates and I, my Jamaican father's resistance set the standard for confronting discrimination.

PROFESSOR JAGBIR JHUTTI-JOHAL

Violence against women

Professor Jagbir Jhutti-Johal OBE is the first female Sikh contributor on the Thought for the Day *rota and it's been really good to have her on board. A senior lecturer in Sikh studies at the University of Birmingham – the first British university to have a course on Sikhism – she has much enjoyed speaking to the wider* Today *audience on the subjects she works with academically in the Edward Cadbury Centre for the Public Understanding of Religion.*

As an academic her teaching and research focuses on Sikh theology, inter-faith dialogue and the Sikh diaspora, nationally and globally. She also sits on the board of the European Society for Intercultural Theology and Interreligious Studies. But her particular focus on Thought *has been in exploring gender inequality. The Sikh Gurus taught that men and women are equal, and should be treated as such, but, as she courageously explains in this* Thought, *discrimination and injustice towards women have not been eradicated in the Sikh community – nor in wider British society. And in many parts of the world it is accompanied by violence too.*

1 September 2021

This week, I was horrified to read that every year 12,000 women are abducted and forced into marriage in Kyrgyzstan. Men kidnap women to avoid courtship and save the payment of the *kalym,* or dowry, which can cost a groom up to £3,000 in cash and livestock. Fleeing brides, like Aizada Kanatbekova, risk further violence and even death. In Afghanistan, it's reported that the

Taliban have asked women to stay at home because 'Our security forces are not trained [in] how to deal with women – how to speak to women and how not to harm or harass women.' They are now prisoners in their homes and there are reports in the British press and elsewhere of Afghan women and young girls being forced to marry Taliban fighters.

Discrimination against women often starts in the womb. This month research was published outlining how countries from South-east Europe to South and East Asia have a skewed sex ratio at birth, and how we are set, worldwide, through pre-natal sex selection to 'lose' another 4.7 million girls by 2030, mainly because of a cultural preference for sons.

The Sikh Gurus raised a forceful voice against injustice towards women and condemned the second-class status of women and the violence that they were subjected to in medieval India. To curb the dowry system, which resulted in female infanticide, Guru Ram Das, the fourth Guru, wrote: 'O my father, please give me the Name of the Lord God as my wedding gift and dowry.'

Sadly, although the Gurus preached, for their time, a revolutionary message on women's equality both social and religious, these teachings have not always translated into practice. In fact, social and cultural traditions that have been part of India's society for centuries continue. The sex ratio in Punjab, the homeland of Sikhs, was, last year, 919 to 1000, and while this is an improvement on the previous decade, it's still a huge cause for concern. Other Indian states fare even worse.

We in the UK might hear this and feel a sense of moral superiority. But we'd be wrong to do so. The UK Femicide Census highlights that a man kills a woman every three days. So, violence and discrimination against women, in all their forms, remain endemic worldwide. The rapid turn of events in Afghanistan has shown just how fragile progress can be. It's only when women, unconstrained by cultural or religious barriers, are given equal opportunities and access to positions of power, so that their voices are heard, that we'll be enabled to live our lives free from violence and misogyny.

VENERABLE LIZ ADEKUNLE

The only person of colour in the room

The Venerable Liz Adekunle is an Anglican priest and former Archdeacon of Hackney in the diocese of London where she was born. She read theology at Birmingham University and did a masters in African Christianity at the School of Oriental and African Studies, University of London. After ordination she did parish work in Hackney and then became Chaplain of St John's College, Cambridge. She has sat on various bodies within the Metropolitan Police and regional police forces advising on ethical and diversity matters. In 2017 she was appointed as a Chaplain to Her Majesty The Queen.

This varied background gave her an understanding of the experiences of black women and men in inner-city London and also of how they are viewed by those of a more privileged background. In this Thought, *Liz reflects on the damaging stereotypes of black people in Britain today and sets out a better vision for the future.*

5 May 2022

It's two years ago this month since the death of George Floyd, a man killed by a police officer in Minneapolis. The incident, captured on phone screens, went viral and spread around the world, as many of us were confined in lockdown.

His death caused outrage at the open injustice. People felt helpless and anxious, and it felt like the world was in flux.

It seemed, if only for a few months, to change so much. The stories and experiences of black people in Britain revealed bias and damaging stereotypes. Actresses, lawyers and authors expressed often through tears and anger a desire for acknowledgement, of not just historical injustice, but also of discrimination that continues today, in subtle and obvious ways in our institutions and communities.

In Viola Davis's new autobiography *Finding Me*, her listed achievements include an Academy Award, a Primetime Emmy and two Tony Awards. She's the only African American to achieve this Triple Crown of Acting. She recalls that early in her career when asked who she was, she replied, 'I'm the little girl who ran from school in third grade because the boys hated me, because I was ... Black.'

I often find myself in settings where I'm the only person of colour, navigating people's hopes and fears at my existence in that context.

The book *The Good Immigrant* is inspired by this question of why society often sees people of colour as bad immigrants, for example job stealers, benefit scroungers and undeserving refugees, until they earn extraordinary achievements by, for example, winning an Olympic medal; when they somehow become good immigrants, with seemingly little in-between.

I long for the day when my appearance isn't a fascination, but my heritage and background an asset, a gift that makes up a rich and diverse Britain. I long for the day when the lived experience of those who've endured discrimination is behind us. I long for the day when people can engage openly and honestly about the existence of prejudice that is learned, inherent and benefits them, but that is wrong.

The apostle Paul proclaimed, 'There is no longer Jew or Greek, there is no longer slave or free, there is no longer male and female; for all of you are one in Christ Jesus.' I long for the day when these radical words about the life and love of Christ – himself an asylum-seeking refugee – create fresh energy, new perspectives and a determination to make Paul's words resound, the day when our stories of injustice no longer threaten our society, but strengthen it.

RABBI JONATHAN WITTENBERG

Roe v. Wade overturned

In June 2022, by a five–four majority, the US Supreme Court voted to overrule American women's constitutional right to an abortion, which had been guaranteed for half a century by the Roe v. Wade case. The Supreme Court had never before withdrawn a constitutional right that so many Americans have relied upon for so long. The decision, drafted by the conservative Catholic Justice Samuel Alito, was met with rage and fear from those women fighting against the ruling and triumphant celebrations from those who had won.

The topic was extensively covered in the news the following day. But Jonathan Wittenberg, the senior rabbi of Masorti Judaism, offered an entirely new perspective on the subject in his Thought. *Among other things he helpfully explained that much discussion on abortion is rooted in a distinctly Christian notion of 'ensoulment' – the moment that the soul is said to enter the foetus – a view which Jews, and others, do not accept.*

The Masorti movement falls halfway between Orthodox and Reform Judaism. It is traditional in its practice, but it interprets Jewish teaching in the light of contemporary knowledge and scholarship. How should the reversal of Roe v. Wade *be viewed? Jewish teaching, says Rabbi Wittenberg, suggests that God always inclines towards compassion. But does this decision?*

27 June 2022

I often listen as people pour out their hearts. Few matters are more sensitive than those concerning pregnancy. So I'm troubled at the Supreme Court of America's overturning of *Roe v. Wade*, allowing each state to legislate on abortion. Anti-abortion campaigners champion the rights of the unborn, but there must also be concern that millions of American women may now have no, or limited, access to abortion. Speaking about this I'm acutely aware that I'm male, but I'm also a husband and father. These matters concern men too.

Judaism does not allow abortion on demand. The Torah's first commandment is to have children. Holocaust survivors often say what mattered most was to create a new family. Judaism is very child-oriented, but it doesn't believe in ensoulment at conception; from the establishment of pregnancy, until birth, in Jewish law a baby is considered like its mother's thigh – her life takes precedence. If she's absolutely at risk, abortion may be mandated; otherwise it may be permitted, on grounds of her health, including mental health. Some authorities interpret this narrowly, others broadly. The Supreme Court's judgement may put that health in greater danger.

Banning abortions effectively means banning safe abortions. Forced into other options women may die. Clinics may face criminal charges if held to assist in abortions. Poor women will suffer unequally, unable to travel to states which allow abortion – journeys which may themselves be criminalised. Fears have been expressed about the levels of surveillance which may be imposed on women.

There are deeply held and serious religious beliefs on the other side of this question which argue that abortion undermines the sanctity of life. But one synagogue in America has already challenged the court's ruling as imposing on people of different faiths a doctrine they don't hold. In a land which separates church and state, this objection is shared by other minorities.

There are further concerns. *Roe v. Wade* understood the 14th amendment as covering rights not specified in the American Constitution, including the right to privacy in matters of contraception, marriage, abortion and sexual orientation. In overturning it Justice Alito wrote that, to be included, such rights must be deeply rooted in American history and religion – in which, at the critical times, women had no legal voice. He deemed abortion not to qualify. I worry what further privacy matters may lose protection.

The rabbis imagined how God makes decisions; God inclines towards compassion, they decided. I fear this ruling inclines in the other direction. Its potential ramifications are being noted with apprehension around the world.

Chapter Five

Religion and Society

BISHOP TOM BUTLER

The Rushdie affair

In 1989 a faultline opened in British society between defenders of free speech and those who were concerned that it had not been exercised with sufficient responsibility. The year before, Salman Rushdie's novel The Satanic Verses *had provoked widespread outrage among Muslims who saw it as a blasphemous slur on the Prophet Muhammad. Protests spread throughout the Islamic world. In Britain, the book was publicly burned. Iran issued a fatwa, placing a death sentence on the author and publishers. Western liberals were outraged in response.*

Bishop Tom Butler, who had been successively bishop of the ethnically diverse dioceses of Willesden, Leicester and Southwark, could see both sides of the story. He had no sympathy with calls to ban the book. But when International Guerrillas, *a Pakistani film about the whole affair, came out in 1990 – portraying Rushdie as a Bond supervillain who is part of a Jewish plot to destroy Islam so he can build casinos, nightclubs and brothels around the world – the British Board of Film Classification banned the film. Tom Butler's sense of fairness and balance were troubled, as this bold* Thought *shows.*

23 October 1990

The Rushdie affair has been given another turn of the screw this week by the decision of the British Board of Film Classification to refuse to pass the Pakistani-made film which shows Mr Rushdie as a debauched plotter against Islam. And this time, I for one am firmly on the side of the Muslim community. The film board may be acting quite correctly within their technical guidelines, indeed they may be acting quite correctly within the law, but if so, then the law seems unfair.

Let's look as the affair as it might seem to the man on the top of the Bradford omnibus. Salman Rushdie writes a book which Muslims believe treats the founder of their religion in an untrue and insulting way. Muslim leaders try to have the book banned and are told that this is not possible within British law. They are further told that it is their duty to keep any protests peacefully within the law. Fair enough.

Then this film is made which, we're told, treats Salmon Rushdie in an untrue and insulting way, and immediately the film is banned, before the courts have even had a chance to decide whether or not it falls within the law. It really doesn't seem to add up to fair and even-handed treatment. It's not as if every docudrama at the cinema or on television about recent history pretends to true accuracy. We are well used to faction – the portrayal of real events concerning real people in such a way that fact overlaps with fiction – and from the snippets shown on the TV news this is clearly the style of the Pakistani film.

Of course there is the danger that such a film will inflame tensions further, but I believe that there is an even greater danger of giving ammunition to those wilder members of the Muslim community who would have us believe that British society is totally hostile to their religion.

Now Christians wouldn't want their faith to be judged totally on statements emerging from some of the noisier leaders in Northern Ireland, and equally I believe that it's unfair to judge a great and civilised religion like Islam on the basis of statements from its more bigoted leaders. It's obvious that, as with Christianity, there are divisions within the Muslim community, and for every hardline leader using rash and angry words, there are moderate leaders urging that Muslims should play a full and constructive part in the life of our country in an open and democratic way.

Such leaders are not helped if it seems that British laws and institutions are weighted against minority groups like their own. St Thomas Aquinas, in his great study on law, spoke of the Law of God, the law of justice and love, overarching all human laws. All societies have a duty to try to see that their human laws and institutions approximate to those of the Law of God, and benchmarks of good laws include balance, even-handedness and fairness. Traditionally, in this country, we pride ourselves on such values; we had better show that we still believe in them.

HRH THE PRINCE OF WALES

A new millennium

As the new millennium approached at New Year 2000, thoughts turned to how such a momentous milestone could be marked. It is the kind of historic occasion it can be hard to believe has fallen in our lifetime to our generation. So when The Prince of Wales agreed to write and deliver the broadcast it felt a great endorsement for the national significance of Thought for the Day.

In this Thought *His Royal Highness beautifully articulates the paradoxical emotions and feelings that come with such landmark events. Everyone wants it to be special, but it can be an anti-climax after all the build-up. Like every New Year it offers that crux of wondering if it will bring hard times or better times. In his* Thought *Prince Charles took us back to the source of the counting of the years, decades and centuries – back to the birth of Christ. And he suggested that the key to success and sustainability in the New Millennium must involve us rediscovering a sense of the sacred in life.*

1 January 2000

I suspect many of us will have been wondering how to approach the millennium, wondering what it actually means in the midst of our daily lives.

I daresay many of us will have decided what it does not mean. Will it, for instance, be an 'experience' – the dawning of an exciting moment when we step boldly across a thresh-old marked 'twenty-first century' and emerge into the golden, promised land of a perennial future where there shall be no more 'wailing and gnashing of teeth', where water flows uphill and the whole of humanity is genetically re-engineered? Or will it, perhaps, provide a sacred moment of reflection as we cele-brate the 2000th anniversary of that unique occurrence when 'the word became flesh and dwelt among us'?

Will it remind us that each New Year represents, as did Christ's mysterious birth, a microcosm of the vital process of renewal that dominates our existence? For although our every-day lives seem to be dominated by linear time, one day following the next and year following year in an unbroken line, each New Year reminds us of the importance in our existence of natural cycles, of events which continually recur. But, of course, there is all the difference in the world between renewing what is old and replacing old with new.

The millennium provides us with an opportunity to abandon the poles of blind optimism on the one hand and total despair on the other, and to rediscover a much older emotion – hope. Hope belongs to a world which recognises the idea of limits; going with the grain of nature and cherishing, and learning, from the best of what we have inherited from the past. In this sense, the dawn of a new millennium should not be the excuse for a bonfire of the past, but a chance to rediscover the profound wisdom of those who have made the difficult journey through this life before us; those who, like Our Lord Jesus Christ, taught that this life is but one passing phase of our existence and that the reality lies within each one of us. Or, as Rilke put it: 'Death is the side of life turned away from us.'

In an era when we are tempted to believe that science knows nearly all the answers it is instructive to recall that Einstein under-stood the close connection between wonder and the sacred. To him the sense of wonder was the most important sense to open ourselves to the truth, the immensity of the mystery and the divinity of ourselves and our world. He wrote that 'a person who is religiously enlightened appears to me to be one who has, to the best of his abilities, liberated himself from the fetters of his selfish desires and is preoccupied with thoughts, feelings and aspirations to which he clings because of their supra-personal value'.

As we enter a new millennium, with all its hopes and fears, I pray that we may come to realise that life is a strange paradox and that the art of living it lies in striking a balance; and that it is a sacred thing to compose harmony out of opposites.

Two and a half thousand years ago Plato was at pains to explain through the words of Timaeus that the great gift of human rationality should not be disparaged. Far from it, he said – it should be exercised to its utmost, but it must not make the mistake of believing it has no limits.

In an age of secularism, I hope with all my heart that in the new millennium we will begin to rediscover a sense of the sacred in all that surrounds us – whether in the way we grow our crops or raise our livestock on the land that God has given us; whether in the way we create places for people to live in the countryside we have inherited; whether in the way we treat disease in our fellow human beings; or whether in the way we educate or motivate our young people.

But to do that we must first of all understand that life is a more profound experience than we are told it is. After all, the likelihood of life beginning by chance is about as great as a hurricane blowing through a scrap yard and assembling a Rolls-Royce.

Perhaps, in the midst of all the celebrations and the hype, deep down inside many of us may feel intuitively – to paraphrase a wonderful passage from Dante – that the strongest desire of everything, and the one first implanted by Nature, is to return to its source.

And since God is the source of our souls and has made it alike unto himself ... therefore this soul desires above all things to return to Him.

ARCHBISHOP ROWAN WILLIAMS

Inside 9/11

The horrifying image of the Twin Towers being struck in 2001 became imprinted in billions of minds. But those who were actually there had very different memories. On the first anniversary of 9/11 Archbishop Rowan Williams generously agreed to write a Thought for the Day *of his own recollection of that day, difficult though that was for him.*

The archbishop was in New York on the fateful day, with just one tower standing between him and the World Trade Center. He was there to deliver four meditations on 'The Shaping of Holy Lives', which were to be recorded for a special broadcast. The recording was scheduled to start at 8.45am. At 8.46 the first plane smashed into the North Tower. The person who organised the recording, Courtney Cowart, later said: 'The programme was never made. Instead, our lives were reshaped forever by what we saw and felt.'

As only the genius of Rowan Williams could, his Thought *took that life-changing experience and put it into the context of the way God sees the world and all that's in it. Rowan offered a profound and heartfelt message of caution as he asked: how should we respond, if our own humanity is to be preserved?*

11 September 2002

I find it really difficult to look at the photos of the Twin Towers dissolving in flame and rubble. I know I'm not alone in that; but for me, they bring back the memory of being, for a while, on the inside of the picture, that day in New York, when I with others was trapped for a period in a neighbouring building. The image from outside is the single dramatic moment, the crash out of a clear sky; but what we are going to remember from inside is the chaos, dark and dust; and the unexpected intimate conversations and touches of the hand between strangers as we waited. And photographs can't begin, somehow, to do justice to what we can't see: the thousands of lives ending dreadfully, the fear and agony, the prolonged anguish of those who lost friends, children, parents. Our minds can't really cope with all that. And if they can't, just gazing at the pictures feels detached and wrong.

Perhaps it's got something to do with how easily we do, in fact, concentrate on dramatic pictures to spare us from the personal reality. The terrorist, the suicide bomber, is someone who's got to the point where they can only see from a distance: the sort of distance from which you can't see a face, meet the eyes of someone, hear who they are, imagine who and what they love.

All violence works with that sort of distance; it depends on not seeing certain things. No one would ever have been able to carry on as a soldier in earlier days without the training not to see or think about an enemy in personal terms. Sometimes what made soldiers break down in an environment like the trenches of the First World War was some moment when they became aware of the humanity of a particular enemy. And one of the disturbing things about religious faith is that it tells us that God never sees at a distance, never sees things only in general. There are no lives that are superfluous, no lives you can forget about.

War may well be getting nearer.* Those who urge caution inevitably get accused of a sort of loss of moral nerve, a willingness to collude with evil. But if the great religious traditions, Eastern and Western, insist on surrounding war with so many questions and conditions, they do so because they know not only that the choice to go to war is at best the lesser evil, but also that there are ways of fighting that increasingly damage our own humanity, changing what we expect of ourselves and others.

With the high-tech military methods we've got used to in recent years, there's a greater temptation to take for granted the view from a distance. And this means that we should see the military option as something to be considered a lot further

* The invasion of Iraq began six months later

down the road than it would have been even 50 years ago. If we don't see the point of this caution, which isn't at all a matter of squeamishness or cowardice, the nearer the terrorist comes to winning, because it means we're getting used to the view from outside as the normal perspective – the distant view that spares us the real cost to our own humanity.

RABBI LORD JONATHAN SACKS

Yom Kippur and the age of greed

In September 2008 the US financial services firm Lehman Brothers went into bankruptcy. Banks around the world began to fall like dominoes. Stock markets plunged. Credit markets were paralysed. Companies began laying off workers. By the start of the first week of October the global economy was on the brink of systemic meltdown. What had driven this process was an era in which financiers had announced 'greed is good' and proclaimed it was greed that drove the world economy.

The distinguished social philosopher and theologian Jonathan Sacks, who was then Chief Rabbi of the United Hebrew Congregations of the Commonwealth, had been arguing for some time that Britain needed to reinvigorate the concept of the common good – and restore a model of citizenship based on us taking responsibility not demanding our rights. Now he saw the global financial crisis as the turning point in which the age of greed could be replaced by an age of responsibility. Rabbi Sacks in this Thought *– written in the midst of a crisis that many feared to be apocalyptic – turns his powerful intellect and profound sense of compassion upon the problem. Before change can happen, he warns, we need to admit what went wrong – and what part we played in it.*

3 October 2008

Next week in the Jewish community we'll observe Yom Kippur, the Day of Atonement, the holiest day of the Jewish year. We'll spend the whole day in synagogue, fasting, confessing our sins, admitting what we did wrong, and praying for forgiveness.

Something like that seems to me essential to the health of a culture. Often we see things go wrong. Yet rarely do we see someone stand up, take responsibility and say: I was wrong. I made a mistake. I admit it. I apologise. And now let us work to put it right.

Instead we do other things. We deny there's a problem in the first place. Or if that's impossible, we blame someone else, or say it's due to circumstances beyond our control. The result is that we lose the habit of being honest with ourselves.

In America in 1863, in the midst of the civil war, Abraham Lincoln proclaimed a national day of fasting and prayer. It was an extraordinary thing to do. Lincoln, after all, was fighting for a noble cause, the abolition of slavery. What did he or those on his side have to atone for?

Yet America was being torn apart, so he asked the nation to set aside one day for reflection and prayer. 'It is the duty of nations as well as of men,' the proclamation said, 'to confess their sins and transgressions, in humble sorrow, yet with assured hope that genuine repentance will lead to mercy and pardon.' It was America's Day of Atonement.

The result was that two years later Lincoln was able, in his Second Inaugural, to deliver one of the great healing speeches of all time, calling on Americans 'to bind up the nation's wounds' and care for those who had suffered during the war and were still suffering.

We're living through tough times globally, and we'll need all the inner strength we have to survive the turbulence, learn from the mistakes of the past, and begin again. The real test of a society is not the absence of crises, but whether we come out of them cynical and disillusioned, or strengthened by our rededication to high ideals.

The age of greed is over. Will the age of responsibility now begin? That will depend on whether we are capable of admitting our mistakes, and renewing our commitment to the common good. Atonement, the capacity for honest self-criticism, is what allows us to weather the storm without losing our way.

PADRE MARK CHRISTIAN

Christmas Eve in Helmand

In her Christmas message in 2009, HM The Queen described the year gone by as 'a sombre one'. She paid tribute to the 13,000 men and women in our forces who were soldiering in Afghanistan – where a series of military operations was conducted to take control of the Taliban stronghold that was Helmand province. The Queen said she was proud of the positive contribution they were making with our allies but spoke, too, of being saddened by the casualties suffered by our forces serving there. With footage from Helmand – and also of the coffins of our fallen troops arriving in Royal Wootton Bassett for repatriation – she described the debt of gratitude owed to them as 'profound'.

Padre Mark Christian, senior chaplain with the British Army out in Helmand, wrote this Thought for the Day *from first-hand experience of being alongside those soldiers. It was a script which could only have been written by someone out there, ministering to the troops, meeting the need exactly where it is. His broadcast on Christmas Eve 2009 was personal, strong and very moving.*

24 December 2009

Every time a soldier loses his life we gather at our headquarters to remember them, to honour and respect them, and to pray for their family and friends. Last week, at the end of one such service, our brigade commander came off the parade and said to me: 'Listen to that, Padre.' I wondered what he was talking about. I listened. I could hear the sound of traffic from the town that surrounds our base, but then I became aware of the laughing and shouting and squealing and the giggling sounds of children playing. The brigadier commented that we wouldn't have heard that three months ago.

I went to the garden outside our church and reflected on the sounds of those children. I allowed my mind to travel home to my children. Another Christmas apart. They are adults now but I miss them, as all of our soldiers miss their families. One of my daughters will give birth to my first grandchild in February. I will miss that too. I reflect on the many, many, conversations I have had with soldiers about the pain of being separated from loved ones. I think of the times I have been privileged to listen as soldiers record bedtime stories for their children.

My thoughts turned to the children I have met in the various places I have served with the army. The orphanage in Bosnia that soldiers volunteered to repair. The ragged slip of a girl that I met in Iraq in 2003. With all of the children of her village, she surrounded the vehicle I was on, to grab one of the sweets I was offering. When all the sweets had gone and the crowd had dispersed, she remained, sitting shyly on a sand hill, looking at me. I made faces at her. She laughed. She slowly made her way towards me and held out both her hands. In each was one of the sweets she had fought so hard to win. She tried to give one back to me. I wept at the generosity of one who had nothing.

I think of the children here. The fact that they would prefer pen and paper to sweets. That they laugh and play as our children do back home when they have the security to do so. They exude hope. They are the future.

Hope. Not just a whimsical wish, but the belief and desire that things will turn out better than they are now.

This evening we celebrate the birth of the Christ child. God's message of hope for us all. A child born in poverty of a single mother becomes our salvation. It is in the birth of this child that our hope rests.

'And this shall be a sign unto you; Ye shall find the babe wrapped in swaddling clothes, lying in a manger. And suddenly there was with the angel a multitude of the heavenly host praising God, and saying, Glory to God in the highest, and on earth peace, good will toward men.'

May God bless you this Christmas and give you peace and hope.

PADRE MARK CHRISTIAN

Lent in Lashkar Gah

Lent can be a difficult season for people to understand. They know about Shrove Tuesday and making pancakes as a 'feast' of sorts. They may know it lasts for 40 days. They certainly know it ends with Easter eggs. Lots of people will also know it as a season to think about 'giving something up'. But this Thought for the Day *from Padre Mark Christian, senior chaplain with the British Army in Lashkar Gah, capital of Helmand province in Afghanistan, shows that Lent for soldiers in a war zone is a very different undertaking.*

There, the ashes thumbed on to the soldiers' foreheads, in a simple communion service for Ash Wednesday, bring home to them the nearness of the danger they live with on a daily basis. It brings into very sharp focus the notion of what sacrifice might mean in this context.

To be a chaplain to men and women in that situation is a special kind of ministering as the padre spells out. The two Thoughts *he wrote for us from the area made an invaluable contribution to the public's understanding and the Radio 4 audience wrote in to express their appreciation. In the end, every soldier knows that one day he may have to reconcile himself to the reality of battle, but Padre Mark made you glad they were not alone.*

18 February 2010

Last night here in Lashkar Gah, in the tent that is our church, we had a simple Holy Communion service, marking our foreheads with crosses of ash. Each mark was made with the words: 'Remember that you are dust, and to dust you shall return. Turn away from sin and be faithful to Christ.'

I am not sure if you could say there's ever a good time to come out on military operations, but the season of Lent reflects the atmosphere here better than any other church season. The men and women serving here live a very simple and basic existence. All the distractions and many of the comforts of home are missing. Everybody works relentlessly, but in the times you do have to yourself, living this life helps you focus on what is important – family and loved ones at home, of course, but also the people around you, who serve with you, and upon whom you depend – sometimes to keep you alive.

At the heart of the Lent theme is sacrifice. A quality that's paramount to any soldier, but especially at a time like this, during a major operation. The concept of sacrifice is so important to the army that it appears as 'selfless commitment' in our six core values.

Every day, soldiers in Helmand put themselves in harm's way for the sake of the security of our nation and to bring peace to Afghanistan. The young rifleman knows that he will be attacked almost every time he leaves his patrol base. Every soldier, in the face of the enemy, understands that he is expected to show 'courageous restraint' – not to open fire if there is any chance of civilians being killed, even if this puts him in greater danger.

The courage, the fear, the sacrifice, the loss of friends and the hard-won successes, among other things, make a tour of duty in Afghanistan an emotionally intensive six months. It changes everyone who serves here – not necessarily in the negative ways that you'll hear on the news or read in the papers – but it deepens our understanding of life because every day in one way or another we reflect on, and are challenged by, issues of morality, mortality, faith and human relationships.

On my recent leave I visited some patients at Selly Oak Hospital. I was talking to one recently injured soldier for over an hour. He was talking about his friends – the ones who had died and the ones he had fought with. About how scared he was, but how he knew he had to go on. At the end of the conversation I noticed that he was holding one of the brigade dog tags that his chaplain had given him. He read from the verse of scripture that is on the back, from Joshua chapter 1 verse 9: 'I will be strong and courageous. I will not be terrified or discouraged; for the Lord my God is with me wherever I go'. He looked at me and said: 'Do you think I have been strong and courageous, padre?' I think you can guess how I answered him.

ANNE ATKINS

Why me?

Anne Atkins has been writing for Thought *since the mid-nineties when she made the headlines with the forthright views in her debut script (see page 142) and, for some, the die was cast on who they thought she was. She read English at Oxford and, after an early career as an actress in the theatre, she turned to writing when she had children. She has written four novels and three non-fiction books but when writing for radio Anne Atkins has a very personal style, which makes her stand out and is much appreciated by her many fans.*

One of the key qualities we look for in contributors to Thought *is the critical ability to bring the genuine article to the microphone. You can't con the audience. Anne always speaks from the heart about what she sees, feels and cares about. Her passions include Shakespeare, ancient Greek, her family, loyalty, music, the simple pleasures and reading the scriptures that guide her Christian faith, to name only a few. She seizes on snapshots of life and draws from them something universal.* This Thought *starts with a tragic loss for her son, but from it forces an exploration of why bad things happen and how we cope with them.*

7 June 2010

'It doesn't make sense,' my son said over and over again, after his first explosion of grief had subsided enough for words. He received a call last Tuesday that his best friend and tutor had died abroad. His last text, still on my telephone, describes the beach bar, asparagus, fresh lemon sole from the bay: 'Life ain't bad.' 'It was going to be a new beginning,' my son said.

'It doesn't make sense.' He never had time to tell him of the place at Cambridge he owes him. Nor of something else far more important.

Vanity, vanity, all is vanity, complains the preacher in Ecclesiastes. Futility, meaninglessness, emptiness. Why? What prompted it? Couldn't someone have stopped it? Who was to blame?

Who caused this, the onlookers asked Jesus of a man who'd been born blind. Was it his fault, or his parents?

You brought this on yourself, Job's miserable comforters kept telling him, of the suffering which smote him repeatedly at random.

'Don't you feel guilty at your daughter's illness?' the therapist asked me. 'You must feel responsible.'

Over and over again we look for reason, or cause, or somebody accountable. Shouldn't we have taken away his gun licence? Why did nobody see it coming? Couldn't anyone have caught him?

Why, why, why? 'The motive-hunting of a motiveless malignity' was how Coleridge described Iago. But why should malignity need a motive? Why do we expect to be able to explain it?

Curiously, we don't hear of lottery winners saying: 'Why me?' though it's just as random and undeserved. It's only of tragedy that we ask: 'Why?' As if we know undeniably deeply, that the world was made to be good not bad, we were created to live not die, we are formed for love not hate. We take fair fortune in our stride as a natural: we only rail against inexplicable evil.

There seems something in the human spirit expecting virtue at the heart of the universe. The Western pursuit of physics was based on a belief in pattern and purpose: 'The works of the Lord are great, sought out by all those that have pleasure therein', as is inscribed above the modern Cambridge Cavendish Laboratory. The same impulse which prompts a man only a few weeks married to agree, with five others, to be locked in isolation for over 500 days, in a quest to reach and understand Mars.

We yearn for goodness, and knowledge, and meaning, and something keeps telling us we will find it. I admire the courage to say: 'This is all there is.' But everything I experience tells me there is more, there will be answers, there is some sense sustaining us.

My son also never told his friend how much he loves him. But I believe with all my heart and based on all the evidence around me, that he now celebrates even more, on a further shore, where the wine and singing is even better, and he no longer needs to be told.

CLIFFORD LONGLEY

Is Britain more secular or spiritual?

A row developed in the run-up to the state visit to the UK of Pope Benedict XVI in 2010. Around 10,000 marchers took to the streets in a 'Protest the Pope' rally organised by a coalition of militant atheists, gay groups, sex-abuse victims, anti-papist Protestants, and Catholic campaigners in favour of the ordination of women. Media coverage ahead of the visit was largely critical, complaining that the cost would be borne by taxpayers. But when hundreds of thousands of people turned out to cheer the Pope the media had to change its tune.

Yet even before that happened one Thought for the Day *stalwart, the Catholic commentator Clifford Longley, had spotted a false dichotomy in much of the commentary asserting that Britain was now a thoroughly secular society. For more than half a century, Clifford has been the doyen of Britain's religious affairs journalists, working on* The Times, Telegraph *and now on the Catholic weekly* The Tablet. *The breadth and depth of that experience, combined with a philosophical and analytical acuity, prompts him in this* Thought *to dissect what we actually mean when we say 'secular'. The result surprised many listeners.*

30 *August 2010*

Here's a bank holiday quiz question. As we congratulate David Cameron and Samantha on the birth of their beautiful baby girl, is our joy at such events 'secular' or 'religious'? You may think that what matters is the joy – and the baby – and not what category we put our feelings in. But it does relate to an issue we are going to hear more about in the next few weeks. Will the state visit of Pope Benedict XVI, just over two weeks away, amount to a dramatic confrontation with Britain's secular society? Indeed, is that a correct – or even useful – description?

A Vatican spokesman, trying to set the stage for the papal visit, said that from Rome Britain seemed a very secular society. But not long ago the Archbishop of Westminster, Vincent Nichols, took a rather different tack. He described British society as a lot less secular than people supposed. Many who did not go to church nevertheless prayed to God when things got difficult. And another Catholic bishop was quoted yesterday saying: 'No one ever defines secularism. If they mean an absence of interest in spirituality, for instance, then I would say that there is plenty of evidence of exactly the opposite.' And that is precisely what opinion polls tell us. If you ask people if they are religious most of them say No; but if you ask them if they are spiritual most of them say Yes. Indeed I put myself in that category – spiritual, yet secular.

This has all got mixed up with our attitude to Church, and in England that means the Church by Law Established. It is still seen as the official religion of the English – or, on the other hand, as the church most English people have stopped going to. But then we can't ignore the fact that, when some tragedy strikes that deeply affects the local community, people turn to the Church of England (or north of the border, the Church of Scotland) for some way of expressing what they feel. Even if the pews are a bit empty most Sundays, there is still that vital chaplaincy role to play. But that is not by any means the limit of God's presence among us.

Matthew Arnold wrote a poem in 1867 called 'Dover Beach', which has provided ever since – I think very misleadingly – our template for understanding such questions. The poem describes, with something like fatalistic dread, the gradual withdrawal of the 'sea of faith' from the shoreline, the beach, using the metaphor of the tide going out. So eventually faith, by which he presumably means the place in society of the Church of England, will have reached the far horizon. That is the model of secularisation which still governs our discussion of these issues, and I think it is a false one. God hasn't gone away – he just isn't where we thought he was.

POPE BENEDICT XVI

Christmas message

What a day for the airline to lose my luggage! I had been driving, in a jumper and jeans, to the hairdresser when my mobile rang. For several years we had been trying to persuade Pope Benedict XVI to do Thought *for the* Day *without success, though we began to hope it might happen after his successful visit to the UK in September 2010, which had been a resounding success with the British public. But no* Thought *materialised.*

But then, quite out of the blue, came that call from the Vatican. It was Monday 21 December. I was told he would record a Christmas message for Thought *at 11am on 23 December in Rome. I turned the car round. I had 40 minutes to pack and get to the airport. There was just one seat left on the last plane out of Manchester before a winter snowstorm descended and shut the airport. But then the airline lost my case. I couldn't go to see the Pope in my jumper and jeans. So the morning before the recording I rushed round the smart boutiques of Rome to find the black dress it was traditional to wear.*

I arrived the next day, with David Willey, the BBC's Rome Correspondent, and the Pope could not have been more friendly and accommodating. It was quite something to at last find myself sitting with Benedict XVI in the Vatican recording the first Thought *ever done by a pope. Written for broadcast on Christmas Eve morning, it was duly recorded and I was back just in time to turn it round for the next day. From the warmth of his personal greeting to the people of the UK in his opening line, it was clear that his visit to Britain had meant a lot to him too.*

24 December 2010

Recalling with great fondness my four-day visit to the United Kingdom last September, I am glad to have the opportunity to greet you once again – and indeed to greet listeners everywhere as we prepare to celebrate the birth of Christ. Our thoughts turn back to a moment in history when God's chosen people, the children of Israel, were living in intense expectation. They were waiting for the Messiah that God had promised to send, and they pictured him as a great leader who would rescue them from foreign domination and restore their freedom.

God is always faithful to his promises, but he often surprises us in the way he fulfils them. The child that was born in Bethlehem did indeed bring liberation, but not only for the people of that time and place – he was to be the Saviour of all people throughout the world and throughout history. And it was not a political liberation that he brought, achieved through military means: rather, Christ destroyed death for ever and restored life by means of his shameful death on the cross. And while he was born in poverty and obscurity, far from the centres of earthly power, he was none other than the Son of God.

Out of love for us he took upon himself our human condition, our fragility, our vulnerability, and he opened up for us the path that leads to the fullness of life, to a share in the life of God himself.

As we ponder this great mystery in our hearts this Christmas, let us give thanks to God for his goodness to us, and let us joyfully proclaim to those around us the good news that God offers us freedom from whatever weighs us down: he gives us hope, he brings us life.

Dear Friends from Scotland, England, Wales and indeed every part of the English-speaking world, I want you to know that I keep all of you very much in my prayers during this Holy Season. I pray for your families, for your children, for those who are sick, and for those who are going through any form of hardship at this time. I pray especially for the elderly and for those who are approaching the end of their days. I ask Christ, the light of the nations, to dispel whatever darkness there may be in your lives and to grant to every one of you the grace of a peaceful joyful Christmas. May God bless all of you!

VISHVAPANI

Mindfulness in Parliament

The news that more than 70 MPs were engaged in mindfulness classes in the House of Commons broke at the end of February 2014. Within days Vishvapani, Thought for the Day*'s principal Buddhist contributor, was sharing with Radio 4 listeners the benefits of his long years of mindfulness practice, having been a Buddhist since the age of 14. Mindfulness is not just at the core of his religious practice; he also teaches Mindfulness-Based Stress Reduction courses for a range of organisations including the NHS, prisons and probation services.*

The MPs and peers, after seven-week-long sessions run by the Oxford University Mindfulness Centre, later set up a Mindfulness All-Party Parliamentary Group of which Vishvapani is now an associate member. Some 300 politicians and 500 members of their staff have now received mindfulness training. The wisdom of ancient religions, he says in this Thought, *has much to offer our stressed-out society.*

28 February 2014

The former Speaker Bernard Weatherill once told a friend of mine that when the Commons was in uproar he groaned inwardly and then turned to his long-standing meditation practice. I like the image of the Speaker, sitting quietly amid the Westminster hullabaloo, noticing his breath and feeling his feet on the floor. It's a long way from the notion that you need to be halfway up a mountain before you can find calm. And I heard on *BBC News* this week that many MPs and Lords are taking mindfulness courses – learning to ground their attention, especially by focusing on the breath and the body.

It's heartening for someone like me, who's long practised mindfulness in a Buddhist context, to see the recent cover of *Time* magazine featuring a meditating beauty and the headline: 'The

Mindfulness Revolution'. This ancient practice now appears to be the latest thing!

Bodies like the NHS and the US Marines believe they can offer mindfulness because it can be tested scientifically and makes sense in a purely secular setting. Mindfulness practices directly address the distinctive challenges of a world where things keep on speeding up and we face ever-more demands. More than ever we need ways to manage our attention.

Buddhism teaches that the mind is malleable and the way we respond to the world around us shapes our experience of it. As the Buddha said: 'Experiences are preceded by mind, led by mind and produced by mind.' Mindfulness is the capacity to pay attention in a calm, open way to whatever's happening, even if it's difficult. Longer periods of meditation are also important because they give you the space to become deeply absorbed, and thankfully it isn't essential to sit with your legs wrapped up like a pretzel.

The demand for mindfulness has taken my own teaching activity out of Buddhist centres and into workplaces and probation hostels; and politicians are exploring if it can be offered much more widely in the health service, education and criminal justice, which are dealing with the mental health consequences of our speedy stressed-out society.

The mindfulness movement may seem a surprising marriage of the secular and the religious. But the growing incidence of stress, anxiety and depression means that mental wellbeing can no longer be taken for granted. It has become a priority for us to understand our minds better and to look after ourselves mentally, just as we do physically. The wisdom of ancient traditions, for which the mind has long been a central concern, is turning out to be more relevant than ever.

ELIZABETH OLDFIELD

Holy Saturday hope and despair

Elizabeth Oldfield is an accomplished speaker, writer and host of the podcast The Sacred. *I first met Liz in 2007 when she was working at the BBC making successful documentaries and talk programmes on religion and ethics for Radio 3 and Radio 4, and she later produced for television too.*

When she left she moved to become Director of Theos, the religion and society think-tank where her passion for intelligent public engagement found full rein in an in-depth research programme covering big issues such as multiculturalism, religiously inspired violence, the ethics of debt and faith-based social action. Its mission, she said as she stepped down after ten years, is 'to make a case that faith in general, and Christianity in particular, is a gift not a threat, a friend not a foe, especially amongst those least likely to believe this'. This Thought for the Day *is about a distinct tension that Christians live with – caught between the despair of Good Friday and the hope of Easter Sunday – a tension exemplified by the 'in-between day' of Holy Saturday.*

4 April 2015

Today is Holy Saturday. It's often overlooked. It's the in-between day, no church services, no special meal, maybe just time to catch up on DIY. But I'm always struck by how profound this particular Saturday is, how it sums up a tension at the heart of human life. The literary critic George Steiner uses the day between Good Friday and Easter Sunday as a metaphor for the psychological experience of atheist and believer alike. He says: 'Ours is the long journey of the Saturday, between suffering, aloneness, unutterable waste, on the one hand, and the dream of liberation, or rebirth, on the other.'

Steiner believes that human lives are Saturday lives – that we must exist in the in-between spaces, the tightrope walk between hope and despair. Looking at the news this week, it isn't hard to find tragedy. The bleakness of Good Friday seemed especially bleak this year, with the groans and cries of people across the world echoing in our ears. It's not just terrorist attacks and plane crashes that can tempt us to despair – it's also the ordinary miseries and small heartbreaks that never make the news.

These Friday things are inescapable. The temptation to throw up our hands, and kill our hopes for more, is strong. Some advise this: at least if you expect nothing you can't be disappointed. Perhaps it's the expectation that's the problem; if we can let that go perhaps we will find peace.

The problem is that hope is persistent. We wait and we look and we long, and far off in the distance, if we squint, we think we can see Sunday coming. Many of us have a hunch that whatever it may look like, the story of history is not, after all, a tragedy.

It's tiring, this holding both hope and despair in our heads. It is like walking a tightrope. There's a longing to be able to fall off in one direction or another, to say, well, the real truth about life is 'it's a misery to be endured', or the real truth is that 'everything's all right, really'. But we can't.

In the Christian tradition, learning to live with this tension is central. Most bad theology is an attempt to close the tension down. Good Friday is real. At least part of the truth about humans, Christians believe, is that when we encounter goodness, truth and beauty, especially when embodied in a man, we cry: 'Crucify him.' But Easter Sunday is also true, when this goodness is shown to be more enduring, more forgiving, more fundamental than we ever dared hope.

And so I'm trying to learn to live well in this Saturday, waiting, walking that tightrope, balanced between the two.

ARCHBISHOP JUSTIN WELBY

Hope and resistance on Good Friday

Sometimes a religious festival takes on an additional resonance because the news establishes a distinct context for an event we usually regard as a feature of the annual religious calendar. Good Friday in 2016 came at the end of a week filled with terror, fear and hate. Three days earlier terrorists had coordinated suicide bombings on three targets in Brussels in which 32 people had died and 300 more were injured in the deadliest attack in Belgium since the Second World War.

Then, on the day before Good Friday, the Bosnian Serb leader Radovan Karadžić – who once was a psychiatrist and poet – was found guilty of genocide, war crimes and crimes against humanity for the killing of more than 8,000 Muslim men and boys in and around the town of Srebrenica, during the Bosnian War.

The Archbishop of Canterbury, Justin Welby, in this Good Friday Thought for the Day *took those terrible events for a reflection upon human cruelty, its motivations and rationalisations – and found an echo of the love of Christ chalked on a Brussels pavement.*

25 March 2016

For me one of the best and most challenging parts of Canterbury Cathedral is the number of memorials to past archbishops. There are saints and, to be honest, villains; the brilliant and the dull. Some were heroes, doing the right thing for the right reason; others acted cruelly and brutally, or in T.S. Eliot's great sentence, put into Becket's mouth in his play *Murder in the Cathedral*: 'They were tempted to the greatest treason: doing the right thing for the wrong reason.' All had mixed motives and characters.

Good Friday, the day on which Christians remember the death of Jesus on the Cross, challenges all our reasons for everything we do, all the motivations we claim for any action. Good Friday has that healthy and necessary aspect that is found in many faiths, of a time for self-examination.

In the week of the attacks in Belgium – and of recalling the horrors and crimes of the Balkan Civil War, with the conviction of Radovan Karadžić – I am struck by the savagery and bitterness, the utterly perverted reasons, of the attackers and perpetrators, carrying out not right deeds but the most deeply wrong ones that could be imagined, and the contrast with the sacrifice of Jesus. He was the one person in history Christians believe to have had only pure motives for all he did, and for me he sets the standard for both actions and reasons.

The nature of hatred is that it is infectious. Terror wins when it causes others to fear or hate. On Good Friday terror and oppression are met by love, with Jesus praying for the forgiveness of those who caused his death. Christians, considering the Cross, see God crucified because of human cruelty and sin.

The mystery of the immense savagery of human beings, of our desire to use power to harm not heal, is one that confounds all attempts to explain it away. The depth of the grip on us held by lust for power and the desire to dominate others is judged by the crucifixion. Before it, we are confronted with our wrong reasons and actions.

But I find myself also confronted with the love of God that goes deeper than our cruelty, of God's reaching out to us that goes beyond our pride and power-seeking. One of the messages chalked on a Brussels pavement this week was: 'Hope is our Resistance'. It is compellingly true. Even on this day, even in this week, I find hope because for me at the end of all things God is over all.

MARTIN WROE

Shakespeare and the Bible

Martin Wroe is ordained in the Church of England and almost every-thing he writes is steeped in a scriptural knowledge, yet it never feels like church jargon. He draws on the questions, phrases and conversational riffs of everyday life, and imbues them with new depth. Martin is a published poet, a master of words and ideas that fall easy on the ear. Such as in this Thought *to mark the 400th anniversary of the death of England's greatest playwright. In it Martin dances through phrases from Shakespeare and the King James Bible – virtual contemporaries in their times of writing – in an offering of sayings you thought you'd forgotten, or which are so melded into our language you have to do a double-take to hear them stand out. For Martin it's about looking for the inspiration needed to live a good life.*

9 April 2016

Take a listen to these expressions: 'Wild goose chase'? 'Wear your heart on your sleeve'? 'Mum's the word'? Are they Shakespeare … or are they scripture? What about: 'By the skin of your teeth'? 'Fight the good fight'? Or 'Eat drink and be merry'?

This month marks the 400th anniversary of the death of William Shakespeare. Only five years ago we marked four centuries of the King James Version of the Bible. No other literary sources give us more of our everyday phrases and sayings. We may think we know little of either, but they speak through us daily.

Language is viral, quietly travelling centuries. Sticky expressions and turns of phrase glue themselves into our conversation. Tripping off our tongue, before we've even noticed.

'So …' is a current example. When did someone decide that the word 'So' must preface our response to a question?

And it turns out that everyone has adopted the phrase 'it turns out' – a recent verbal tic for explaining a twist in the tale you're telling.

Yesterday I enquired of a twentysomething in our house about the expression 'bae' – spelt B.A.E. – which, it turns out, has nothing to do with British Aerospace – it's short for babe. Maybe you'll notice it, now I've mentioned it. Soz – as … we … now say.

As communication migrates online, the acronym flexes its uppercase muscles. DIY, RSVP and AWOL are eclipsed by LOL, OMG and GPWM. That last is Good Point Well Made – BTW – By The Way. Doubtless, many of these will bite the dust, in the twinkling of an eye. They carry all the stickability of the cockney translation of the Bible where Jesus miraculously feeds 'five thousand geezers' with 'five loaves of Uncle Fred and two Lillian Gish'.

Purists can find the use and abuse of language a thorn in the flesh. They'd prefer that the original – Shakespeare or scripture – was set in stone. But language won't be trapped, that's how it survives. And the Bible will always be one of those places we come from – even if we can't remember being there – every time we suffer from a broken heart or reluctantly concede that someone we trusted is a leopard who cannot change his spots.

Yes, some phrases no longer mean what they once did … but they stick around because they ring true.

Sometimes truth trumps accuracy. The great Jewish novelist, Elie Wiesel, could have been talking about Shakespeare, or about the parables of Jesus, when he said: 'Some stories are true that never happened.' And some words remain true, even as their meaning evolves.

'The grass withers, and the flower falls,' reads the Bible. 'But the word of the Lord endures.' And the word of William Shakespeare too.

AKHANDADHI DAS

===

Weinstein and Diwali

Just one week before Hindu contributor Akhandadhi Das wrote this Thought, *the* New York Times *published a story detailing decades of allegations of sexual harassment against the film mogul Harvey Weinstein. In the days that followed a stream of women came forward alleging sexual coercion and rape. Weinstein's own company sacked him. His wife left him.*

Akhandadhi Das, a Vaishnava teacher and theologian, was forcibly struck by the parallels between the Weinstein saga and one of the stories at the heart of the great Hindu festival of lights, Diwali. It tells of a demon king named Ravana who, after a long history of sexual predation, finds the tables turned against him. Akhandadhi recounts the story in some detail and the parallels with the Weinstein saga become clear. So too does the fact that sexual harassment is all too often about a disparity of power, wealth and influence. Hinduism, it turns out, had its own #MeToo moment – but thousands of years before ours.

12 October 2017

As Hindus prepare for the Diwali festivities next week, I suspect many may have noted the odd parallel between the reports of Harvey Weinstein accused of sexual predation and the character and behaviour of Ravana, the anti-hero of the Diwali story.

Ravana was powerful, intelligent, charming and charismatic. Though he was used to winning over any woman he fancied, he understood he'd be destroyed if he forced himself on a woman against her will. However, he was ruthless in gaining such compliance. He utilised what Hindu texts call the tools of persuasion of the rich and powerful: *dana* and *danda*. *Dana* are generous gifts – and Ravana bestowed them liberally upon the objects of his desire as well as to his lackeys and sycophants. And, if that failed, he turned to *danda* – threats to punish anyone who rejected him or who raised dissent.

Initially, Ravana had his 'people' encourage the beautiful Sita to submit to their leader with presents and promises. But, when Ravana directly approached Sita, she threw straw on the ground in front of him. This 'casting of straw' had several meanings. It was a gesture of etiquette and a reminder of social formality between them. It also suggested that Ravana and his wealth were no more to her than dried-up chaff. And, it contained a plea for Ravana not to treat her with contempt and disregard, like straw in the street.

Ravana reacted to her rejection by threatening that if she didn't acquiesce to sharing his bed within one month he would kill her mercilessly. It was then, in Sita's darkest moments, a friend came to encourage her to be strong in her suffering and resolve. Help was on hand.

But, it wasn't until someone closest to Ravana turned on him that the balance swung away from the tyrant. His brother, Vibhishan, finally challenged him: 'I have supported you as our leader; I love you as a brother, but to my shame I've tolerated your heinous activities. Now, I must offer myself to those who will bring you to justice.'

Clearly, not all of Ravana's story may be applicable to Mr Weinstein. But, I think it has broader relevance to how we, as a society, try to deal with the issues of sexual harassment that may occur and be overlooked wherever there is disparity of power, wealth and influence. How can vulnerable women feel more confident to 'cast straw' in front of predators? What support can we offer that delivers actual protection? And how do we encourage those in the know to speak up sooner rather than later.

As Ravana's widow commented on the inevitable downfall of her husband: 'May the tears of innocent women never fall on the ground in vain.'

BISHOP PHILIP NORTH

Oxfam on Shrove Tuesday

In 2011 Oxfam was contacted by a whistleblower who reported that some of the aid agency's staff had been paying young girls for sex in earthquake-devastated Haiti. The charity investigated and sacked four aid workers, allowing three others to resign. Seven years later a newspaper got hold of a copy of Oxfam's internal report into the affair – and accused the charity of a cover-up. The Conservative government swiftly cut the agency's funding. Donations from the public fell by almost £4 million.

Thought for the Day regular Philip North is always very mindful of the people who have no voice to speak for themselves. He was alarmed at who would end as the real victims here. Before becoming Bishop of Burnley he had served as a Church of England priest in disadvantaged areas in Sunderland, Hartlepool and London. He is a member of the Company of Mission Priests, men who consecrate themselves to the Church's mission, free from the attachments of marriage and family. They work primarily in big housing estates and inner-city areas but also in Africa.

In this Thought, given on the eve of Christianity's penitential season of Lent, Bishop Philip, a man with a heart for social justice, reflects on the self-righteous indignation of the rich – and laments its impact upon the world's poorest people.

13 February 2018

Until the news broke about the behaviour of a group of their aid workers in Haiti, it was hard not to be impressed by the sheer goodness of the development work undertaken by Oxfam. The charity places its staff in the most troubled regions, it offers practical help and support to the world's poorest, and through its research and communications it is a passionate voice for justice.

Why then have the recent revelations of staff using prostitutes done Oxfam quite so much damage? I think it is because of the widespread cultural abhorrence of hypocrisy. If a charity claims to stand up for truth and justice and fairness, people understandably feel extremely shocked when its staff are undermining those values through their moral choices.

But it all gets messy when we seek ways to express our anger and disapproval. As a result of the news some individuals may be thinking of stopping their donations to Oxfam. Government has also suggested that it may halt its own funding. But who would ultimately suffer as a result of these decisions? It won't be those known to have taken sexual advantage of the vulnerable because they have left Oxfam's employment. As so often, the poor will end up paying the cost of the sins of the rich – because the victims will be Oxfam's beneficiaries. It will be the hungry and the thirsty, and that sits ill with me.

Perhaps today offers a more productive way to think through such situations. It's Shrove Tuesday, which brings with it pancakes, carnivals, high jinks and fun. But the word 'shrove' comes from the old English 'shriven', which means to be forgiven. On this day the church bells would ring loudly to call the faithful to confession. Today, as they prepare for Lent, Christians are called to take stock of their lives, accept their own fault and hypocrisy, and reset their moral compass through the gift of God's forgiveness.

While the actions of those Oxfam staff in Haiti are reprehensible, there is a danger that we rush to condemn others precisely in order to deflect the need for the sort of introspection that Shrove Tuesday demands. Sadly it's all too easy for anyone to lose track of the values of the organisation of which they are a part. The imminent appearances of churches, among them my own, and other organisations in front of the Independent Inquiry into Child Sexual Abuse will be stark reminder of that.

It's not surprising that many people at the moment are calling for stronger moral leadership. But Shrove Tuesday reminds us that moral leadership only has substance when we start by looking honestly at ourselves. Let the one who is without sin cast the first stone.

PROFESSOR ANNA ROWLANDS

True north

Anna Rowlands is a highly respected political theologian and author. I had talked to her a few times about doing Thought for the Day *and always caught her over-busy. But there was a brilliant opportunity after she had moved to Durham University's Theology Department where she is now the first St Hilda Professor of Catholic Social Thought and Practice. The* Today *programme were taking an outside broadcast team up to the north-east for a live edition of the programme from Gateshead in front of an audience. The BBC was partnering 'The Great Exhibition of the North', a massive undertaking involving 10,000 artists, scientists, inventors and designers to tell the story of how the north's innovators shaped our present, and how they are inspiring our future.*

What could be better than a northerner speaking with passion and personal knowledge to a live audience in the room who would definitely know the difference? Outside broadcasts always give a more integrated feel to the place of Thought *in the* Today *programme. Anna spoke, setting out the paradox that the north embodies the heartbeat of the nation and yet is routinely neglected by the powerbrokers in the capital. It was a classy debut to a delighted audience who enjoyed hearing an authentic description of their lived lives. The enthusiastic applause conveyed she'd done them proud.*

23 June 2018
North is the position we set our compass to. North, as Peter Davidson writes, is 'the direction taken throughout history by the adventurous, the curious, the solitary, and the foolhardy'.

North, for Stuart Maconie, is both 'something powerful (like Newcastle Brown Ale) and something vague (like most Oasis lyrics)'.

For those of us who live in the north we don't live with generic ideas of the north, we live rooted in particular places. In a sense, we each live with our own north – a north made up of collections of past memories, tied irrevocably to particular places, people and times. And the reality of the north is the people and the places we make our lives with.

The events planned for the Great Exhibition this summer showcase the creativity that has always been part of our northern story. Yet the exhibition is taking place in a region – the north-east – that now has the lowest wages, highest-use food bank and largest free school-meal entitlement in the country.

Schools tell me that they struggle not only with the impact of low wages and insecure work but also with a chronic lack of self-esteem and a sense of powerlessness among families.

It seems to me there is a paradox: people feel simultaneously done-to and yet ignored, peripheral to flows of power and capital and yet trapped by systems that limit and contain their aspiration. Both immense cultural vibrancy and cultural frustration marks 'the North' of today.

When St Paul writes about the common good he uses the image of a body made up of its many parts. The common good is often spoken of as if it is a slightly sterile process of consensus building. For St Paul the common good is closer to an artistic process through which we fashion a social body. Art and innovation, like the wider common good each contributes to, is built on a fragile process through which we venture, fail and venture again.

The common good in this case is neither a true art nor a true politics nor a true Christianity if it frustrates the participation of those who are seen as the least respectable, least honourable and least valuable.

Here's the uncomfortable edge to Paul's teaching: 'the eye cannot say to the hand I have no need of you, nor the hand to the feet'.

The common good can never be reduced to the greatest good for the greatest number, discarding the least.

The challenge is to look at where – and more to the point in whom – you place cultural value, and then look again. Viewed this way, among those who are culturally discarded, here is the heartbeat that would enable the social body to thrive.

LORD INDARJIT SINGH

The martyrdom of Guru Teg Bahadur

Indarjit Singh was a longstanding contributor to Thought for the Day *who began writing for the slot in 1984, only finishing 35 years later in 2019. For much of that time he was the main public voice of the Sikh community in Britain. Born in Rawalpindi in the British Indian province of the Punjab he came to England with his parents a year later. He had a career in civil engineering before serving in local government in London.*

As Founder/Director of the Network of Sikh Organisations (UK), he regularly represented the Sikh community at civic occasions, and took a prominent role in the inter-faith movement both nationally and abroad. In 1989 he received the prestigious Templeton Award for services to spirituality and was made an OBE in 1996 and a CBE in 2009. He was created a life peer in 2011, taking the title Lord Singh of Wimbledon.

In this Thought *Lord Singh celebrates two events which, separately, honoured two Sikh Gurus. He recalls in more detail the martyrdom of Guru Teg Bahadur who paid with his life for defending the religious freedom of others.*

28 November 2018

Last weekend was, for Sikhs, a bit like Christmas and Easter rolled into one. Celebration of the birth anniversary of Guru Nanak, who taught the need for responsible living centred on the rights and concerns of others, was followed next day by the commemoration of the martyrdom of the 9th Guru, Guru Teg Bahadur who in 1675 gave his life in the defence of human rights.

The Mughal ruler Aurangzeb, in his determination to extend Islam to the whole of the subcontinent, was forcibly converting large numbers of Hindus in Kashmir. In desperation the Hindu leaders asked Guru Teg Bahadur to intercede on their behalf. They said, we know that you and earlier Sikh Gurus have always stood up for the rights of all people, will you appeal to the Mughal emperor to stop this forced conversion?

The Guru knew that such an appeal would almost certainly cost him his life. But, true to Sikh teachings on freedom of belief, he set off for Delhi. The emperor refused to change his policy and instead offered rich gifts to the Guru to convert to Islam. When Guru Teg Bahadur refused, he was publicly beheaded in the centre of Delhi. His crime, defending the right to freedom of belief of those of a different religion to his own.

The universal right to freedom of belief is emphasised in the UN Declaration of Human Rights, written in the aftermath of the Second World War. We all applaud its lofty sentiments, but all too often put these below trade and economic interest. For example, questions have been recently asked about the selling of arms to Saudi Arabia in the light of the killing of the prominent journalist Jamal Khashoggi and the ongoing conflict in Yemen.

Guru Teg Bahadur set the bar high when, on a cold winter's day, he gave his life in the defence of human rights and gave stark reality to Voltaire's famous words: 'I may not believe in what you say but will defend to the death your right to say it.' Yet, in the Sikh view, fundamental human rights will continue to be ignored unless those in power and authority are prepared to put these rights well above the false lure of short-term economic gain.

ARCHBISHOP DESMOND TUTU

Rainbow family Christmas

Over the past 30 years I've produced the Thought for the Day *contributions of many exceptional pastors, leaders and thinkers, including those who have reserved their own place in history. Archbishop Desmond Tutu is one of those people.*

I first met him in 1990. It was an amazing experience to encounter at first-hand his energy and exuberance for life, for people, and for his faith. He was already revered around the world for his leadership of black South Africans during the apartheid era for which he had received the Nobel Peace Prize in 1984. All those years of the struggle hadn't diminished his basic belief that human beings were created for fellowship, to form a human family, and to love one another.

When, in 1993, the black activist Chris Hani was murdered by a white racist, Desmond immediately understood the threat it posed to the negotiations to end apartheid and bring about majority rule. Pleading for calm and for no revenge he declared: 'We are the rainbow people of God! We are marching to freedom! Black and white together.' When he agreed to write a Thought for the Day *in December 2018 his Christmas message underlined that fundamental rainbow vision of the world.*

28 December 2018

When we are young and sit down with a bunch of crayons to draw a picture of our family, mum might be purple, dad orange, and grandma blue with a green Mohican. They may look a little garish, but they exude love, compassion, interdependence, dignity and security. The sun is shining, flowers are blooming; perhaps there's even a rainbow in the sky.

This is the human family, God's family; God-carriers made for goodness – all of us.

As we grow and are exposed to prejudice, pride, greed and envy, the picture changes. We disavow our interdependence and common humanity, and become increasingly conscious of perceived differences, superiorities and inferiorities. In this distorted context discrimination becomes justifiable, and the irrational becomes rational. We become fearful and mistrustful of members of our family who don't look like us, dress like us, worship like us … Prejudice and hatred become defensible, to some.

In the Gospel according to St Matthew, Jesus is asked which of the commandments is the most important of all. Jesus responds that the first and greatest commandment is to love God, and the second is to love your neighbour as you love yourself.

In the Gospel according to St Luke, Jesus is challenged to identify this 'neighbour' whom we are exhorted to love. Jesus replies with the parable of the Good Samaritan. It is a story about a traveller responding humanely, at some risk to himself, to a distressed sibling from an unloved branch of the family. I have always been enchanted by this story because it is an antidote to discrimination and insecurity. It tells us that the essence of our humanity is more powerful than prejudice.

Although framed in the politics and prejudices of the Holy Land many centuries ago, it speaks with great clarity to many of the greatest human challenges today: to the people who seek to build higher walls to keep 'other' members of the family out … to the legions of predatory men preying on women and girls … to the consumptiveness of the rich at the expense of the poor …

When we invest in loving our neighbours, in hearing their voices and upholding their dignity, we are investing in God and in a secure coexistence for us all.

I'd like to wish my fellow Christians – and everybody – a peaceful and blessed Christmas. Please lay an extra place at the table, and invite a neighbour in. God bless you all.

JASVIR SINGH

The 550th anniversary of Guru Nanak

Hostility between India and Pakistan has been, sadly, a feature of international politics for seven decades. But in the late 1990s they attempted to set aside their differences to set up a visa-free corridor to enable Indian Sikhs to visit the birthplace of the founder of their religion just across the disputed border inside Pakistan. Yet negotiations kept stalling. Then in 2018 Imran Khan became prime minister in Islamabad and, just three days before the anniversary of Guru Nanak's birth, the pilgrimage corridor finally opened.

Jasvir Singh is a British barrister specialising in landlord–tenant and family law who founded City Sikhs to provide an important new voice for progressive Sikhs. It now has over 7,000 members and a wide array of social inclusion projects with stakeholders including charities, corporates, faith and inter-faith groups. He has worked with similar initiatives to bring together Londoners of the capital's nine main faith communities. He was made an OBE in 2017 for services to social cohesion. Jasvir embodies the mutual respect that, in this Thought, *he describes as being at the heart of Guru Nanak's vision – and that is today needed more than ever.*

12 November 2019

Sikhs around the world are today marking the 550th birth anniversary of Guru Nanak, the founder of the Sikh faith. Although the celebrations have lasted much of this year, the last week alone has seen the Dalai Lama praising the teachings of the first Sikh Guru and the Vatican remarking on Guru Nanak's message of universal fellowship. However, the most remarkable aspect of the anniversary is undoubtedly the opening of a new border crossing between India and Pakistan specifically for Sikh pilgrims.

Guru Nanak spent his final years preaching in the town of Kartarpur. His teachings on the oneness of humanity were ground-breaking, and Hindus and Muslims flocked to him as disciples. According to legend, there was an argument between the two groups about whether the Guru should be cremated or buried after he passed away. The Guru told both to leave flowers in his room and whoever's were still fresh the following day could do as they wished. When his followers entered his room in the morning, the Guru's body had disappeared while all of the flowers remained unwilted. The Hindus and Muslims agreed to share the flowers and bedsheets among themselves. Half were cremated. Half were buried.

Due to the Partition of India in 1947, the town of Kartarpur found itself a couple of miles inside Pakistan. The trauma of partition was acutely felt by Sikhs, who have prayed ever since to be allowed unrestricted access to worship at the birthplace of Guru Nanak and all other gurdwaras and shrines in Pakistan.

Those prayers were partially answered this weekend, when the prime ministers of Pakistan and India opened the Kartarpur Corridor, a joint project costing millions of pounds allowing visa-free access for Indian Sikhs to the holy shrine. A Hindu PM and a Muslim PM coming together in the memory of Guru Nanak's teachings of oneness: its impact cannot be overstated. India and Pakistan, two nuclear states, have been at loggerheads for the last 72 years, they've gone to war several times, and yet their reverence and respect for a humble spiritual teacher born five-and-a-half centuries ago has helped the two nations come together to discuss how best to honour the Guru's memory.

Living in these deeply divided times, the idea of even meeting with people with opposing views and beliefs can seem daunting and challenging. However, Guru Nanak's encounters with others were based on mutual respect, even if he vehemently opposed their customs and practices.

Guru Nanak said: 'As one who is centred on the Almighty, look upon all with the single eye of equality; in each and every heart, the Divine Light is contained.' Five hundred and fifty years on, that idea of considering all as equals in society, while respecting and acknowledging our differences, is as necessary and timely today as it's ever been.

CHIEF RABBI EPHRAIM MIRVIS

Toxic politics at Rosh Hashanah

When the Supreme Court ruled in 2019 that it had been unlawful for Boris Johnson's government to prorogue the House of Commons, to cut short debate on Brexit, the prime minister was incensed. In Parliament, Mr Johnson spoke of 'sabotage' and 'surrender'. His opponents replied with high-octane rhetoric accusing him of being 'unfit to serve'. Next day the Speaker of the House, John Bercow, reprimanded politicians on both sides saying: 'There was an atmosphere in the chamber worse than any I have known in 22 years.'

Chief Rabbi Ephraim Mirvis took up the matter the following day on Thought for the Day. *He was the first United Synagogue rabbi to host an address by an imam in his synagogue and as a Jewish leader he's made much of reaching out to other faiths. So he was well-placed to argue for the importance of civility in discussions of difference. On the eve of Rosh Hashanah, the Jewish New Year, and the celebration of the creation of our common humanity, he said, the ancient rabbis had a useful principle on disagreement to offer to our times.*

9 September 2019

'Toxic' – that was how Speaker John Bercow, yesterday described the culture in the House of Commons. Reflecting on how passions were inflamed on both sides, the speaker stated that the atmosphere had been worse than any he has known and he urged MPs to 'disagree agreeably'.

When it comes to our politics today, civility is often left at the door and people define so much of their identity by what and whom they are standing against, as opposed to what they stand for. An aversion to complexity and the demise of nuance have made compromise harder than ever to achieve and, most worryingly, when tribalism inspires hate speech, hate crime is only one step away.

For millennia, Jewish tradition has treasured healthy disagreement – it has been the lifeblood of our religious practice. The best-known Talmudic adversaries were the great sages, Hillel and Shammai. They disagreed on virtually everything – but they engaged in what we call a '*machloket l'shem Shamayim*' – an argument for the sake of Heaven. This was because neither of them ever allowed their disagreements to become debased or personal.

And why does our religious practice today follow the view of Hillel and not Shammai? It's because Hillel and his students would always respectfully present the differing perspective of Shammai before teaching their own strongly held view.

This coming Monday and Tuesday, Jewish communities around the world will be celebrating Rosh Hashanah, our New Year. It is the anniversary of the creation of humanity. The Yiddish word for a human being is *mensch*. Colloquially, to call someone a mensch is to pay them the ultimate compliment – conveying the highest attributes of decency and dignity.

I believe that now, more than ever before, our challenged world needs to understand and internalise what it means to be a mensch. A mensch passionately fights for what they believe is right without ever compromising on courtesy. A mensch debates the substance of an issue without seeking to destroy the opposition. A mensch is slow to anger and quick to learn from others – including those with whom they may profoundly disagree. And a mensch puts humility and responsibility before their own reputation.

It was nearly 55 years ago when Martin Luther King Jr noted that human beings have mastered the complexities of flying through the air like birds but haven't learned the simple art of living together. When will we learn?

REV. DR ISABELLE HAMLEY

Looking out for the invisible people

Isabelle Hamley grew up in France and, although she has ministered in England for over two decades, Bastille Day still looms large on her calendar. It is the French national holiday that marks the storming of the fortress once used to house the enemies of the king. Its fall marked the start of the French Revolution, which ushered in the values of liberté, égalité, fraternité *on which modern democracy is founded.*

Rev. Dr Isabelle Hamley, at the time of this Thought, *was Chaplain to the Archbishop of Canterbury. Previously a probation officer – as well as a theologian at the universities of Leicester and Nottingham where her academic interests included individual and corporate identity – she has a deep concern for those who are victimised and marginalised. In this* Thought *she begins, in her characteristically acute and insightful manner, by asking about the people the king of France did not see. Then she goes on to ask who are the people who are invisible to us, those for whom we have no regard?*

14 July 2020

Today is 14 July, which for a French woman immediately says Bastille Day, bank holiday and fireworks. It takes me back to my school days: we always got told that on the day the Bastille prison was taken by the people of Paris, King Louis XVI wrote the word 'nothing' as his diary entry. Of course, historians tell us that his diary was only concerned with recording the royal hunt. But still. It tells us something of the king's field of vision, his priorities, what he saw and what he didn't see, or chose not to see.

It is so easy to get trapped in a bubble, an echo chamber of those who look at, and comment on, the things we see already, and be oblivious to invisible people and events around us. It takes effort to extend our field of vision, and willingness to be made uncomfortable. The best advice I was given on becoming a priest was 'always pay particular attention to invisible people'. Go out of your way to see those who are marginalised, those who are quiet, those who are excluded, those who simply never make it to a place where they are seen. If you don't actively search, you will not see.

In the gospels, Jesus is particularly good at doing this. In a beautiful story, a wealthy, well-known city official, Jairus, seeks healing for his young daughter. In the same narrative, a woman, excluded from society because of a chronic illness, reaches from behind to touch him, hoping not to be seen. Jesus heals both. But he heals the daughter of Jairus behind closed doors, making the visible invisible. In contrast, he heals the nameless woman in front of everyone, and enables her to be seen and received back into society.

It is of course much more comfortable not to see everything. People, systems and places that are invisible can make us uncomfortable. Whether it is a homeless person, an isolated elderly neighbour, someone with chronic illness, seeing them challenges us to ask, why are they often invisible to me? And what part do I play in keeping them invisible?

It would have been agonising for Louis XVI to see his world falling apart, and the way in which his own privilege had sustained an unjust, oppressive system that sowed the seeds of its own destruction. Truly looking, and seeing, is a dangerous act. It calls us either to denial and complicity, or to action that will change both ourselves, and the world around us.

BISHOP JAMES JONES

Nick Cave and the supremacy of love

Every faith marks the great moments in the year in religious festivals that punctuate the stages of our life's journey, and provide us with rituals for right living and good death. Thought for the Day *marks these as part of its mission to explain the nation to itself – an increasingly important task as our country becomes more diverse in its range of faiths and cultures. The challenge lies in commenting on their significance for a particular faith in a way that connects with the wider Today audience.*

Good Friday can be among the hardest to handle, which is partly what makes this Thought *from Bishop James Jones so special. The many years he's been writing for* Thought for the Day *have given him a great breadth of experience of many eventualities. He is a wordsmith who relishes plucking examples and experiences from all corners of life to illuminate his theological points.*

His use here of a Nick Cave love song that talks of an interventionist God was inspired. Does God intervene? This is one of theology's most difficult topics and Bishop James handles it with a deft assuredness, counterpointing Cave's lyrics with the words of Christ on the Cross – and sharing with the listeners the trauma of his own grandson's illness. There is something both profound and moving in this message of love.

10 April 2020

On *Desert Island Discs* last month Daniel Radcliffe chose a song by Nick Cave, 'Into My Arms'. A love song, it begins with the sonorous line: 'I don't believe in an interventionist God / But I know, darling, that you do'. That division of belief goes to the heart of the spiritual response to our current crisis of health and wealth.

Some feel there's no point to asking God for help. 'What will be will be.' Others will be on our knees begging God to protect our loved ones and to vanquish the virus.

The Christian faith was born out of a belief in an interventionist God – that the One who made the world would rescue it out of the mire of so much that was now bad.

Although today – Good Friday – feeds this belief it also fuels disbelief. The cry of Jesus from the cross 'My God, why have you forsaken me?' looks like evidence for those who doubt that God has either the will or the power to intervene. If he couldn't rescue his own child what hope is there for us?

Later on in Nick Cave's song he concedes: 'But I believe in Love / And I know that you do too.'

Beneath any arguments about whether or not God intervenes there seems to be a universal conviction about the primacy of love. It's shared by people of all faiths and of none. Kind signs of it are now spreading to surprising places like seeds in the wind blown by the storm of the virus.

Like many people I've prayed to God in difficult times. Last summer our six-year-old grandson had a tumour removed from his brain and is now undergoing 12 months of therapy. And yes, we are praying for God to intervene.

At such a time philosophical arguments evaporate in the heat of love – love for him, for his family and in the hope that God too loves him with all his heart. That's the love that we cling to in such a crisis. It's the same love that energised the life of Jesus.

At the end of Good Friday after the questioning and the thirsting, after the giving and forgiving, after the promise of paradise and the struggling for breath, and just before he declared that it was 'finished' Jesus sighed, 'Into your hands, Oh Lord, I commend my spirit'. Into your arms.

It was his last testament to Love which in our present crisis is our best hope.

REV. DR SAM WELLS

Evil v. sin

'Evil has returned,' said the president of Ukraine, Volodymyr Zelensky, in an emotional address to mark the anniversary of the surrender of Nazi Germany in the Second World War. He was speaking on Ukraine's Day of Remembrance and Reconciliation in which his nation commemorated, ironically, fighting on the same side as Russian soldiers against Adolf Hitler. 'Darkness has returned,' he said, 'in a different form, under different slogans, but for the same purpose.'

Sam Wells is Vicar of St Martin-in-the-Fields. Situated in the heart of London it has a long history of ministering to the homeless. He is also a former Research Professor of Christian Ethics at Duke University and is Visiting Professor of Christian Ethics at King's College, London. From these backgrounds he weaves together weighty theology with the compassion and care of a pastor. He brings both to bear here in this Thought *in which he explores the nature of evil.*

17 May 2022

The war in Ukraine is a challenge not just to Kremlinologists and military strategists. It's a challenge to all of us, to face some indigestible realities. A thousand civilian bodies have been discovered in Bucha region – many buried in shallow graves.

All's fair in love and war, they say. But it's not true: the 1949 Geneva Conventions cover non-combatants in war, and 196 countries subscribe to them, including Russia. You don't get to massacre unarmed local people, whatever your commander says, however intoxicated with violence you've become.

People start sentences with: 'Here we are in the twenty-first century …', thus disclosing a belief that evil is something humanity should grow out of. There's no question the notion of war crimes and the existence of an International Criminal Court are healthy steps. But evil itself doesn't seem to be going away.

I draw a distinction between sin and evil. Evil isn't sin with a loud voice: they're qualitatively different. Sin is where you've transgressed. You know it's wrong, but you tell yourself a false story – everyone does it, no one will notice, it's only a small thing, look at all the good things I've done that outweigh it, I'm not a bad person. But evil has an alternative logic: you tell yourself what you're doing is actually good. Your story has dispensed with guilt and shame and replaced them with pride. I'm not shooting innocent people in the back; I'm denazifying a whole country. I'm not doing it behind the bike sheds; I'm doing it in the village square.

We've had two years to observe how a virus works. Evil is like a virus. It tells a false story that justifies sacrificing other people for a hideous false god. Sin is living in a world without God, without good and bad, without judgement. But evil is creating a whole new and demonic god, and reshaping your entire life to assert that terrible things like cruelty and murder are actually noble. Evil on a national scale creates a mythical story that appeals to a grotesque past that needs honouring – and projects a phantom future where those who slaughter so-called enemies will be rewarded.

To defeat evil takes more than weapons. It requires a very different kind of story. Jesus told stories and lived a story that said the truth will set you free. To overcome evil you have to discredit the story that makes it seem good. You can't destroy evil, any more than you can a virus. You can only tell and live a better story.

Chapter Six

People

BISHOP LORD RICHARD HARRIES

Mary Bell

Mary Bell was a name synonymous with the phenomenon of a 'Killer Child'. The name of the 11-year-old girl from Newcastle became infamous after she was convicted in 1968 of strangling two younger boys. After Mary was released from prison on licence in 1980 she collaborated in writing a book with the journalist Gitta Sereny, who had covered her 1968 trial. The book detailed how Mary was abused by her prostitute mother and her mother's clients. Sereny's thought-provoking biography – of someone who was considered to have committed an evil crime of unparalleled horror – brilliantly delved into the mind of this complex and damaged human being. But it was widely denounced by the press because part of the book's royalties were paid to Mary.

Bishop Richard Harries was one of the first people I worked with on Thought for the Day *back in 1989 – by which time he was already a very experienced broadcaster. As a new producer I learned a lot from him. In this* Thought *he demonstrates his ability to weigh the complexity of an argument in a way that at once appeals to the listener's sense of fairness, and at the same time gently challenges them to rethink their automatic initial reactions.*

4 May 1998

A book about Mary Bell, a child murderer, who had herself been terribly abused as a child, will be published tomorrow. Sadly, the debate about this and the controversy over released paedophiles seem to totally lack any Christian dimension. But the Christian view of existence has truths that are crucial to these issues.

First is the fact that there is a darkness in all of us; one that we are very reluctant to acknowledge. When things go wrong, whether at home or nationally, our instinct is to blame other people. So, in the Genesis story, Adam blamed Eve and Eve blamed the snake. Worse than this, we project our unacknowledged fears on to others. So we get scapegoats and witch-hunts and the whole hue and cry of the popular press. For example, it is, of course, vital to take the greatest possible care in discharging convicted paedophiles into the community. But to demonise them, as has happened, ignores the fact that most child abuse is perpetrated by someone already known to the victim.

Then we ourselves are never in a position to make a final judgement about whether a person could or could not have acted differently. We have to make provisional judgements about who is at fault – the whole criminal justice system depends upon it – but the full truth is another matter. Mary Bell was herself terribly abused as a child. And about someone else who has been vilified it has been said: 'In the lost childhood of Judas, Jesus was betrayed.' Only God knows the pressures people are under. Only God knows whether I have done better or worse in my circumstances than Mary Bell or Judas Iscariot in theirs.

Then, hard though it is to take in, the Christian faith asserts that there is no one who is beyond the scope of Christ's redemption. He came to save all who will be saved. On the cross, one of the criminals turned to Jesus and said: 'Lord, remember me when you come into your Kingdom.' Jesus replied: 'Today you will be with me in paradise.'

This scene haunts Samuel Beckett's play, *Waiting for Godot*. An important part of the background of this play for Beckett was some of Saint Augustine: 'Do not despair; one of the thieves was saved. Do not presume; one of the thieves was damned.'

Demonising a person or particular group of people is always deeply unhealthy. The Christian faith bids us instead to look at the seeds of evil in ourselves and put our trust in the one who came to save us. Criminals need to hear Augustine's words: 'Do not despair.' Some of us, perhaps, are in no less need of hearing his other words: 'Do not presume.'

CANON ANGELA TILBY

A Naked Civil Servant

Quentin Crisp died aged 90 in Manchester on the eve of a sell-out tour of his one-man show, but that fame and appreciation came to him late in life. British-born in 1908 this writer, raconteur and actor found fame at 59 when – the year after homosexuality was decriminalised – he published The Naked Civil Servant, *an account of his years of flamboyant life in London. Before becoming well-known, he was an artist's model paid by the Department of Education, hence the title of his memoir. He finally found happiness when he moved to New York aged 72, remaining one of its most celebrated resident aliens for the rest of his life.*

Angela Tilby, who is now a canon emeritus of Christ Church Cathedral in Oxford, is instinctively empathetic and is adept at exploring why life is so much harder for some people than others. In this Thought *she suggests it's usually as much to do with the way they are treated as the way they behave. Angela reverses the spotlight and throws the questions back to those who do the judging, rather than those who are judged.*

24 November 1999

Quentin Crisp died on Sunday – the 'stately homo of England' as he rather grandly styled himself. From the obituaries his picture surveys us with weary amusement. The made-up face framed by the lilac hair and battered trilby, dainty shirt and chiffon scarf. His arched eyebrows seem to be asking us if we are still shocked by his antics. He was 90 and for years had dreamed of death. He said he wanted the fame of being murdered, though he wasn't. Instead, he'll be missed.

Inside Quentin Crisp was a serious question: *Who would you be if there was no praise or blame?* He tried to live the answer to his question: to imagine, in an age which hated effeminacy, that there was no finger-pointing mockery; at a time before gay rights, that he was nobody's victim. He defined his task in life as being resolutely, defiantly himself. For this he was ridiculed and beaten up, ejected from homes and denied jobs. He learned to bear injustice and to go on flaunting his peculiarities until *we* learned to be more tolerant. Over the years people began to see in him, not bravado but real bravery, something almost akin to saintliness.

The question he asked is important, perhaps the most important question there is. *Who would you be if there was no praise or blame?* All the spiritual traditions tell us to know ourselves and yet our self-knowledge is often constructed from other people's opinions. We want to be praised and fear to be censured, and while we are pulled between the two, our sense of self fluctuates between self-approval and self-hatred. Even God becomes part of the cycle of praise or blame; looking after us when we're good, bashing us when we're bad.

There's a popular spiritual experiment in which you try to write two obituaries of yourself. One you write as if you were your greatest enemy; the other as a sympathetic friend. As you compare and contrast the two accounts you begin to realise that they are not only written *about* the same person but *by* the same person. You are those two selves. You are your own judge and your own advocate. With that insight comes freedom. I think Quentin Crisp went through a version of that process when he decided to live flamboyantly, as a figure of disgrace.

It's a paradox that what he shows me is something about *grace*. Grace is not a reward for goodness, nor a rescue from badness. It is simply that dangerous freedom to be who you are. In religious language, a justified sinner. Or perhaps that most inconceivable of heroes – a naked civil servant.

REV. JOEL EDWARDS

Martin Luther King

Every Thought for the Day *contributor has to prepare themselves for a phone call, late in the day – or even very early next morning – which tells them they have to abandon the script they have carefully prepared and start again. It was after 7pm when Rev Joel Edwards got that call on 15 April 2013 to tell him that two terrorist bombs had gone off among the crowd watching the Boston Marathon. Hundreds had been injured and three people were dead.*

Joel Edwards has a special place in Thought for the Day *history as the first member of the African and Caribbean Evangelical Alliance to join the* Thought *rota. He had arrived in Britain aged eight from Jamaica and took great pride in his Black Pentecostal heritage but saw his vocation as bringing Christians of all backgrounds together. After leading a congregation in east London, he first became the general secretary of the African and Caribbean Evangelical Alliance in 1988 and seven years later he became the first black leader of the whole Evangelical Alliance UK. It was not an easy task, serving as the spokesperson of thousands of evangelicals who did not always agree on theology, politics or culture. But Joel was a man who lived every moment of his ministry in the light of the gospel in which he believed. His warmth, the sincerity of his faith, and his hope that all things were possible, made working with him a joy.*

His original script had reflected on it being the 50th anniversary of Martin Luther King's 'Letter from a Birmingham Jail', one of the most important written documents of the civil rights era. Much of his original thoughtful reflection now had to be left aside. And yet, as you will see, it informed, and added depth, to what was broadcast next morning.

16 April 2013

As we have been hearing this morning, the city of Boston was victimised by calculated evil when two bombs were detonated at the finishing line of the Boston Marathon, killing, injuring and maiming innocent bystanders yesterday. In an instant, the courage and companionship of strangers who became friends along the track, the adulation and endorsement of friends and families, were all blown apart in a moment of inexplicable madness. And as intended, the conspiracy of maliciousness stole the headlines.

In the aftermath of the carnage, America and the world will wade through the implications of the disaster, evaluating and reassessing our security, rebuilding hope and calming fears. In the coming days, we will wait to hear of loved ones whose lives will have been changed forever.

And yet again we are left with deeper and disturbing questions. For once again, we have been confronted with evidence that in the twilight zone of the human condition, lurks a devastating capacity for destruction. But as we reflect on these things, we simply mustn't surrender the significance of yesterday's marathon. The Boston race held in memory of American Independence was a gathering of people from around the world who came together to join in America's celebration of patriotism. In our anguish we cannot afford to be traumatised into forgetfulness.

So it's worth remembering that 50 years ago today, Martin Luther King Jr, the Baptist preacher and civil rights leader, wrote his famous 'Letter from a Birmingham Jail'. King, who struggled against the incomprehensible cruelty of a segregated America, would have understood the ubiquitous spirit of the Boston Marathon. His modern epistle betrayed the mind of a theologian, philosopher and pastor wrestling with a world of possibilities disfigured by injustice. From the narrow confines of his prison cell in Alabama his letter remains a powerful and timely reminder that we are all involved with each other.

Martin Luther King was clear that injustice in any one place is a threat to justice everywhere. Humanity is bound together in a single destiny by a web of mutuality which none can escape. Whatever affects one of us, affects us all. As prayers are offered, these words are worth remembering in our marathon run against terror.

BISHOP TOM BUTLER

Nelson Mandela

Bishop Tom Butler was well travelled. Like many Anglican bishops he served on church and charity boards, which meant getting involved in places from Iraq to Africa to inner-city Britain, encountering both the high and the humble – whose stories he drew on over a long and distinguished period in which he was a Thought for the Day *stalwart. Here, the morning after the death of Nelson Mandela, he tells the story of an inspiring meeting with the great man who – after decades imprisoned for his leadership in the struggle to end white-minority rule in South Africa – set about building a post-apartheid reconciliation in the early 1990s.*

On his release Mandela had stood before a cheering crowd and told them: 'Your tireless and heroic sacrifices have made it possible for me to be here today. I therefore place the remaining years of my life in your hands.' In this Thought *Bishop Tom offers a glimpse of what Nelson Mandela meant by that. This beautifully paced retelling of 'one day in the life' was a fitting tribute to the dedication and duty of one of history's great heroes. On the morning it was broadcast, one line was, sadly, cut for time. It was: 'As Tutu has said: Forgiving is not forgetting. It is actually remembering and not using your right to hit back.'*

6 December 2013

So Nelson Mandela has died after a time of courageous resilience typical of him. When he emerged from 27 years in prison in 1990, many were fearing the toll that those years might have made on his character and leadership. They needn't have worried. With an iron discipline which remained with him unto death, he had used the years behind bars to plan for the future, which he always believed would come, when all the peoples of South Africa would be free to vote for the government of their country.

On and around his release, he not only threw himself with heart and mind into negotiations with the De Klerk government, he also taught his own ANC colleagues how to win respect and power through sticking firm where necessary, and making concessions where useful. The fruits of his efforts came in 1994 when he was elected president of his country.

In a small way I saw him at work during these years. I had been chairman of the Luthuli trust, a charity raising money to educate in the universities of Britain and America the children of ANC leaders like Mandela imprisoned or in exile. The moment that Nelson Mandela was released from prison, however, the money was diverted to South Africa, and we were in the situation of not having the funds to enable several hundred students to finish their studies and get them back home to help in nation building.

The Nationalist government was still in power and I asked for £200,000 from their ambassador in London. 'Not unless you get the signature of Nelson Mandela,' he said. I went to Johannesburg and had three meetings with Nelson Mandela. The first was at eight o'clock in the morning and his secretary told me that he had already been at work for two hours. The last was at half past ten at night and I left him working at his desk. During the meetings I was cross-examined by a man who had lost none of his forensic skills; he was courteous, focused, intentional, with a mind like a ticking clock, unhasting and unresting. I got his signature and the money, and as I flew back to London, pretty exhausted, I told myself that South Africa was going to be in safe hands. I was right.

Nelson Mandela didn't wear his religious faith on his sleeve, but on release from prison he stayed with his long-standing friend Desmond Tutu, then Archbishop of Cape Town. The archbishop has spoken of Mandela's long 27 years of incarceration as a time not only when suffering ennobled him, but as a time when the tribulations purified the dross and deepened his spiritual resources. Certainly forgiveness and reconciliation became Nelson Mandela's hallmarks, symbolised powerfully by his insistence that his white jailer from Robbin Island attend his installation as president. May he rest in peace and rise in glory.

REV. PROFESSOR DAVID WILKINSON

Luis Suárez the biter bit

During the 2014 World Cup, Luis Suárez shocked the football world by biting an opponent, Giorgio Chiellini, during a game in which Suárez's Uruguay were playing Italy. He was not penalised by the ref on the pitch but the television cameras caught him out. Suárez had form; he had been suspended for biting for seven games in 2010 in Holland and again in 2014 for ten games while playing for Liverpool. In the end the football authority FIFA slapped a four-month suspension on him and sent him home from the tournament.

Rev. Dr David Wilkinson is a theoretical astrophysicist and professor of theology at Durham University but he is also a scholar of contemporary culture. In addition to learned tomes such as Christian Eschatology and the Physical Universe *he has also written on 'The Spirituality of* Star Wars'. *David always came to our morning production conversation with at least four ideas and I was delighted when one of them was the idea of tackling the Suárez incident. I knew he would deliver it with a sense of mischief. But he also drew from it some lessons on morality and the difference between the letter and the spirit of the law.*

26 June 2014

Is biting a defender worse than spitting at them, or indeed a manager head-butting a member of the opposition? Luis Suárez has seemingly done it again, provoking headlines of '*Jaws 3*', a storm of condemnation from a majority of pundits and the need for FIFA to act quickly for the sake of the World Cup.

If found guilty of biting Giorgio Chiellini, then Suárez faces a lengthy ban. In a post-match interview Suárez said that 'situations arise on the pitch' and therefore there was 'no need to make a story out of it'. Now, of course there's always been a certain amount of dark arts in cricket, rugby and football, although Norman Hunter* biting your legs was never a literal description.

FIFA's disciplinary proceedings will explore an infringement of codes and then if proven how such infringement should be punished. Yet there is a bigger picture here than just whether certain actions cross the boundary of the outer edge of acceptability on a football field. And that picture is certainly bigger than maintaining the FIFA brand with corporate sponsors or a possible transfer to Barcelona.

The bigger picture is more about the spirit of a game, the way it respects laws rather than simply pushes them to the limit. It takes into account that behaviour influences the next generation, and that we have a responsibility for the legacy of a beautiful game.

Often sport can be a small window into our wider culture. It seems to me that there is a tendency to concentrate on the outer edge of the law, judging what is right or wrong by degrees, rather than seeing the principles at the centre – whether it be in the banking crisis or phone hacking or tax avoidance.

Jesus was often confronted with such a tendency. Some teachers of the law, so concerned with being right with God, drew circles of acceptability around what you should do on the

---

* The tough-tackling 1970s Leeds player nicknamed 'Bites Yer Legs'.

Sabbath or who you could eat with. By contrast Jesus was never concerned with those outer limits, he was more concerned to point to God's love, mercy and justice as the source and inspiration of moral behaviour. He was also committed to the individual who needs help, as has been suggested for Suárez.

It is possible to try and shape behaviour by continually legislating, policing and condemning – and my own Christian tradition has not been immune from that. But I want a society which celebrates and promotes the bigger picture rather than just the limits of acceptability. Just because it's not illegal, doesn't mean that it is good. After all, I want footballers who know not to bite opponents, rather than a world where it is compulsory that they wear gumshields.

PROFESSOR MONA SIDDIQUI

Raif Badawi and Saudi piety

The fate of the human rights blogger Raif Badawi, arrested in Saudi Arabia in 2012 and facing barbaric punishment, was truly shocking. He had been sentenced to ten years imprisonment with 1,000 public lashes – 50 a week for 20 weeks – for the crime of establishing a forum to encourage debate on religious and political matters in Saudi Arabia. A week after the first whipping of 50 lashes in January 2015 hospital doctors in Jeddah declared that his injuries had not healed and he was in poor medical condition.

This Thought *from Mona Siddiqui was broadcast the morning that the second flogging was due to be given. It felt a very important statement at the time of broadcast, coming as it did from Mona who is a specialist in Islamic jurisprudence (*fiqh*) and ethics – and was the first Muslim to hold a chair in Islamic and Interreligious Studies at the University of Edinburgh. But it was also important to Mona herself to express her horror at what was being meted out in the name of Islam. Her voice matters – she is also*

Dean International for the Middle East at the University of Edinburgh –
and this Thought for the Day *was an early part of the international*
outcry that followed the first flogging. We couldn't have known at that point
what would happen and the outcome looked very grim.

16 January 2015

What does insulting Islam mean today – seemingly everything
from provocative cartoons to having a website championing for
free speech. The Saudi writer Raif Badawi has been sentenced
to ten years in prison and 1,000 lashes – 50 per week – for setting
up a website calling for a more liberal and free society in Saudi
Arabia; he was arrested in 2012 and his blog shut down.

Today he will receive the second round of lashes after
Friday prayers, despite international condemnation of torture
and human rights violations. As so often the cry of 'God is
great' will be followed by an act of violence. The world will
watch as we become increasingly desensitised to the levels of
brutality perpetrated by Islamists and states of all creeds and
colours. Saudi Arabia isn't the only country to violate international laws but it does so often with an air of chilling certainty
that its punishments reflect piety.

If globalisation has made the world a smaller place, never
before have cultural values seemed so far part. I believe we
should speak up not out of any moral high ground but rather
if we stand for any kind of universal human dignity, we can't
remain silent. After all, it's the appeal of a certain puritan-
ical and violent Islam that is being played out on the streets
of Europe; and what happens in distant lands affects us over
here. It's one thing for leaders to march together defending
free speech, and however welcome that is – it's quite another to
stand up for it in the face of autocratic states.

And yet this is the real challenge because one country isn't
supposed to dictate to another how it should manage its laws;

political realities make it very difficult to intervene in the culture of another country. Over the last few years, writers and artists have spoken out against the destruction of all that Saudi Arabia considers an insult to its ideas of true Islam; and yet in the end we have been helpless to do anything. Today we can plead that Raif Badawi's crime is pardoned. If we remain silent in the assurance that forgiveness will just happen, it won't.

'God is great' is heard all the time but it seems to me that the words 'God is merciful' are gradually disappearing from the streets and in the pulpits. A merciful God is of no value to those for whom mercy means weakness. 'Je suis Raif' is springing up over social media but we don't need another hashtag to appreciate that the demand for a more open society can only ever be a good thing, wherever we live.

In Raif's own words, his government's 'hold over people's minds and society shall vanish like dust carried off in the wind'. But if this does happen, it may already be too late for Raif.*

FRANCIS CAMPBELL

Why Pope Francis is different

When the first pope from the poor world visited the richest country in the world it was bound to be a study in contrasts. Pope Francis landed in the United States, arriving rather pointedly via Cuba, which prompted reporters to ask him if he was a communist. 'Maybe I have given an impression of being a little bit to the left,' the Pope said but then offered to recite the Creed to prove his politics were rooted in Christianity. Practising what he preached,

---

* In fact, Badawi's floggings were suspended after the outcry. He was released at the end of his ten-year sentence on 11 March 2022 but remains under a travel ban preventing him from leaving Saudi Arabia for another ten years. His wife and children had already fled to Canada where they were granted asylum in 2013.

Francis insisted on driving around Washington, DC in a tiny white Fiat car – the smallest in the motorcade.

One Thought for the Day regular was best-placed to explain that the Pope's lifestyle was not just personal modesty. Francis Campbell, born a Catholic farmer's son in Northern Ireland, had risen to the top in the British civil service – working for Prime Minister Tony Blair in 10 Downing Street before becoming head of the Foreign Office policy unit. En route he had been British ambassador to the Vatican. In this Thought he draws on that varied experience to throw some light on what lay behind the simple leadership style of this unusual pope.

26 September 2015

This time last week I was in New York amid all the flurry of activity ahead of Pope Francis's arrival in the city – from the construction workers on Madison and Fifth filling in the potholes, to the scaffolding around St Patrick's Cathedral being hastily dismantled. The Pope's ambassador showed me all the preparations he had in place to host the Pope during his stay. It was all so reminiscent of events here in London five years ago ahead of Pope Benedict's state visit to the UK. As a former ambassador to the Vatican I know from experience that there is no diplomatic manual for visits of the Pope; they are unique regardless of the context.

Yet despite the modern protocol that accompanies state visits, it is somewhat counter-cultural that the world's oldest office – the papacy – which is not a democracy, is giving such a powerful and somewhat unique lesson in leadership. Francis's informal and simple style is connecting with people far beyond the Catholic fold. His message of mercy and forgiveness and of solidarity is one which is both challenging and reassuring in equal measure, both within and outside the Catholic Church. He is forcing people to think and to reappraise. But his leadership style also gives tangible expression to deeply held principles.

The image of the Pope's little Fiat car, amid all the hustle and bustle of a huge security motorcade, is striking. No doubt

Francis's scaling back of security to get closer to people has given the US Secret Service many headaches, but it is both symbolic and constant. It also challenges many other leaders who perhaps enjoy the trappings of office – and where security can become a welcome barrier between leader and people and brings rights of privilege over the rest of society.

Francis has a prophetic leadership style rather than a calculating one. He is not thinking about how a situation can play to his advantage or how he can get to the next level. In a temporal sense he *is* there – and so the papacy brings an immense freedom as an office. It allows a prophetic voice to come forth in a way that few other leadership offices can safely permit. But that only answers part of the question about why Francis's style and message are still captivating so many.

That prophetic voice, to be truly prophetic, has to be authentic, consistent and sincere. It has to speak truth in times of harmony and disharmony. In Francis's case the message is not his, but Christ's and delivered in a rather unique, direct and simple style. People seem to be responding. They are looking at the words and then his actions – they are seeing a consistency, not a contradiction.

Francis is showing other leaders in all walks of life that the 'servant leader' with the prophetic voice is more appropriate to our age than the privileged and calculating leadership styles of the past. His example may be as powerful as his message and be his lasting legacy.

BISHOP NICK BAINES

Who is Martin Luther?

Nick Baines, the Anglican Bishop of Leeds, has a gentle Liverpudlian accent, is happy to refer to himself as a 'Scouser', and is one of the few people who can do irony and humour on air and pull it off. There's something about his distinctive delivery that gives itself to sending up the pompous or the vain. This Thought *was delivered in the run-up to the 500th anniversary of the Reformation, the sixteenth-century religious movement that altered the course of world history for ever.*

Bishop Nick was preparing to give a lecture in Erfurt, the city that contained the monastery which was the original home to Martin Luther who kicked off the whole Reformation by fixing his famous Ninety-five Theses *to the door of Wittenberg Castle Church. It's the kind of topic that most of the* Today *audience will know all about but on* Thought for the Day *we need to connect with every listener without taking anything for granted. Nick begins his* Thought *in a vein of humour but then makes it clear that he does not find anything very amusing contemplating the outcome of religious illiteracy and historical ignorance.*

29 August 2016

I went into a bookshop last week to get a book I'd seen reviewed and, on a first look around the ground floor, couldn't find it. So, I went to the assistant and asked if they had the new biography of Martin Luther by Oxford academic Lyndal Roper. The conversation went something like this:

'You mean Martin Luther King?'

'No, I mean Martin Luther.'

'I've never heard of him. Who is he?'

'He was a German monk who set off the Reformation in Europe.'

'A German monk? He's probably in "Religion".'

Eventually I went upstairs anyway and found it myself under 'German History'.

Well, I was a little alarmed about this. Not so much because of the religious illiteracy it demonstrated, but the historical ignorance. When I tweeted this exchange, a friend reminded me of the occasion when someone went into a bookshop and asked where he could find Oscar Wilde. The answer? 'He's not in today.' Other funny comments followed.

Call me old-fashioned, but it is impossible to have any understanding of the modern world – especially modern Europe – without some reference to the German monk. And for me this is personal: I will be speaking in Luther's Erfurt at the end of October this year to kick off the 500th anniversary of the Reformation in Europe.

The challenge this presents is this: which histories need to be known if we are to know who we are and what got us to where we are? I lived and worked in the Cold War, so inhabited a divided Europe: my kids did not, and for them the Soviet Union is as remote as the Boer War. Yet, some histories shouldn't be ignored.

Luther was a complicated man: intense, argumentative and bad-tempered. He said some terrible things about Jews (which in turn had terrible consequences even four centuries later) and wasn't exactly a proto-feminist. He challenged one political power only to find himself colluding with others. He was brave, disciplined and sharp as a knife. He changed the German language forever, and shaped what became the modern world by following up on an idea: that God loves us anyway.

In other words, Luther was a complex human being – just like the rest of us. We don't have to ignore his faults or take him out of his times in order to make him palatable to twenty-first-century sensibilities. Praise him or damn him, we still have to take seriously what he did at the time he did it.

Essentially Luther was empowered by one simple discovery: we can never be perfect, but we can be liberated by knowing we are freely loved by God. 'Grace' it was called. It changed him, and he changed the world.

We see around us plenty of anger, strife and disputation. Surely it wouldn't be a bad thing to rediscover grace. And also to rediscover history.

CATHERINE PEPINSTER

Pinter, Bakewell and truth

Catherine Pepinster has a long track record of striving for a combination of accuracy and fairness in her journalism working as a writer and editor on secular newspapers such as the Independent *and in religious journalism as editor of the Catholic weekly* The Tablet. *So it's unsurprising that both accuracy and fairness find a place in this* Thought.

Other people's relationships make for good theatre, particularly if, like Harold Pinter and Joan Bakewell, the two lead characters are both luminaries in their chosen field. After a seven-year clandestine affair in the 1970s both later wrote contrasting plays about their relationship – his Betrayal, *and hers* Keeping in Touch. *In this* Thought *Catherine gently guides the listener through the alternatives to ask: can both be true? She unfolds a fascinating line of argument, and then broadens the debate by speaking of those priests who refused to be silent under oppressive regimes and paid with their lives. Most of us will never have to go that far but if we couldn't speak for ourselves, who would we trust to speak for us?*

22 April 2017

This afternoon literary history will be made on this radio channel when two plays are broadcast. The first, *Betrayal,* by Harold Pinter, tells the story of an affair between Jerry and Emma, who is the wife of his best friend Robert. The second by Joan Bakewell is being performed for the first time. What is intriguing is that Pinter based his play on the eight-year long affair he had with Bakewell in the 1960s. It now emerges that Joan Bakewell wrote her own play after the premiere of *Betrayal,* distressed by Pinter's account of their relationship, put it in a drawer and forgot about it until now. Joan Bakewell has indicated that it matters to her to put the record straight by giving her version of events. In other words, she wants what she believes is the truth to be heard.

Truth was central to Harold Pinter's acceptance speech when he won the Nobel Prize in Literature. He described the search for truth as what drives a writer but said that in drama there is never just one truth. This fluidity is highlighted by these two plays being broadcast side by side this afternoon. Can both be true? Whose version of events should we trust?

Since the Enlightenment, the notion of truth has developed as something that can be understood entirely objectively, rather as if a dispassionate observer gazes at it down a microscope. For the Christian, truth is more something that is understood through attentiveness to the other. It is self-centredness that cramps perspective, thwarts honesty and leads to betrayal.

And yet being a follower of the truth can demand more than that. In his Nobel speech, Pinter changed tack and spoke not just about the truth being elusive but about people he admired for standing up for a truth that wasn't fluid at all. One was a priest who served in Nicaragua, whose parish was attacked and church burned down by the US-backed Contras, another was a group of six Jesuit priests murdered in 1989, and the third was Archbishop Óscar Romero, assassinated as he said Mass, all of them in San Salvador, all defenders of people against human rights violations.

Pinter interpreted this sacrifice by the priests as their countering of certain politicians who were intent on manipulating power in the name of their so-called truth. A Christian interpretation would see the priests' actions as witnessing to an absolute truth – the love of God for his people.

This obligation to speak up, though, is not so much a lack of choice but a form of freedom – freedom from the compromises that others demand of you. As Christ said, the truth will set you free.

REV. LUCY WINKETT

A note from Albert Einstein

Everyone loves a fascinating snippet. A little-known fact about one of the most famous men in history always goes down very well. A pub-quiz winner. It's not hard news but it is the kind of thing you would remember and mention to someone else. Light and shade, happy and sad, or a maxim to live by from the greatest scientist of the twentieth century: they all have a place on Thought for the Day. *It's what keeps it human among the relentless seriousness of the news.*

Lucy Winkett, Rector of St James's Piccadilly, in London, is good at taking hold of this kind of story and finding the kernel at the heart of it that speaks at a deeper level to lots of people. How interesting that a world-renowned scientist is not looking for success or fame, but just enough to be happy in himself. And that begs the question, if Einstein could gather his thoughts on happiness so quickly and succinctly, could we do the same?

26 October 2017

A small handwritten note was auctioned this week in Jerusalem, and was expected to fetch between $5,000 and $8,000. To everyone's astonishment it went for over $1.5 million. The note was short, on generic hotel notepaper from the Imperial Hotel Tokyo, and was written in 1922 in lieu of a tip for a hotel worker by the guest who wrote it. The note wasn't an IOU; the guest wrote this: 'A quiet and modest life brings more joy than a pursuit of success bound with constant unrest.' Albert Einstein wrote this note to a courier, not long after he had been told he was nominated for the Nobel Prize in Physics.

Even today, the name Einstein is a byword for genius. We use it defensively – 'I'm not Einstein' we say – when some flaw in our logic is exposed, or when we have come to the edge of what we can understand. His ability to see what baffled previous generations is, for those of us who are not scientists, exhilarating.

And it's this symbolic meaning of Einstein that struck me as I thought about this note, written in a moment for an anonymous courier when Einstein was far from home. His subject was not physics – but joy. That's what he chose to say in that transient moment in a hotel lobby. He wrote about joy.

A lot is said these days about the opposition between science and faith. That logic trumps belief in a way that is final, triumphant and conclusive.

But this great scientist himself, just before he died, even spoke of God. He wrote to a friend: 'If God has created the world his primary worry was certainly not to make its understanding easy for us.'

He seemed to value not just the pursuit of knowledge, which is what he is famous for, but the wonder of living and the endless questions that raises. From this I learn that my struggle to know more, mostly reveals to me the true extent of what I don't know. And as I accept this, so my wonder deepens, my sense of adventure intensifies, and the world becomes not a less but a more mysterious place.

For someone as distinguished as Einstein to say that the pursuit of success, in his words, doesn't bring joy, is a voice from the frontline of intellectual endeavour. And in a world obsessed by success, it's hard to put into practice. But as Einstein also wrote in his own hand, in another note auctioned at the same time: 'Where there is a will, there is a way.'

REV. ROY JENKINS

Jamal Khashoggi and the price of silence

The murder of Washington Post *columnist Jamal Khashoggi was particularly gruesome. He was assassinated by agents of the Saudi government*

*who lured him into the Saudi consulate in Istanbul on the pretext of provid-
ing documents he needed for his forthcoming wedding. Once inside he was
suffocated and dismembered by 15 Saudi assassins. His final moments were
recorded by Turkish intelligence who later released transcripts of the killers'
chilling conversations during the horrible act.*

*The world was outraged. Major global organisations announced they
were pulling out of 'Davos in the Desert', a big conference designed to
boast Saudi Arabia's modernisation. Good, said Rev. Roy Jenkins, in this*
Thought. *Roy is a Baptist minister who has been a campaigner against
human rights abuses since his student days. He founded Christians Against
Torture as long ago as 1981. Drawing on all that experience, Roy, who
is one of* Thought*'s most uncompromising and trenchant voices against
injustice, asks whether international indignation will persist in the face of
the multimillion-dollar deals the Saudis have on offer.*

20 October 2018

There was a grimly prophetic ring to Jamal Khashoggi's final
newspaper column published this week. The Saudi journalist,
whose killing has created a storm of protest, referred to a fellow
writer imprisoned for comments which displeased his country's
rulers. 'Such actions,' he wrote, 'no longer carry the consequence
of a backlash from the international community.' Instead, they
'may trigger condemnation quickly followed by silence.'

Well, the indignation has been loud, for sure, with an embarrassing string of high-profile withdrawals from the glittering
global event designed to showcase the nation's modernisation:
the movers and shakers now have more pressing engagements.

But how soon before the condemnation is 'quickly followed
by silence'? Multimillion-pound deals, with their promise of
jobs and influence and profit, can have a powerfully quietening
effect. How do you balance their allure against the need for
people to be allowed the basic right to speak truth to power?
Will anything change?

Whether they wander out of a desert in cloaks of camel hair and present themselves to a ruler in person, or publish tracts, or newspapers, or web blogs, prophets are rarely welcome. 'They tell the prophets to keep quiet,' wrote Isaiah in the Old Testament. 'They say: Tell us what we want to hear. Let us keep our illusions' (and today they might add, 'our contracts').

Martin Luther King hauntingly observed that, ultimately, we will not remember the words of our enemies but rather the silence of our friends. What value our initial indignation at a wrong, if we don't go on speaking up?

It's never, of course, the responsibility of people who've been on the receiving end of abuse, but of those who know – and choose to say nothing. This discomforting issue faces the entertainment world, business, education, the aid sector, religious organisations and parliament itself.

And all of us, I suppose, know far more than we'd like on all kinds of injustice which might make us want to scream in fury – from oppression, hunger and disease across the world, to the poverty and inequity which diminish many lives in our own communities.

The need can overwhelm us. I've long been helped by the words of the Methodist preacher and broadcaster Colin Morris, who died earlier this year. He said: 'Being finite and fitfully loving humans, we can only really feel for a few … Only God can love them all. The most we can do is to take hold of the near edge of one of these great issues – and seek to act, at some cost to ourselves.'

For me, then, the question is always: who represents the edge of need nearest to us? And how should we go on speaking for them?

BRIAN DRAPER

Vera Lynn

Brian Draper, formerly of the London Institute for Contemporary Christianity, is a freelance writer, speaker, retreat leader and mindfulness practitioner. He comes into contact with people of all faiths and none, and from all walks of life, helping them to see the world from a creative and engaging spiritual perspective – all of which has honed his skills for being able to strike just the right tone on Thought for the Day.

When Vera Lynn died, only a month after the 75th anniversary celebrations for VE Day, it felt to many people as though they had lost someone they knew, almost as if she was one of their own. She had been a national figure in the lives of at least three generations. It's not often someone can fill the need as perfectly as she did in a time of national crisis during the war years. And for the rest of her life she projected the same warmth and humanity that had meant so much to people. She deserved all the accolades that flowed in when her death was announced. Hearing Brian Draper's tribute coming out of the radio was particularly moving.

20 June 2020

I loved what Sir Cliff Richard said this week of the time he guided Dame Vera Lynn to the stage, through crowds of veterans, for the 50th celebrations of VE Day in 1995. 'They were reaching out to touch and get a smile from Vera,' he said. 'I heard the words: God bless you … thank you … we love you.'

Of course, many of those first hearts to be captured by the Forces Sweetheart have long since gone ahead of her.

But the fact that her most iconic song, 'We'll Meet Again', is cherished not just by the class of '39, but by their children's children, shows the power of a song to move us.

How revolutionary, in a way, that it gave a nation of buttoned-up Brits the words to say. As Dame Vera said, '[It was] a very basic human message of the sort that people *want* to say to each other but find embarrassing to put into words.'

And how fascinating, the song was almost banned for sentimentality. 'As I saw it,' she said, it 'was reminding the boys of what they were really fighting for, the precious, personal things.' A more feminine, spiritual complement, perhaps, within the context of conflict. And a reminder for us, beyond any present jingoism, to ask: what are *we* fighting for?

For the song does reach to us. Offering hope and resilience, as referenced by the Queen, within the isolation of lockdown; and being carried on the air of the VE Day celebrations this May. I remember, that night, stepping outside to hear a distant trumpeter play its tune; people sang, and cheers arose, along with goosebumps on my arm.

It's not *just* that it connects us evocatively back to the war, but that it resonates with our universal longing for homecoming and reunion. And for me, in a sense, it begs an immortal question: '*Will* we meet again?'

When the journalist Cole Moreton dared to ask Dame Vera, in her final interview, whether she thought we *would*, beyond death, she replied, 'I think there has to be something. What it is, I don't know. I wasn't brought up to pray. It's a difficult subject.'

That's where her music does the talking, like a psalm. But, as someone who *was* brought up to pray myself, I think of Jesus' promise to the thief on the cross, that they will be reunited that very same day. And I hope Dame Vera wouldn't mind me saying that her song enriches my faith in such a promise for us all. In the words of the veterans, God bless you, Dame Vera. Thank you. We love you. Until that sunny day …

BISHOP JAMES JONES

Anthony Walker

Whenever there's a new Jimmy McGovern drama scheduled there is invari-ably media coverage because of the strong stories the Liverpudlian dramatist chooses to write about. The killing of Anthony Walker was no exception. In the run-up to the televising of the drama Anthony, the mother of the murdered young man, Gee Walker, was interviewed on Today. *The element of faith was at the heart of this story so that this* Thought, *rather than being a theological reflection, is more a sharing of a lived faith experience.*

James Jones, who was Bishop of Liverpool for over a decade, has his own story to tell about the Walker family too: the horror, the loss, his support for Gee. This is, of course, the role of the pastor and priest. Yet for Bishop James it also becomes personal. It's about the violence on the streets of his adopted city; how a mother tries to reconcile herself to her loss; and how much does society really care? These raise theological questions and he puts them very directly. But they also open up for him the need to ask why such killings repeatedly arise and how their coverage affects the public response. Why do some hit home, and others don't? Like Jimmy McGovern, Bishop James does not leave Anthony where he fell.

27 July 2020

On Thursday this week it'll be the 15th anniversary of the murder of Anthony Walker, and tonight on BBC One Jimmy McGovern's play *Anthony* will tell the story of the life he never got the chance to live.

I led Anthony's funeral in Liverpool's Anglican Cathedral and last year on Good Friday I interviewed his mother Gee Walker here on Radio 4. When I asked her to describe him she said: 'He was just every mother's dream child. Thank God, he gave me everything I ask for. Tall, dark, handsome. Sensitive. Loved me, loved God, loved people.'

Gee wanted him to be a preacher, Anthony wanted to be a lawyer. He used to taunt his teachers with a cheeky grin: 'Go on, miss. Smile. Have a nice day!' He was fit and strong. No one would mess with him. Except one night on 29 July 2005 Michael Barton and Paul Taylor hurled racist abuse at him and his friends at a bus stop in Huyton and Taylor sank an ice-axe into Anthony's head.

When Gee got to the hospital and insisted on seeing him she told me all she had to do was to follow his blood. 'His blood led me to him.'

By this time Gee had got hundreds of people all over the world praying for Anthony but 'he never regained consciousness' and died. When I asked her: 'What did that do to your faith?' I didn't expect what followed. 'That increased my faith because I realised that now all I've got is God.'

I wish I could replay the whole 60 minutes we recorded. Or better still, see the full three score years and ten that Anthony should have lived. For he had the faith and the values of his mother.

As I've looked back over the last 27 years and the deaths of Stephen Lawrence, Damilola Taylor and Anthony Walker, I've wondered why it's taken the killing of an unknown man in Minneapolis to make us in this country 'take the knee'. Why did not the murder of three of our own black teenagers drive us to our knees?

As I've watched Anthony's mother – her willingness to forgive, her refusal to be consumed by hatred – I've wondered if we've presumed too much on the decency of the Lawrences, the Taylors and the Walkers.

On this programme Gee Walker said she hoped the play tonight would 'honour' Anthony. Unlike a statue it'll make him come alive, breathing life back into his wounded body. It'll be a vindication – and a Resurrection.

CHINE MCDONALD

George Floyd

The deaths of black citizens at the hands of white police officers have become a sad and terrible commonplace in recent times. But one inspired a global protest movement, perhaps because the killing of George Floyd – pinned under the knee of a white policeman for 9 minutes and 29 seconds as he pleaded repeatedly 'I can't breathe' – was caught on the camera of a mobile phone and went viral around the world. One year on, demonstrators took to the streets again to mark the grim anniversary.

Chine McDonald, who has brought a distinctive new perspective to the Thought for the Day *rota in recent years was well-placed to reflect upon the event and its resonances. Born in Nigeria, she moved to the UK at the age of four and read theology and religious studies at Cambridge University before training as a newspaper journalist. She then headed up community fundraising and public engagement at the international development charity Christian Aid before publishing* God Is Not a White Man – And Other Revelations. *In this* Thought *she talks about the importance of remembrance.*

25 May 2021

Today, people all over the world will engage in acts of remembrance to mark a year since the murder of George Floyd; lighting candles, saying prayers, kneeling and sitting in silence for the length of time in which Derek Chauvin knelt on his neck.

We know what happened next – the spread of the Black Lives Matter movement and a reckoning with racial justice across our institutions. I heard someone recently describe now dividing time between 'before George Floyd' and 'after George Floyd'.

There was a sense – at least in the weeks that followed – that we could never be the same again.

Last week, I spoke at an event with Patrick Ngwolo – George Floyd's pastor – and asked how he felt about the legacy of his friend's death. He broke down as he remembered again the cruelty of watching Floyd's execution – a prolonged and agonising death, while crying out for his mother.

Remembrance is important, but it can also be painful. Philosopher Friedrich Nietzsche wrote that life would be more joyful for all if we engaged in 'active forgetting'.

It would be easy for me here to recast George Floyd as a Christ-like figure, whose death and sacrifice is ultimately for the good of us all. To show that black death demonstrates that where the world has been a place of injustice, oppression and violence for black people, there will be justice and peace in the world to come.

But why shouldn't justice begin now? Why can't there be life in all its fullness before death?

George Floyd was not a martyr who willingly laid down his life, but a victim of a pervasive system of oppression, centuries-long in the making, that sees black people as lesser.

Christians believe Christ died once and for all people. But black people have seen the brutalisation of the bodies of those who look like them time and time again. Today we remember George Floyd, but the annual calendar is marked with too many memorials to slain black men and women. We keep remembering. Because we have to.

Collective memory – memorials, statues, commemorations – help us make sense of today. We look back so we can move forward. The ritual of remembrance is an important space through which we can engage in transformation.

In the Last Supper, Jesus instructs his followers to continue to eat the bread and wine in remembrance of him. This act is not an empty gesture; but intended to be a place of remembering, before rebirth and then renewal. Through remembrance, transformation is possible. This transformation happens not in isolation, but in community.

As many light candles today to remember George Floyd, let's remember to 'fight racism with solidarity'.

Chapter Seven

Science, Nature and COVID

AKHANDADHI DAS

When man and nature clash

The Sea Empress oil spill was one of the worst environmental disasters in British history. On 15 February 1996 the oil tanker hit rocks as it entered the Milford Haven estuary in south-west Wales and was holed below the waterline. Severe weather hampered attempts to bring the vessel into port. Over 72,000 tonnes of oil was released into the sea along one of Europe's most important wildlife and marine conservation areas, the Pembrokeshire Coast National Park. The clean-up took over a year to complete.

The Vaishnava theologian Akhandadhi Das was living in Wales at the time as the news was filled with reports of thousands of oil-coated seabirds and devastated local tourist and fishing industries. What was on display, he reflected in this Thought *– drawing on the teachings of a renowned Hindu holy man – was more than just a catastrophic environmental disaster. There was also the recognition that our rampant consumer mindset was driving our lifestyle so hard that the natural world would increasingly become a casualty of our need to obtain and transport the things we think will make us happy. Looking back, Akhandadhi's insight was well ahead of his time.*

22 February 1996

It is ironic that, in the same week scientists reported adverse changes to the Gulf Stream caused by global warming, we are then faced with another environmental disaster, also related to a man and nature clash. The sea, it seems, struck back – only to spite itself. Although, the *Sea Empress* has now been rescued, its lost cargo of crude oil will do no good to the wildlife of the Pembrokeshire coast. And dispersing the slick by chemical treatment further exacerbates the questionable cocktail that was once saltwater.

The huge slick isn't just oil – it is liquid consumerism. Oil is drilled and transported to fuel our insatiable cravings for more products and services – and to have them now – in the belief that happiness is increased through endless material acquisition. Prahlad, a renowned Hindu saint, did not share this belief. He warned: 'Ideas devised by greedy and materialistic minds fail to satisfy our expectations of pleasure. Rather such "solutions" to life's problems bring more severe problems in their wake.'

We may look back to the dirty era of nineteenth-century industry and persuade ourselves that our current technology is somehow more benign. Yet we are doing more now to dese-crate the natural world – indeed, we have ample potential to make it totally uninhabitable. We must certainly apply our intel-ligence to consider methods of lifestyle, industry, agriculture and transport which are truly sustainable. After all, if human brain power can put a man on the moon, why can't it resolve our basic needs on earth which are disrupting the ecosystem for future generations? But intellect alone is not the answer.

The satirical story of one young man eager to live simply and eschew materialistic life illustrates the tendency. This budding ascetic was advised to be satisfied owning a single loincloth. After a while, he thought that having a second cloth would be advantageous and, surely, no hindrance. However, this spare cloth was attacked by mice and so the young man got a cat to guard it. Then he got a cow to provide milk for the cat; then a wife to care for the cow and, before he knew it, he was back in his old job working to pay the mortgage.

In an age when personal fulfilment is God and economic growth the religion, self-control and an honest appraisal of our real needs are not virtues. Perhaps, it requires a revolution of our concept of happiness to plug the gushing flow of liquid consumerism.

Once, a king berated a brahmana youth for not taking advantage of his generous offer of land and wealth. The brahmana replied that 'if I were not content with the simple possessions I now have, what certainty is there that I would be satisfied even if you gave me the whole world? Contentment,' he said, 'is internal satisfaction gained by enriching the heart. It isn't endless acquisition at the expense of Mother Earth.'

REV. PROFESSOR DAVID WILKINSON

The Large Hadron Collider and the Big Bang

The Large Hadron Collider at CERN was built to allow physicists to test different theories of particle physics. It created huge excitement both among experts in astrophysics and ordinary listeners who were simply fascinated by the human endeavour to find out what really happened in the first moments of the universe. Its search to find the Higgs boson – which the tabloid press dubbed 'the God particle' – was a moment the media were desperate to capture.

Rev. Professor David Wilkinson is Principal of St John's College at Durham University. He's a professor in systematic theology and also has a PhD in astrophysics; he's an expert in star formation and is a fellow of the Royal Astronomical Society. His many illuminating contributions to Thought for the Day *on the interaction between science and religion have brought a new dimension to listeners' appreciation of the synergies and compatibility of the two disciplines. This* Thought *begins with a nod to the fireworks on Southwark Bridge at the celebration of the 2008 Mayor's Thames Festival in London.*

10 September 2008

To add to the many bangs of fireworks over the last few days, a number of news sites have reported a number of mini Big Bangs created at the Large Hadron Collider at CERN. For some, the thought that scientists were now moving into the realm of God has the same effect of loud rockets on the neighbour's dog. However, we need to step behind the headlines, and the horror of some religious people, to see what is really going on.

After a successful time of colliding protons into protons at record energies, the Large Hadron Collider on Saturday moved on to accelerate and collide together lead atoms stripped of electrons. It is hoped that the energies achieved by this will allow the study of a quark-gluon plasma, which would have occurred in the first instants of the universe's existence and then evolved into the matter that makes up the universe today. In particular, we hope that it will allow further study of the strong interaction which binds quarks into bigger objects such as protons and neutrons.

The energies, although far higher than what we have produced before, are still a long way from the initial moment of the Big Bang itself, so we are not in danger of producing loads of universes in our own backyard. However, there will be those who still fear that such science is trespassing into an area which should be left to God the Creator. After a talk on the Big Bang I did last week, I was approached by a teenager who asked: 'Why do we need to know about such things anyway?'

It is an important question, not least when such vast sums are spent on colliding bits of lead. We do know that investment in this type of pure science has long-term benefits, as our understanding of the fundamental laws of nature can open up new applications in a surprising and fruitful way.

Yet as a Christian, trained as an astrophysicist, there is a further reason, why I will be following the results of the collisions this week. The more I get to know about the elegant scientific laws which lie behind the universe, the more I see them as a reflection of the faithful sustaining activity of a Creator God.

For the Christian understanding of creation is not about a god who lights the blue touch paper and goes off a safe distance to leave the Big Bang to itself, but a God who holds the whole scientific process in the palm of his hand, and then invites us to wonder at the beauty not just of the universe but also the science. We may not all need to know about such things, but if we do want to know we are invited by God to keep asking the questions, and keep doing the experiments.

JASVIR SINGH

The Beast from the East

Jasvir Singh was born in London into a Sikh family and has dedicated himself to explaining the culture of his heritage to the land of his birth. Despite his busy practice as a barrister, specialising in family law and landlord–tenant relations, he devotes much of his spare time into inter-faith and inter-cultural relations. He is the co-founder of South Asian Heritage Month, vice-chair of the Faiths Forum for London, and also set up the organisation City Sikhs to provide a voice for his younger co-religionists.

Now a regular contributor to Thought for the Day, *he has become expert in applying the insights of Sikhism to the wider British cultural context. This* Thought *was prompted by the severe weather front in which an Arctic polar vortex brought a blast of cold Siberian air to Britain, causing widespread heavy snowfall and temperatures as low as minus 14°C. Jasvir here compares Britons' constant preoccupations about the weather with Sikh wisdom on how to cope with the things that cannot be controlled in life.*

2 March 2018

Snowdrifts on roadsides. Rubbish bins flying around in blizzards. The country coming to a standstill. I can only be talking about one thing. The Beast from the East and now Storm Emma. The Siberian winds have caused schools to close, left people stranded on motorways overnight, and has tragically resulted in fatalities. For many of us commuting to work, the weather has been something to endure. However, it's also transformed Britain into a beautiful winter wonderland, with people making the most of it, building snowmen, having snowball fights, and one intrepid individual even trying to ski along Oxford Street.

As Brits, we obsess about the weather in a way that no other country does. For us, talking about it is a national hobby, come rain or shine. In some respects, it's an acknowledgement of the power that the elements have had on our islands for millennia, and shows our understanding that there's little we can do to influence them.

Regardless of our beliefs, we all understand that there are still many things in our lives that we can't control ourselves, and that there are forces far bigger than us, including weather fronts. The natural world has an uncanny ability of showing us who's boss, even when we think we've finally conquered it.

It reminds me of a couplet written by Guru Nanak over 500 years ago: 'We are all within the Divine's command. No one is beyond that command.' It's the idea that we are not the masters of all that happens to us, and that there will be times when we can do little more than accept the circumstances we find ourselves in. The famous legend of King Canute sitting on the shore to show his courtiers that he couldn't stop the tide from coming in is a good example of how we can't always have power over our surroundings, no matter how powerful others think we are.

We may not be able to control what happens around us, but we are in charge of how we react. When my grandmother sadly passed away a few weeks ago, the poetic phrase that my family used over and over again was that she'd 'breathed all the breaths that she had been given'. It reflected our acceptance of what had happened, that her death couldn't have been prevented, and that we should be grateful for the long life she'd lived. In our deepest grief, we knew that we couldn't do anything more than mourn her passing and talk about our memories of her.

Life can be chaotic at times, and it may take a while for normal service to be resumed. Even in the most challenging situations, sometimes all we can really do is accept what's happening around us, that we can't control everything. But I believe that navigating life with both humility and purpose might just make it easier to weather any future storms, no matter where they may come from.

VISHVAPANI

The Buddha and the Burning House

The signing of the Paris Agreement on Climate Change in 2015 was widely hailed as a major achievement. But three years later, when 3,000 diplomats and observers met in Bonn to measure progress on implementation, the talks looked like ending in stalemate. Poorer nations said they were fed up with how rich countries were dragging their feet over carbon-cutting commitments – and not keeping their promises to fund the developing world in its fight against global warming.

Thought for the Day's Buddhist contributor, Vishvapani, reacted to news of the looming stalemate by recalling a parable from the teaching of the Buddha. Its central image – of children trapped inside a burning house – seemed all too apt. But so too is its central message that a carrot, rather than a stick, is the key to motivating us to build a better relationship with the planet.

11 May 2018

The 2015 Paris climate change agreement was an inspiring example of the world coming together to tackle a shared problem. But talks in Bonn on implementing the deal stalled this week with poorer nations saying that the richer ones prioritise their own economic growth above reducing emissions or helping developing countries.

The image that evokes our situation most vividly for me is the Parable of the Burning House that's found in the Buddhist text *The Lotus Sutra* and is as well known in the Far East as the Good Samaritan and the Prodigal Son in the West.

A group of children live in a crumbling mansion, oblivious to its decay because they're caught up in playing with their toys. Then a fire breaks out and their father, who's outside the house, sees what's happening. There's no way for him to carry the children out, so he calls to them that they must escape; but the children just keep running around.

Scientists who sound ever louder alarms about the consequences of global warming must feel like that father. Economic growth pays for our services and lifestyles and isn't a game; and many of us do our bit to live sustainably. But in thinking of our culture and economy as a whole there's something compelling in the image of those children, entranced by what's in front of them and ignoring the wider dangers.

In the parable, the father's solution is to tell the children that outside the house are new toys, much better than their old ones, and they come running to him. In the original setting the father represents the Buddha and the toys he offers are the riches of spiritual practice; but perhaps there's a further resonance with the climate crisis.

Fear alone can't sustain the slow and difficult changes that will reduce global emissions. We also need compelling images of a sustainable society that's more attractive than the current one, and countless initiatives around the world focus on doing that.

And I think that individually we also need a vision of a meaningful life in which we find satisfaction in zero-emission pursuits like friendship and appreciating beauty, and love of nature for what it is, not what it can give us. Art has a place in that and so do ancient sources of wisdom, perhaps including the Buddhist tradition, that speak to our hearts like the cries of the father in the parable. First he made a cry of anguish; then he made a cry of inspiration.

PROFESSOR MONA SIDDIQUI

Reassessing Ramadan

Every faith community in the country had to adjust to the rules and restrictions which COVID brought in. Religious worship had to be modified in the same way working patterns and socialising were affected too. That created dramatic changes – for some festivals in individual faith communities more than others. The bigger the festival the more intrusive the changes were.

Mona Siddiqui is Professor of Islamic and Interreligious Studies at the University of Edinburgh where her research areas include Islamic jurisprudence and ethics. Speaking to a general audience on Thought for the Day *she has always been skilled at explaining not just the rituals of Islamic worship but also the reasoning behind them. COVID prompted Mona to take a fresh, and deeper, look at a subtle shift that had been occurring in recent years in attitudes to Ramadan – the Muslim month of fasting, alms-giving, prayer and reflection. COVID, she concludes in this* Thought, *was an opportunity to return to its original vision.*

24 April 2020

As we all make adjustments at this time, most major religions have quite rightly tried to change how their communities take part in worship. The fear of contagion and our heightened vulnerabilities have forced many of us to rethink what exactly is important to us in our lives and in our faith.

For Muslims, today marks the beginning of the month of fasting, Ramadan. A month which for many is both joyous and difficult even in normal times, will this year present unique challenges. The main principles of the month – abstention from food and drink from dawn to dusk, increased worship, and prayer and the intention to do better and live better – these things will continue to guide. But the current lockdown will create a different rhythm to the day – there won't be any communal *iftars* or evening meals with wider families, neighbours and friends. There won't be any daily gatherings for the longer night-time prayers, as mosques remain shut. Indeed, when so much of normal life has been suspended, many who would normally fast, may not feel they are able to cope this year because of the extra anxiety.

Our current upheaval and the unravelling of so many norms and expectations, is causing many to rethink the world order. Whereas some call for more global cooperation, others see greater value in self-efficiency. These questions around the world economy, trade and culture also give us an opportunity to rethink the purpose of religious ritual itself. Because it's been said for some time, that in many Muslim-majority countries especially, Ramadan too is slowly transforming from a religious ritual to a holiday marked by relative consumption; that consumerism means this most sacred month is increasingly being promoted as a product.

Maybe relative isolation and less activity will help guide the faithful back to what's really important – prayer for forgiveness, self-reflection, gratitude and betterment of character. The chance to stretch our imagination, to appreciate the worth of all human life, to carry out greater acts of kindness and charity, to see and feed the hungry even more, to be there for those who are struggling, frightened and vulnerable. These are the real blessings of the month. As the poet Rumi wrote: 'If you wish mercy, show mercy to the weak.'

Religious ritual shouldn't be functional, an external marker of difference and hierarchy. All ritual should engage people's internal life and challenge them to think more deeply about what their faith requires from them. This year faith demands much greater hope and compassion. And for me the ethical principles of Ramadan shouldn't just be confined to 30 days but be the basis for the whole of life.

HANNAH MALCOLM

Not just a walk in the park

Listening to people as they are experiencing the difficulties of grief, among other things, is something Hannah Malcolm understands from both a professional and a personal point of view. Hannah is an ordinand at Cranmer Hall at Durham University and the winner of the 2019 Theology Slam competition. She recently edited a volume entitled Words for a Dying World: Stories of Grief and Courage from the Global Church, *which advocates making greater efforts to learn from the grief of people who have different experiences to us … 'in order to make our understanding of this kind of grief richer'.*

In this Thought, *Hannah spoke, just a month into lockdown, about her daily walk in the local park, something the vast majority of the audience would recognise. For Hannah it was a lifeline. In a brave and open admission of the struggles she was having with her mental health – exacerbated by the lockdown rules – she turns her* Thought *into a confessional conversation with the listener about why these walks provide solace and uplift her. The Radio 4 audience responded in their droves. Hannah had clearly articulated something much appreciated and shared by many others.*

25 April 2020

Six weeks ago today, my spouse and I began strict social distancing due to his underlying health condition. Suddenly I was forced to drop many of the coping mechanisms I've developed over more than a decade of mental illness: the company of others, highly structured days, communal prayer and worship, a recently begun course of trauma counselling, and extended time outside.

In her book *The Wild Remedy*, Emma Mitchell describes her own struggle with mental illness and her pursuit of wellbeing through a year of carefully recorded encounters with the living world. Like Emma, I find particular reprieve in the company of other creatures.

But unlike Emma I don't have a garden, and I don't live in the Cambridgeshire Fens. I live in Moss Side, one of the most densely populated areas of Manchester. Our nearest green space is our busy local park. Walks there are fraught: my spouse's health makes him vulnerable to COVID-19, and we anxiously try to avoid all the other people who are anxiously trying to avoid us.

But it is also one of the few places where I find peace from my own thoughts. There is a cluster of blossoming fruit trees near its centre, and I slow down my government-approved dog walk just enough so that I can lift up my head to smell their fragrant flowers and hear the hum of bees. It is not a cure. But for a while it soothes the dizziness and dread that I struggle to shake from my limbs. I feel human again.

This park has become a lifeline, and I am acutely aware of the ways my mental and spiritual wellbeing are bound to each other. Franciscan theologian H. Paul Santmire suggests that Jesus' words – behold the lilies of the field – were not just a convenient example to illustrate a point, but a commandment to his followers: you ought to contemplate the world around you. Live with it. Learn from it. Let it do its work. Let it heal you.

I have not found silver linings in this pandemic, or in my struggle for sanity. This lockdown is not likely to make me a better person. I believe that it is one thing for each of us to find meaning in our own suffering, and quite another to find meaning in the suffering of others. I do not seek meaning, but I do seek survival. And more than ever before, I am attentive to Jesus' instruction: 'Consider the birds of the air. Consider the lilies of the field. Your Heavenly Father cares for them, and He cares for you.'

PROFESSOR TINA BEATTIE

The Tale of the Two Wolves

Tina Beattie is a Christian theologian and writer, who was Professor of Catholic Studies at the University of Roehampton in London where she was also Director of the Digby Stuart Research Centre for Religion, Society and Human Flourishing. She held both posts until August 2020, since when she has written her first novel. A great storyteller, in this Thought *Tina takes a well-known fable in which two wolves represent the alternative forces with which human beings struggle all the time. She reflects on how it's possible to influence the outcome, and whether our view of ourselves will be the stronger deciding factor. It is universally applicable, but it spoke directly into the uncertainty of the time she wrote, as COVID took greater hold on the country.*

11 May 2020

Despite the prime minister's announcement last night of certain changes, this time of extended confinement confronts us with our deepest fears and hopes. I've been reflecting on a well-known story about an old man telling a child that there are two wolves always wrestling inside us. One is darkness and despair, the other is lightness and hope. 'Which wolf wins?' asks the child. 'It depends which one you feed,' replies the old man.

Today we see evidence of those opposing impulses all around – in altruism and solidarity on the one hand, and in selfishness and aggression on the other.

These conflicting human urges fuel a debate that has divided Western philosophy – are we naturally violent and selfish, or are we naturally good and sociable? Dutch writer Rutger Bregman sets out evidence in favour of the more positive interpretation in his new book, *Humankind: A Hopeful History*. In an interview, he argues that, though we are 'the cruellest of species ... our secret superpower is our friendliness and ability to cooperate'.

He refers to William Golding's dystopian 1954 novel, *Lord of the Flies*, which describes the anarchic violence that erupts when a group of boys is stranded on an island. Bregman contrasts this with a true story of what happened when six schoolboys from Tonga were marooned on a small island for more than a year in the 1960s. By the time they were rescued, the boys had created a supportive community which was a model of ingenuity, solidarity and care.

Bregman is the secular son of a Protestant pastor. He acknowledges the formative influence of his father's Christian faith on his ideas. Christianity also recognises those two wolves struggling within us – our capacity for love and generosity, and our capacity for violence and hatred. Whether we draw our values from a religious or a secular tradition, only a shared commitment to feed the one and resist the other will give us the vision we need to create a better world out of the challenges ahead.

As Bregman points out, the way we understand ourselves can become a self-fulfilling prophecy. In other words, what we choose to believe about human nature may influence who we are and what we become. So which wolf are we going to feed? How we respond to that question may shape the future when this is over.

BISHOP GULI FRANCIS-DEHQANI

On science, faith and not knowing

Bishop Guli, the Bishop of Chelmsford, lived through danger and uncertainty in the Iranian Revolution before her family fled Iran and arrived in the UK when she was still a teenager – following an assassination attempt on her father, the Anglican Bishop in Iran, and the murder of her brother. After university, she worked as a religion producer for the BBC before training for the ministry. Previously, as Bishop of Loughborough and then

Leicester, she worked with many diverse communities – understanding well the marginalisation of those from an ethnic minority background, particularly in the Church.

In this Thought *she brings that wide experience to bear, looking at what can be done, rather than accepting the view that nothing really changes. Two months into lockdown she explores how we view science and how we view faith, and finds striking similarities in how we experience them. She concludes that the journey may be different but there is much to be shared and celebrated.*

19 May 2020

There's a widespread belief that science and religion are incompatible. That science is about facts while religion dabbles with ideas that can't be proven. Certainly in the current pandemic it's scientists we look to for solutions but sometimes I wonder if we burden them with unreasonable expectations.

There's often talk of following the science as if it's a single identifiable entity – a magic bullet that'll provide the solutions. In truth, it's rather that there are scientists striving to better understand a new and unknown virus. It's no surprise then that there's disagreement, for example, about whether or not to wear masks, when to ease lockdown or send children back to school.

I heard Professor Brian Cox speaking recently reminding us that there's far more that scientists don't know compared to what they do know. Referring to the twentieth-century physicist Richard Feynman, Cox said the most valuable thing about science is that it teaches us to embrace uncertainty and doubt – and that not knowing is to be welcomed rather than feared. And this, for me, takes us into the territory of faith.

There are those who dismiss faith because it can't provide clear answers to the existence of God or the problem of suffering or any number of other questions. But for my way of thinking, if science is a mindset – a desire to know and understand more about nature – then faith too is a mindset – a desire to know and understand more about the creative force behind the universe, what many people call God.

The priest and poet Mark Oakley describes belief in God as stemming from a place of intuition, a sense of awe, surprise, wonder, beyondness, epiphany, perhaps not unlike the starting place for many scientists. Thus faith emerges and then begins a journey of gradual discovery. There'll always be more that's unknown about God than those things which are discovered but this not knowing, what we might call mystery, is to be embraced and welcomed not feared.

In the end it'll be scientists who find a way to lead us out of this pandemic. Out of the not knowing we hope and trust clarity will emerge – a cure, a vaccine, some kind of treatment. Meanwhile, for those who choose it, the gift of faith is an invitation. For Christians it is an encounter with the loving presence of God through the person of Jesus Christ. This is not just in the hope of a better future but in the very darkness of suffering and the uncertainties of life.

REV. MARIE-ELSA BRAGG

Collared doves and climate change

In a rich and varied career Marie-Elsa Bragg has studied philosophy, Christian theology and Jewish mysticism. She has been a spiritual director for over 20 years, 18 of them in the Ignatian (Jesuit) tradition. She was also a duty chaplain at Westminster Abbey for ten years.

Marie-Elsa has a distinctive mix of calm and enthusiasm when discussing ideas for Thought. *She brings to the process all her exposure to the wide range of people from different walks of life, traditions, religions and experiences of faith she has encountered when leading workshops and retreats. Marie-Elsa is half-French and half-Cumbrian and she has a long connection with Sénanque, the Cistercian monastery local to her family in Provence, and with the local Christianity and literary tradition of the Lake District – where she discovered and nurtured her passion for the natural world in the landscape, the wildlife and fauna, and the rhythm of the seasons.*

Marie-Elsa's writing has a striking poetic quality. In this Thought *she imaginatively traces the migratory journey of six collared doves nesting near her home through a landscape of the ecological damage human beings have wrought on this beautiful earth. Can we still find our way back?*

27 June 2020

In the last few months six collared doves have nested under the roof of my closed local church. I've been watching them squeeze into the cracks and gutters, white wings fluttering, bringing sticks or food to their young. Sometimes I've walked so early that I don't know if I see the male who's out in the day or the female is out at night.

They'll have flown over 300 miles from somewhere in Europe to nest and this year they'll have flown through skies that increasingly had less pollution as planes and cars stopped. In April carbon dioxide emissions plunged by a global average of 17 per cent. But even so, they'll have flown over seas containing thousands of tonnes of plastic garbage – or rested where previously there was forest, and may now have parched earth which has released its carbon, and is in dire need of the regenerative farming and rewilding that Prince Charles talked about yesterday.

My great-grandfather used to take a canary down the mines for warning. And the warning of the turtle doves in the UK is that their count is now so low they are hardly seen, along with the nightingale and cuckoo.

On Thursday this week the Committee on Climate Change released their report where they advised the government to plan for a minimum 2°C rise in global temperature, with consideration of 4°C. Scientist Johan Rockström describes 4°C as the loss of all reefs and not millions but billions of lives. I can hear the voice of Greta saying: 'Listen to the science; our house is on fire.'

The UK, of course, has international legal obligations under the Paris Agreement. But as the home of the Industrial Revolution, and a high-emitting country, there must also be the intellectual resource and moral compass for us to lead the way forward.

Amid the science and the moral humanitarian reasoning I can also hear the voices of Dorothy and William Wordsworth asking us to remember to think from the imagination of our souls: one impulse from a vernal wood can teach us more of man, of moral evil and of good, than all the sages can.

During lockdown the churches have been closed and so I found a small circle of trees in a local wood to pray in. For me it's a church of its own and if we can't see religion as not just in partnership but a part of nature, then we're missing the wonder of creation and the profound and unifying relationship God has with each part.

Change must come, yes from science, but also from the imagination and love of our souls. Only then can we find the full connection we have to this remarkable gift of life.

REV. DR ISABELLE HAMLEY

The long haul

It was patients, not doctors, who first uncovered the phenomenon that came to be known as Long COVID. After initially mild symptoms, a chronic condition sets in which can go on for many months. Symptoms can include fatigue, breathlessness, headaches, chest pains, palpitations and dizziness. The condition was first noted on social media by a sufferer in Italy in March 2020. In June the hashtag #LongCovid became increasingly prominent across Europe. One of the first people to publicly report it in the UK was Rev. Dr Isabelle Hamley and she did so in July on Thought for the Day.

Isabelle, who is currently Theological Adviser to the Church of England's House of Bishops, was previously an academic whose areas of research included faith and mental health. Here she uses her own prolonged illness to reflect upon the relationship between physical, mental and spiritual health. She ends with some particular advice to any listeners who have friends or family suffering from this extended condition who need accompanying for the long haul.

7 July 2020

Like many long-term COVID sufferers I count the days of illness. Today is day 108. When I first became ill, I had a bit of a cough, a bit of a temperature, so I followed the advice and didn't worry too much. I trusted the early narrative that said: 'COVID is a mild illness for the vast majority of people. The small proportion of patients, many with pre-existing conditions, will need hospitalisation but most of you will be just fine in a couple of weeks.'

I learned to my dismay that for me, as for tens of thousands of others in the UK, this wasn't the case at all. I developed pneumonia. Three months on, I still struggle with severe chest pain, debilitating fatigue, muscle aches and regular relapses. I cannot go back to work full time. No one can tell me when or if I will get better.

And so the announcement on Sunday that the NHS is setting up a service to aid long-term recovery was met with enormous relief by many of us. I hope it is the beginning of a new narrative about COVID. Narratives matter. They shape our expectations of ourselves and how we relate to others.

As I started going out for a very slow walk every day, I would invariably meet kind people who said: 'How are you? You must be getting better by now.' How confused and disappointed they were when I wasn't able to give good news.

Understanding COVID as a long-term chronic condition is a much harder narrative to hold. It requires us to learn to live with pain, uncertainty and fragility. It requires us to do something human beings often struggle with, to walk with others for the long haul.

One of my favourite stories in the Bible is that of Job. Job goes from being incredibly fortunate to losing everything. His wealth, his loved ones, his health. To begin with, his friends gather round and mourn with him, but after a week they have had enough. They start to look for a way out, explaining away what happened, finding meaning in Job's continued plague, even blaming him.

The Book of Job is deeply realistic. Human beings need meaning and certainty to make life manageable. The friends are fighting their own battle with fear. Job is fighting his with meaninglessness and trauma.

Job never finds out why he suffered; instead he meets with God face to face and finds solace in his presence. This is an invitation for us to consider how we hold each other's pain, and prepare ourselves to walk alongside loved ones, not for a week or two, but for the long haul.

RABBI JONATHAN WITTENBERG

Hannukah in COVID

In this Thought *marking the yearly festival of Hannukah, Rabbi Jonathan Wittenberg recalls how his grandparents would light the candles in a menorah and leave it to shine through the front windows of their home. That tradition has a dual purpose. It's about understanding the stories that have been handed down which bind the generations, but it is also to remember the sacred nature of the light passed on in the teachings of the mystics.*

Jonathan Wittenberg is the Senior Rabbi of Masorti Judaism in the UK. His 'Topical Talmud' sessions at the North London Synagogue attract young people looking to reconnect with Jewish learning through discussions that resonate with their lives today. It is Rabbi Jonathan's contemporary take on his Jewish roots that he brings to Thought for the Day. *His script here ends with a precious memory from his own childhood that speaks of a kindness that has never been forgotten.*

15 December 2020

Happy Hannukah – the Jewish festival of lights. In my teens I would often light the candles with my grandparents. I'd watch their reflections in the window as they burned on the eight-branched Hannukah candelabrum, and the reflections of the reflections. They felt like testaments of hope spreading through the darkness, affectionate messages, fingers reaching out to touch across generations.

With dusk early and nights long, lockdowns and tier rules, though essential, feel hard to bear. Loneliness cuts deep wounds and despair can follow. I feel for older people; what's Hannukah or Christmas without all one's family and friends? I feel for young people; where's the safe world with a place for all?

It's a tough time to find hope – which is why it matters so much.

Hannukah commemorates Maccabean victories long ago. But the rabbis weren't interested in the wars; instead, they told the story of the light.

When those Maccabees regained the ravaged Jerusalem Temple, they searched the ruins until they found one single jar of oil. Insufficient as this quantity was, they lit the menorah, which burned miraculously for eight days.

The accuracy of this account may be doubtful, but not the truth it expresses. However broken our world, we should try not to give up. There is sacred light in everything, the mystics taught; though hidden, it is present in all life.

However small a source of light we find, we should kindle it. Once we do so, the lamps of hope, courage and kindness always burn far longer than we imagine. They reach across the darkness, inspiring others who in turn remotivate us. The scientists who found the COVID vaccines in which we all hope surely had dispiriting days, yet their stamina kept burning.

Yesterday, the Jewish and Uyghur communities lit Hannukah candles in solidarity, determined that the sacred human spirit would overcome oppression, internment, slavery and degradation.

But it's not just in major concerns; hope burns in every act of kindness. I was five when my mother died and have few memories. But I recall how afterwards my father took me for a walk, passing a small garden centre. The owner must have enquired because I saw my father shake his head. The man disappeared for a moment, returned, bent down and, smiling, gave me a primrose.

I don't know if you're alive, garden-centre man, but your light still burns on the Hannukiah in my heart.

REV. LUCY WINKETT

The smile of a snowman

As well as being a stimulating and insightful writer for Thought for the Day, *Lucy Winkett, who is Rector of St James's Piccadilly, is a very good broadcaster. It's not always easy to make the message of a* Thought *cut through, given that the audience can variously be still waking up, making breakfast or finding someone's homework at the same time.*

Fortunately Lucy, who was previously a professional soprano, has the kind of delivery that draws you in and makes you want to listen. In this Thought *the mix of an opening story, with a shot of whimsy, is juxtaposed with the serious business of the coronavirus pandemic. The way she weaves that together is an example of the creativity her* Thought *itself advocates to help people cope with the distress of those COVID days. It is a message of resilience and hope.*

28 January 2021

Yesterday, I went for a walk in the park. A melted snowman, built at the weekend, had become a small pool of ice. But the button eyes and the twig that had been its smile were still in place somehow. So I picked up the stick and I have it in my pocket. To anyone else it's a twig. Ordinary, unremarkable, like millions of others in the park. But to me now it's the smile of a snowman.

I've found myself holding on to it like a relic, like a medieval Christian holds on to a piece of the True Cross. While a mixture of bewilderment and devastation stalks these pandemic days, I carry a symbol that connects me to a deeper truth about human life: that other unknown Londoners – there were many such snowmen – were, it seems, determined to be creative together in the middle of so much distress.

It's been hard to take in what the archbishops called yesterday the 'enormity' of the number dead from COVID. Beyond 100,000 now. Every number has a name. Every life mysterious, precious and, as Christians would say, made in the image of God. Every one.

Statistics and data are crucially important in a crisis dependent on science to get us through. But our soulful selves find meaning not so much in the data but between the cracks of the numbers, in stories and signs: where grows enough faith and strength to be able to face the reality of living and the inevitability of dying, and still say that God is with us, even when it's hard to see how.

Psychologists will tell us that it's absolutely normal for people going through trauma to experience utterly contradictory things all at the same time. We feel both fury at, and sympathy with, decision makers; frustration with, and gratitude for, law enforcement. We feel a disorientating mixture of sadness, guilt and relief, grief and comfort; we feel energised and exhausted; all at the same time in the course of one day, in the course of one hour of one day.

I am asked as a Christian to recognise daily life as fundamentally Christ-like; a human life haunted by grief and shot through with miracles.

And at a time of such destruction to search for signs of creativity … even in the fallen branch of a tree in a park that connects me with the people who imagined it as something else entirely. In itself a sign of resilience, faith, solidarity and hope.

REV. DR JANE LEACH

The ethics of vaccine equity

Safe and effective vaccines against COVID-19 were developed in record time. But they were distributed mainly in affluent industrial countries. The global failure to fairly share vaccines took a toll on some of the world's poorest and most vulnerable people. In February 2021 the UN secretary-general declared: 'At this critical moment, vaccine equity is the biggest moral test before the global community.'

Jane Leach is a Methodist minister and academic who specialises in pastoral theology. She had hands-on experience as a minister of local congregations before becoming Principal of Wesley House, the Methodist theological college in Cambridge where she was previously Director of Pastoral Studies. She is particularly interested in helping churches develop a culture of support and accountability for their leaders. In her contributions to Thought *she brings a clarity and a directness that is always effective. Characteristically she brought all these influences to bear on this* Thought *in which she focuses on a global issue via the death of a single individual.*

8 February 2021

Have you had your vaccine yet? Talking to family and friends this week, mercifully, almost everyone had nothing to report … unless they'd had their vaccine. Comparing vaccine notes has become the new national sport, and despite worries about how well current versions will cope with new variants of the virus, the prospect that the adult population of Britain will all have received at least one dose by June is certainly news that lifts the spirits.

Posed in a different context, though, the question: 'Have you had your vaccine yet?' takes on a different complexion. Last week I was part of a global meeting of the International Association of Methodist Schools, Colleges and Universities. In groups we were asked to compare notes about our national vaccination programmes.

We heard from our colleague from the Democratic Republic of Congo that conversation is pointless because nothing is available. We heard from our American colleague about the low uptake among black, Hispanic and indigenous communities that have little trust in the healthcare interventions of their government. We heard from our South African colleague working in a teaching hospital where the fight is on against the new South African strain. And I began to feel uneasy as I realised that I would have to confess to the vaccine privilege of the UK, and even to the row over alleged vaccine nationalism in the context of post-Brexit trade.*

We had already begun our meeting mourning the death of the brilliant, entrepreneurial, strategically minded and stead-fastly honest Professor Munashe Furusa, Vice-Chancellor of the Methodist University in Zimbabwe, taken by COVID at the age of 59; and now it became painfully and personally obvious

---

* Britain and the EU had fallen out over the supplies of vaccines. Britain was accused of withholding vaccines from the EU, which in turn was accused of stopping the export of vaccines to Australia and elsewhere.

to me that vaccinating me by May might be at the expense of my international colleagues and of some of the vulnerable people among whom they work.

In the Methodist community – worldwide – the word 'connexionalism' is often on our lips. It implies not so much being part of a single polity in which all are subject to the same discipline, as being part of a transnational community in which all have obligations of duty and friendship to one another. Yet, even within such a connexion, it takes work to focus on, and respond to, the needs of neighbours far away.

The *Financial Times* on Saturday highlighted the connections between all countries and all peoples as it described the global COVID landscape as the race between vaccination and new mutations. It argued that, not only is it a moral obligation but a practical necessity for those countries with the means to ensure the vaccination of those countries without – for, in truth, none of us will be safe, until all of us are safe. This is undoubtedly true, but for me, it's the moral question that remains. The question asked of Jesus, by a lawyer who was trying to limit his sense of connection and obligation, 'but who is my neighbour?'

POPE FRANCIS

God's plan for the world

Perhaps the most radical vision to tackle global warming, far to the left of any mainstream political party, is the one set out by Pope Francis in his 2015 encyclical Laudato si'. *It was a prophetic critique of humanmade climate change and the pollution of the planet. Behind the ecological problems lies a more fundamental economic and political crisis, he says. The Pope attacks the unexamined assumptions of modern consumer capitalism – which indulges the affluent but excludes the world's poorest people.*

*The cry of the earth and the cry of the poor are one and the same,
declared the man who has rejected a papal palace to live in two rooms in
a Vatican hostel.*

*On the eve of the global environmental summit held in Glasgow in
October 2021, Francis – the first pope to come from the developing world
– chose* Thought for the Day *as the platform from which to urge world
leaders to take 'radical decisions' that would offer 'concrete hope to future
generations'. His message, produced by Helen Grady and Julian Miglierini,
was recorded in Italian and broadcast on the eve of the summit with a
voiceover in English.*

29 October 2021

Climate change and the COVID-19 pandemic have exposed our
deep vulnerability and raised numerous doubts and concerns
about our economic systems and the way we organise our societies. We have lost our sense of security, and are experiencing
a sense of powerlessness and loss of control over our lives. We
find ourselves increasingly frail and even fearful, caught up in
a succession of 'crises' in the areas of healthcare, the environment, food supplies and the economy, to say nothing of social,
humanitarian and ethical crises.

All these crises are profoundly interconnected. They also
forecast a 'perfect storm' that could rupture the bonds holding
our society together within the greater gift of God's creation.

Every crisis calls for vision, the ability to formulate plans and
put them rapidly into action, to rethink the future of the world,
our common home, and to reassess our common purpose.
These crises present us with the need to take decisions, radical
decisions that are not always easy. At the same time, moments
of difficulty like these also present opportunities, opportunities
that we must not waste.

We can confront these crises by retreating into isolationism,
protectionism and exploitation. Or we can see in them a real

chance for change, a genuine moment of conversion, and not simply in a spiritual sense.

This last approach alone can guide us towards a brighter horizon. Yet it can only be pursued through a renewed sense of shared responsibility for our world, and an effective solidarity based on justice, a sense of our common destiny and a recognition of the unity of our human family in God's plan for the world.

All this represents an immense cultural challenge. It means giving priority to the common good, and it calls for a change in perspective, a new outlook, in which the dignity of every human being, now and in the future, will guide our ways of thinking and acting.

The most important lesson we can take from these crises is our need to build together, so that there will no longer be any borders, barriers or political walls for us to hide behind.

Some days ago, on 4 October, I met with religious leaders and scientists to sign a Joint Appeal in which we called upon ourselves and our political leaders to act in a more responsible and consistent manner. I was impressed by something said by one of the scientists present at that meeting. He told us: 'If things continue as they are, in fifty years' time my baby granddaughter will have to live in an unliveable world.'

We cannot allow this to happen.

It is essential that each of us be committed to this urgent change of direction, sustained by our own faith and spirituality. In the Joint Appeal, we spoke of the need to work responsibly towards a 'culture of care' for our common home, but also for ourselves, and the need to work tirelessly to eliminate 'the seeds of conflicts: greed, indifference, ignorance, fear, injustice, insecurity and violence'.

Humanity has never before had at its disposal so many means for achieving this goal. The political decisionmakers who will meet at COP26 in Glasgow are urgently summoned to provide effective responses to the present ecological crisis and in this way to offer concrete hope to future generations. And it is worth repeating that each of us – whoever and wherever we may be – can play our own part in changing our collective response to the unprecedented threat of climate change and the degradation of our common home.

REV. DR MICHAEL BANNER

The water of life

Moral theology can often busy itself with abstruse issues, says Thought for the Day *regular, Rev. Dr Michael Banner, Dean and Fellow of Trinity College, Cambridge. This can blind it to the pressing problems of the real world. Dr Banner should know. He was previously the F D Maurice Professor of Moral and Social Theology at King's College, London and Professor of Public Policy and Ethics at the University of Edinburgh. But he has also served on numerous public bodies concerned with animal testing, military weapons, environmental pollution, ethical investment and good business practice.*

In this Thought *he draws on the breadth of his theological theory and practice as he turns his acute ethical eye on one of the greatest problems of our time – the future of the planet and our role in it. Here he focuses on a new House of Commons report into the state of England's rivers and the cavalier, almost wilful, manner in which we are despoiling our waters with microplastics and other pollutants. How we treat our water, Dr Banner suggests in his characteristically quizzical style, is a symbol of a more general disregard for our planet – which is leading us to sleepwalk towards disaster.*

14 January 2022

'Son of man, eat your bread with quaking, and drink your water with trembling.' So the word of God instructs the Old

Testament prophet Ezekiel. And he certainly would drink the water with trembling if it had been drawn from an English river.

A report from the House of Commons Environmental Audit Committee says that no river in England can be given a clean bill of health. 'Rivers are in a mess,' the MPs declare: 'A chemical cocktail of sewage, agricultural waste, and plastic is polluting . . . many of the country's rivers.' It being breakfast time, I won't dwell on the slurry and sewage, but I can probably safely mention the plastic – plastic pollution is now 'ubiquitous' in English rivers says the report, with reefs of wet-wipes being a particular, and rather unpleasant, hazard. In one stretch of a river in the north-west, there were 500,000 fragments of plastic for every square metre of riverbed – 'many, many more times the number of insects'.

In the world in which Ezekiel wrote, that of the ancient Near East, the Canaanites, Egyptians and peoples of Mesopotamia venerated storm gods – for water was very plainly the stuff of life. The God of the Hebrew Bible is pictured, in the Psalms, as planting his footsteps in the sea and riding upon the storm, and water is his most precious gift. 'I will pour water upon him that is thirsty, and floods upon the dry ground' – so God promises Israel through the words of another prophet.

So what's up with Ezekiel? Why is he directed to drink his water with trembling? He is told to do so, so that his actions can be a warning sign, a piece of street theatre if you like, for his audience – the people of Jerusalem – who are complacently ignoring a looming catastrophe of epic proportions, namely invasion and exile at the hands of the Babylonians. It is time they were trembling.

Though it has no power to compel anyone to action, the Environmental Audit Committee makes a host of recommendations in its report, but drinking water with trembling is not among them. It surely is fear and trembling, however, which we need to learn to feel, if yet another environmental report which makes for grim reading is not to be well, just water off a duck's back.

Perhaps living among 'our clouded hills', we have less sense of the preciousness of water than did the peoples of the arid ancient Near East. Yet if our rivers are suffocating, as they are – as raw sewage, slurry from poultry farms and wet-wipes drive the life out of them – this is surely a telling sign of a looming ecological and environmental catastrophe of epic proportions which we ignore at our peril.

HANNAH MALCOLM

The swifts return

Hannah Malcolm, public theologian and environmentalist, is training for ordained ministry in the Church of England. She grew up in a family where, she says, 'climate justice and faith were never seen as antithetical'. Her grandfather was Sir John Houghton, the distinguished atmospheric physicist who was co-chair of the Intergovernmental Panel on Climate Change's scientific working group, which shared the Nobel Peace Prize in 2007. He was also an evangelical Christian, so seeing the place of climate science in Christian engagement with the world came naturally to Hannah. She knew from a young age that climate breakdown was a very serious problem – and that adults make a lot of bad choices.

On Thought for the Day *individual contributors regularly mark the seasons, the special days in the calendar both religious and secular, and national events and commemorations. But here, Hannah Malcolm shares a personal moment of joy, freighted with a deeper meaning, when she notices the annual event that means a great deal to her: the swifts have returned.*

11 May 2022

Like many others I have spent the last couple of days with my eyes trained upwards, hoping for my first sighting of a returning swift. Each year the beginning of May marks the end of their long migration from Africa, and each year I wait anxiously for a first sight of their safe return. And then, yesterday morning, I was rewarded with a sudden swooping flash past my window, the dark curve of their wings joyful against the blue spring sky.

In this country our relationship with birds is complicated. Millions of us tune into *Springwatch*, and we spend more than twice as much on bird food as the rest of Europe put together. But we also tear down hedgerows, net our buildings, and make liberal use of pesticides. Last week the BBC reported on a 75-year-long study of great tits which found that the changing climate has pushed egg-laying up to three weeks earlier than usual.

Birds are considered a good indicator of the state of wildlife in the UK, and their numbers have consistently declined over the last half century. As our ability to manage our environments increases, we are remaking the world in our own image. We can look around us and see where humans have intervened to protect and sustain ecologies, and where humans have intervened for the benefit of a few powerful people. When the world feels like it's growing more chaotic and the future feels threatened, it is easy to give up investing in the fates of these other creatures – to see them as insignificant, or even a barrier to our own flourishing.

Last Sunday was the feast day of Julian of Norwich, a fourteenth-century mystic who lived through hunger and plague, political upheaval and violence, and personal suffering. A woman who wrote in the vernacular, her life was insignificant in the hierarchy of the Church. But during an illness which brought her close to death, she had a series of visions about the love of God for creation.

In perhaps the most famous of those visions, she sees a tiny thing in the palm of her hand, the size of a hazelnut. She is told that this tiny thing is everything that is made.

Julian is astonished that something so small could keep on existing. But then comes the response: it lives, and will keep living, because God loves it. Julian sees that littleness and fragility are not at odds with ultimate significance.

As the sky fills with swifts returning for another spring, I am reminded that it is not foolish to delight in these little creatures. Perhaps in doing so we might learn to love the world as though it is not ours to control.

Chapter Eight

Life, Death and Faith

BISHOP TOM BUTLER

Diane Pretty and assisted dying

Diane Pretty was a British woman suffering from motor neurone disease who became the focus of an intense debate on assisted dying in 2002. As the disease progressed she decided she wanted to end her own life – but was unable to because she was paralysed from the neck down. If her husband helped her he would be liable to be prosecuted, so Diane asked the British courts to guarantee him immunity. They refused, saying that the right to life did not include a right to decide when and how to die. Then the European Court of Human Rights ruled that the ban on assisted suicide in the UK could be justified to protect vulnerable people.

Bishop Tom Butler, a scientist by background with a PhD in electronics, started doing Thought for the Day *in 1988. His theology was always tempered by his experience of the wide range of people he has met in his ministry. Diane and her husband were deserving of great sympathy, he declared in this* Thought. *But then, recalling the many conversations he had had with old people in care homes and hospitals, he set out why he thought the courts were right.*

30 April 2002

I was once visiting a ward in a nursing home caring for some very frail elderly people. They were predominantly female, but as I stood and found my bearings an old man beckoned me across. I regarded this as a gesture of male solidarity and went to hear what he had to say. 'You're standing in front of the television,' he complained.

The world occupied by sick elderly people can be a worrisome place, and it's not easy, when you've always led an active life, for your care now to be totally in the hands of others. And more often than not there are things to worry about with home and family, if you still have a home and family. I've lost count of the number of times an elderly person has said to me: 'I don't want to be a nuisance. It would be much better if I didn't live much longer.'

People say these things, and they partly mean them. They don't want to be a nuisance to their children and grandchildren. They don't want to see their house sold and their savings used on costly care for themselves. But when frail people say that they don't want to be a nuisance they are also very often, I believe, looking for reassurance. They are wanting to know that they're still valued and loved. They're wanting to hear that their wisdom and experience still matters. They're wanting to be assured that their life is still worthwhile.

That's why I for one am rather pleased at the decision of the European Court of Human Rights to refuse Diane Pretty's request for her husband to be immune from prosecution if he assists her in committing suicide. Of course, Diane and Brian Pretty have our compassion and sympathy. Theirs is a very hard case. But hard cases make poor law, and if the law wavers over assisted suicide or indeed euthanasia then very many vulnerable elderly people of the type that I've mentioned will feel themselves to be under great moral pressure no longer to be a nuisance to those around.

Law and religion see eye to eye on this. Human life is a gift from God which must be respected. We don't have the authority to take away life, even our own. The judges in Strasbourg are quite right, therefore: human rights legislation protects the right to life, not the right to death. Of course, the Prettys like all of us have the freedom ultimately to follow their conscience, having weighed up the rights and wrongs of their situation, but none of us can escape the consequences of our actions even when we feel that we are following our conscience. There are no post-dated moral cheques in this sacred journey through life and death.*

---

* Diane Pretty died a month later in the care of a hospice.

REV. DR COLIN MORRIS

Life is cheap

Colin Morris was a brilliant broadcaster. His wonderful northern accent, combined with a very direct and distinctive style of delivery, was guaranteed to get your attention. He knew exactly how to write for speech and could glide between challenge and intimacy. But, most of all, he was fearless and always completely in command of his material. It was all part of his virtuosity on Thought for the Day.

This Thought, *for example, begins in Sudan, a country the audience knew he understood from personal experience where, he's now told: 'Life is cheap.' His subsequent illustration is to prove that it's certainly not. The description of the physical mechanism in the action of tossing a coin is detailed and scientific. Then comes an instruction to cost the process, so you'll know what it's worth – with its beautifully pitched jibe about the cost of Wembley Stadium, which had opened a month earlier. And the theological ending delivers something you really weren't expecting.*

9 April 2007

A few days ago I heard a television reporter in the Sudan say: 'Life around here is cheap.' We knew exactly what he meant as we observed the prone and emaciated bodies lying around him. But it's not true. Life is incredibly expensive. Do something very simple. Toss a coin in the air and catch it.

What precisely did you do? Well, someone who knows about such things explained to me that you sensed the energy of the toss and triangulated the position of the coin throughout its flight with your binocular vision. You shut out distractions from your other senses that might have diverted your attention, then you brought into action an extraordinary signal mechanism which triggered off one set of muscles after another in a sequence of ground-to-air control processes so effective that you caught the coin without consciously thinking about it.

Now ask an expert in micro-electronics what it would cost to put together a device which can do that and miniaturise it so that it will operate for three score years and ten in an ultra-microscopic part of you. I guess you wouldn't have much change out of the cost of the new Wembley Stadium.

Then there's the hand that caught the coin. The most costly modern robots are crude compared to the flexibility, strength and sensitivity of the human hand. How much to create a human hand that can play Mozart or paint the *Mona Lisa*. Life cheap?

We've only got to look in a mirror and realise we are staring at a fantastic investment of billions of years of evolutionary pain, in which countless species went to the wall, to make us who and what we are. You would regard it as lunacy to put your foot through the radio which is transmitting my voice because you disagree with me (after all, you've only got to put up with it for two and a half minutes), yet that radio is a Stone Age implement compared to the walking miracles we are busy maiming, starving and killing across the world because they think and behave differently from others.

Our society is rapidly losing our sense of self-worth. After all, long before there was any argument between the evolutionists and the creationists, the psalmist wrote that we human beings are just a little lower than God – I love the gentle irony of that phrase – 'just a little lower than God'.

If you're not disposed to be religious, then just toss a coin and catch it. And that's nothing compared to your capacity to do a thousand things more important. Such as giving and receiving love. And that was precisely the point Jesus was trying to get across 2,000 years ago.

PROFESSOR MONA SIDDIQUI

Our children's inheritance

Since Professor Mona Siddiqui wrote this Thought *in 2013 the down-turn in the economic climate, and the increase in buying up second homes in numerous places around the country, have made it even harder for young people just starting out to get on the housing ladder. Many students leaving university go straight back home and find themselves living with Mum and Dad for the best part of their twenties.*

In this Thought *Mona shares the story of her own family's experience and the advice from her mother that has stayed with her throughout her adult life. Though, in fact, this is more than just advice – it is a whole mindset, informed by personal faith, of how to counter financial worries about the future. Any idea that this is simply a question of 'looking on the bright side' would be wrong. It's much more than that.*

When her mother had to face caring for a husband who had had a stroke that left him disabled for several years before he died, she showed a resilience from the start that was noticed by Mona. Her mother's confidence was placed in the knowledge that there is something more important than money. This wisdom, Mona says, has been her legacy.

18 December 2013

The Institute for Fiscal Studies reports that people born in the sixties and seventies will be the first generation since World War II to be worse off in their retirement than their parents. They'll have smaller pensions, probably not own their homes, and have very little savings. Their only salvation it would seem lies in getting a decent inheritance from their parents.

Indeed many people will receive an inheritance and feel reassured for themselves and their children. From a purely monetary angle, this might be true. But we shouldn't under-estimate the resilience of the human spirit and its ability to focus on what is important in life, notwithstanding financial worries.

Before my father died, he'd lived with a stroke for several years. He had been the sole breadwinner in the family when we were growing up. But now this man, who had worked so hard his whole life, could no longer provide care; he needed care himself. When I think back to those early weeks I still remember my mother's resilience and focus in dealing with the financial impact of his illness, as well as the emotional. She kept things afloat in a way that eluded us all but her advice was always: 'Be prepared for whatever life throws at you and be grateful for the blessings you have rather than anguish about what you don't have. God is merciful and God provides.'

My parents, like many of their generation, had come to the UK with very little money and it was my father's medical career which made our lives in every way. Yet I can't remember them having any anxiety about leaving us an inheritance of any sort. They had instilled in us the importance of education, generosity and they had taught us to cope and manage our lives – in some ways that wisdom was really our inheritance. Working hard for your family, bettering yourself, and with it the lives of your children, wasn't just a matter of economics or personal gain – it was an attitude to life that demanded staying optimistic and hopeful in the bleakest of times.

Maybe it is difficult to stay optimistic in the current economic climate and many of us may feel quite vulnerable in all kinds of ways. But no report and no prediction should paralyse us into thinking that our fate has been sealed and that our individual mindset and attitude don't matter.

Money will always be important – and what the state does, matters – but we can shape our children's destinies in so many ways. It's natural for parents to want to leave their children something. But rather than raising them to be hopeful for an inheritance from us, we should raise them with a sense of self-worth and purpose which will keep their lives meaningful whatever they face.

CLIFFORD LONGLEY

The Angels of Mons

Clifford Longley was a Thought for the Day *contributor with a huge range. Twenty years of writing a weekly column on religion, morality and culture in* The Times *– plus years more as a leader writer for the* Daily Telegraph *and a panellist on Radio 4's* Moral Maze *– gave him a wealth of material on which to exercise his shrewd analytical brain. Here he turns his attention to myth and modern memory in an unusual* Thought *on a legend that sprang up after the Battle of Mons, the first major action of the British Expeditionary Force in the First World War.*

Surrounded by Germans, who outnumbered them five to one, some 4,000 Commonwealth soldiers fought their way through and then managed to find their way back through the darkness to their camp. One over-imaginative writer compared this unlikely success against overwhelming odds to the English victory at the Battle of Agincourt. And so the rumours began that our troops had been miraculously saved by a host of angelic warriors described as phantom longbowmen who had halted the German troops. The tale, Clifford suggests, tell us something unexpected about the spirit of England.

1 September 2014

One hundred years ago today, the British Army was engaged in what became known as the Retreat from Mons. Pushed back by overwhelming odds, exhausted British soldiers suddenly saw, or thought they saw, a host of angels sent by God to protect them.

The legend of the Angels of Mons came to be widely believed in the early years of the war, though there is no contemporary evidence for it. But belief in the intervention of divine providence at moments of national peril was strong at the time, thereby demonstrating, as one historian drily put it, the importance of religion in warfare.

For me the best book about the First World War was by the American literary historian Paul Fussell, called *The Great War and Modern Memory*. It could have been subtitled 'How the British Got Their Famous Sense of Humour'. Its underlying theme is how the next four years witnessed an explosion, not just of shells and bombs, but of irony. It transformed our culture and language. Irony, in all its manifestations, came to infuse the very soul of the nation. It was the way we coped with the otherwise intolerable. And it still is.

Irony here means that things ain't quite what they seem, and while we all know this, it's a kind of shared secret. It says that behind real events, and our real perception of them, lies another meaning which may contradict the first. Indeed, at its extreme it may show that reality itself is close to farce, albeit of a very dark kind.

'Oh, It's a Lovely War' was a popular music-hall song of the time, before it later became the basis for a famous musical play and a film. That's the kind of irony that Paul Fussell was writing about. Interestingly it is irony suffused with anger. It is very British.

The legend of the Angels of Mons could not possibly have happened much later in the war, because it would've been killed off by irony. At best there would have been a satirical song about it, pure trench humour, that the troops could merrily sing as they marched to their probable deaths.

Irony also came to infuse the British sense of religion, and indeed may be one of the major underlying factors behind the gradual slow process called secularisation. It offers a kind of warning sign – danger, never take anything too seriously.

But I feel it now works in the opposite direction. In a secular world we are bound to act as if, to coin a phrase: 'This is all there is.' Yet at some level, deep down, we know this is only true ironically: there is more to life than nuts and bolts. What that something else is, irony cannot begin to say. So perhaps it's best left unsaid. But we haven't completely forgotten it's there.

MARTIN WROE

My football team: being Us not I

It's interesting how people choose to describe themselves. Although Martin Wroe rarely talks head-on about being a priest in the Church of England, that doesn't detract from how serious he is about the teachings of the faith he lives by – and encourages the rest of us to consider. He's aware many people feel disconnected from formal religion and he looks for ways to draw us into a connecting that is authentic and profound.

This Thought *captures the end of a nail-biting season for the teams in the Premiership. The prospect that Leicester City might win the title 'against all the odds' was the kind of situation Martin relishes. So he used that to talk about one of the sacrosanct gatherings of male activity – the football team he plays in. They may not talk intimately about their lives, but they share more in the unsaid than can ever be described. Martin is a people person. You can often recognise yourself or those you love in the situations and characters he introduces us to in his* Thoughts.

30 April 2016

The football season is reaching its climax. Should Man Utd or Spurs lose this weekend, then 5000/1 outsiders Leicester City will become Premiership Champions. Can a team bereft of superstars, who narrowly avoided relegation a year ago, really do it?

On Thursday my own team conceded a last-minute equaliser and were held to a draw. Eleven-all.

We've been playing now for 20 years. Fourteen of us, seven-a-side. Some people have moved away. Some retired hurt. Knees, ankles, pride. It's about fitness, fun, competition – but mainly it's about community.

Men are different on a football pitch. The mild-mannered academic is the midfield enforcer, channelling his inner Roy Keane.

The gentle hospice nurse, wiping the lips of the dying by day, reveals a killer instinct in the penalty box.

In our heads we're 21 ... though some of us can't quite recall 51.

Underneath it all is Dylan Thomas's rage against the dying of the light. We know how a perfectly weighted pass can post-pone the falling dark. We know what's coming, how the light fades every week.

Recently we wept through the funeral of one of our finest players. Another friend, after a stroke, must now watch us from the sidelines.

Football measures our days. It's thrilling drama captures us, as players or fans. It dares us to believe that the implausible is not always the impossible. That Leicester might actually do it ...

Like great literature or art or music, sometimes sport says the unsayable – the thing none of us dare put into words. And it can bind communities close in the darkest days. Witness the dignified fortitude, at this week's Hillsborough verdict, of those families who lost their loved ones.*

And little compares to the quality of deep silence in a packed stadium, on a matchday near Remembrance Sunday. For all our competition and conflict, we notice that in the end it's about Us, not I. About the team not the player.

---

* On 26 April 2016 an inquest jury found that 96 Liverpool football fans who died in the Hillsborough Stadium disaster were unlawfully killed. The behaviour of the fans in no way contributed to the disaster, which was blamed on the construction of the stadium along with 'errors and omissions' by the police and ambulance services.

If Claudio Ranieri's Leicester do pull it off, Gary Lineker – as threatened – will present *Match of the Day* in his boxers.

But more significant will be the witness to the words of a rival manager, Arsène Wenger. 'The act of playing for the team,' he said, 'makes every individual stronger.'

Paul the Apostle would have agreed. In one of his early team talks he said: 'In humility, count others more significant than yourselves.'

And in another: 'The body has many parts – limbs, organs, cells – but no matter how many you can name, you're still one body.'

When the whole is greater than the sum of its parts – when it's about Us, not I – sport transcends itself. On some days it has a sacred quality. At the first match following the funeral of our friend recently, we all stood quietly on the centre circle. Heads bowed. Reverent. And then we kicked off …

BISHOP GRAHAM JAMES

Coping with sudden death

Graham James retired as a bishop in 2019 after a rich and varied career in the Church of England, where he remains an honorary assistant bishop in the Diocese of Truro. Following parish ministry, he was Chaplain to the Archbishop of Canterbury until 1993 when he was consecrated as a bishop at Westminster Abbey to serve first in Truro before being installed as Bishop of Norwich in 1999.

The Thought for the Day *audience will remember Bishop Graham for his calm and thoughtful approach to the vicissitudes of the news. The memories and anecdotes he drew on were often people-focused. In this* Thought, *in the face of a grim air crash, his first thought is for the families of the 66 people who died – but he directs his empathy to one single individual, as a way of bringing home the reality of sudden death. He then recalls his many visits to the bereaved over his years as a priest and recounts the different ways people have faced losing a loved one. Sudden death, he concludes, brings a grief hard for others to imagine.*

20 May 2016

Good morning, though there isn't much that's good about it for the families and friends of those who died on EgyptAir's flight MS804. Whatever the cause turns out to be, their grief and bereavement will not be moderated. Perhaps one of the most tragic stories is that of a young man from Chad currently living in France whose mother had just died. He was on his way home to grieve with his family. In Thomas Hardy's novel *The Return of the Native*, one of the characters says: 'The fates have not been kind to you.' That's how it must seem for that family.

Although the bereaved know that learning the cause and the details of the plane's last moments will not assuage their grief, they will want to know what happened. Love isn't a generalised feeling. We love people in particular and in every circumstance of their lives, even in and through the moments of their dying. On many funeral visits I've listened to spouses and partners offer me a minute by minute account of how their loved one died. By describing it they are not denying its reality but often thankful that the person they love did not die alone. Sometimes we say that we'd like to go quickly, but most religious traditions ask for deliverance from sudden death. It's included in a petition in the Litany in the Book of Common Prayer.

It was as a young priest more than 20 years ago that I came to know Philip Toynbee, for many years the doyen of literary reviewers. He moved to the Welsh countryside and found himself a near neighbour of an Anglican contemplative community of nuns, the Society of the Sacred Cross. It was an unlikely match between someone who'd been fairly bohemian and sisters following the religious life, but they became very close. When Philip was dying of cancer I recall him doubting whether to have a final operation. It was a risk. He didn't want to die on the operating table. He said, 'That would deprive me of the proper stages of dying, and I want to learn all I can from it.'

Rare is the person who approaches their death like that. But the deprivation of sudden death and the infliction of sudden grief are both greater than we may imagine. Perhaps today, as we remember the victims and families of the EgyptAir crash, we may cast our net of sympathy wider to include all visited by sudden death or sudden grief.

DR CHETNA KANG

Anger management

Dr Chetna Kang here combines the insights of her Hindu faith and her decades of practice as a psychiatrist to make the Thought for the Day *audience think in a different way about the issue of anger. The example she uses, of the varied reactions we all experience when driving a car, instantly hits home. Dr Kang insists that optimal mental health does not include being 'happy' all the time but rather allowing ourselves to feel (rather than fear) the full spectrum of human emotion.*

In this Thought *she draws on the Hindu spiritual teachings contained in the books such as the Vedas. In the most prominent of the Hindu scriptures, the* Bhagavad Gita, *the deity Krishna suggests there are six major ways in which the mind blocks spiritual progress: anger, greed, lust, envy, illusion and madness. Mind control is key to spiritual advancement. Here Chetna, who in her professional life conducts seminars on whole person-centred care, explains how anger works – and how we can learn to manage it.*

6 May 2017

There isn't a day that goes by where irrational and extreme acts of anger are not in the news. Such as the tragic death of the young lady who died as a result of a dispute with her neighbour over a ball. Hearing about events like this, however extreme, can serve to remind us of times in our day where we might express our anger in a way that is out of proportion with the trigger. Flying off the handle for things like crumbs on the carpet or having to wait in a queue longer than expected are familiar scenarios for many. I'm personally no stranger to mumbling under my breath at the driver in front of me who decides to stop for everyone the morning I'm most short on time!

Anger can manifest in different ways, the most obvious being when we externalise and express it. Less obvious is when we internalise it, hold on to it and then quietly, with hostility allow it to seep into our interactions. However it manifests, anger ignites our physiological stress response and in my work as a psychiatrist I see many patients who suffer with mental and physical illnesses exacerbated by unresolved anger.

Anger feels powerful and intense, and we're often advised not to make any decisions when angry. In the *Bhagavad Gita* Krishna includes anger as one of the six enemies of the mind and describes it as an emotion that manifests when our desires are not met or when their fulfilment is threatened. From that frustration or fear, anger arises and then leads to bewilderment, which disables our mind's ability to find the clearest way forward and connect with our inner wisdom.

I find we often don't stop long enough to think about what it is that we actually want from a situation and get so consumed by the emotion of anger we end up making assumptions and misplacing blame. There is no point in me getting annoyed at the driver in front of me, I just want to do the school run on time and, if I had left earlier, I am sure I would see their act of letting everyone in as kindness rather than a cause for my delay.

Anger might feel at the time like a visceral reaction, but I really think that if we can learn how to deal with it better, anger becomes more of a choice. We make the choice to be angry based on our perception of a situation. It is something we create by holding it, feeding it and allowing it to develop and grow the more we give in to it. Soon some reactions become so habitual that they become part of our character. I think if we want to improve the quality of our lives and move away from the damaging effects of anger, we need to be more honest with ourselves in identifying where and when we let it get the better of us.

CANON DR GILES FRASER

The martyrdom of Colonel Beltrame

When Lt Col. Arnaud Beltrame, just 44, was shot and killed after an Islamist gunman took over a supermarket in France, tributes poured in from his family, friends and colleagues, from all across France but also from the wider world. After the initial shock of such incidents, Thought for the Day *tries to find something to say that will offer a deeper perspective.*

Two days after the news had broken Giles Fraser, then parish priest of St Mary Newington in London, was scheduled to write. He knew exactly what he wanted to say on that Monday morning, which was the beginning of another Holy Week for Christians. That this man was special, there was no doubt. He was brave 'beyond the call of duty', to quote the testimony of his brother. But as Giles explains in this Thought, *Arnaud Beltrame should be remembered for another part of his life too – a part that was very important to him and very important to the hostage whose place he volunteered to take.*

27 March 2018

As police officer Lieutenant Colonel Arnaud Beltrame walked into that French supermarket last Friday morning he must have known there was a good chance he was walking to his death. Beltrame had swapped places with a hostage to secure their release. And later, responding to the sound of shots inside, his police colleagues stormed the supermarket and the terrorist shot Beltrame through the throat.

On this programme yesterday, the French ambassador described Beltrame as a 'Christian martyr'. Now, some people might have been a little surprised by this description given that martyrdom, in recent years, has come to be associated more with suicide bombers and terrorists – more like the man who had taken the hostage than the one who had saved her. But the ambassador was right. In Greek, martyr means 'witness' – it's not about religious violence. A martyr is someone who witnesses to their faith, who demonstrates faith in action, even to the point of death.

Originally from a secular background, Beltrame found faith in his thirties, received his first communion in 2010 after two years of preparation, and regularly attended Mass at his local abbey. Father Dominique Arz, the national chaplain of the French police force, said of Beltrame: 'The fact is he did not hide his faith, he radiated it. We can say that his act of self-offering is consistent with what he believed. He bore witness to his faith to the very end.'

That was last Friday. This coming Friday, of course, the church bears witness to the original and archetypal martyrdom of Christianity – the crucifixion of Christ. And it is hardly a stretch to understand Beltrame's choice of action as something directly inspired by the story of Good Friday. 'Greater love hath no one than this, to lay down one's life for one's friends' was how the ambassador described it, quoting from St John's Gospel.

For many millions of Christians, the cross is understood very much like that of a hostage swap – Christ exchanges places with humanity, thus to absorb all the horror and violence of the world. The cross is the offer of love in exchange for hate, whatever the cost, whatever it takes. And that's why the cross is the central image of Christianity. It's the pivot on which the Christian narrative turns, a representation of love, absolutely not a celebration of death – even though death is sometimes the cost of love.

The early Christian theologian Tertullian famously wrote in the second century, 'The blood of the martyrs is the seed of the Church'. In other words, it's through acts of self-sacrifice that other people come to understand what Christianity is really all about.

So, in my view, Lieutenant Colonel Arnaud Beltrame was indeed a Christian martyr, a hero of selfless commitment to other people and a witness to the courage and love that is exemplified by the cross. May he rest in peace and rise in glory.

CHINE MCDONALD

Miscarriage, God and pain

Chine McDonald, who moved to the UK from Nigeria at the age of four, has written movingly about her own pregnancies. Her first labour was not straightforward; she later wrote that it was 'by far the hardest and most painful thing I have ever done; I thank God that we got through it and were soon able to meet our son.' The 'we' in that sentence is instructive. She later confessed that she had asked her white husband to take the lead in all the interactions with the medical staff after learning that black women in the UK were four times more likely to die during pregnancy and childbirth than white women. 'I used my husband's whiteness to keep me safe,' she wrote. Of her second pregnancy she confessed she found the first few months 'brutal emotionally and physically'.

The pain of all those experiences surfaces in this Thought *in which she accompanies a friend through the trauma of a late miscarriage. Chine read theology at Cambridge University, trained as a newspaper journalist and then worked for Christian Aid followed by the think-tank Theos, where she is now Director. But it is her direct experience of helplessness and despair that suffuse this* Thought. *Then there is only one solution she can offer.*

28 March 2019

Two weeks ago I sat with a dear friend who had recently experienced the trauma of a late miscarriage. In those moments, it's impossible to find the words that might in any way soothe the visceral grief that comes when such great hope becomes utmost despair.

Those who have experienced baby loss speak of the emptiness that follows, after months of waiting in expectation, growing and bonding with a baby and dreaming of what they might become. I can't imagine the pain.

Nine stillbirths happen every day – one in every 225 births. Mothering Sunday this weekend will be extremely painful for some mothers without their babies.

This week the government announced that coroners in England and Wales may be given new powers to investigate stillbirths. This move is designed to prevent more baby deaths and help bereaved parents gain answers to what went wrong.

Some years ago, when working as a local newspaper reporter, I occasionally attended inquests and saw up close the pain of bereaved families having to relive their loved one's deaths. While some saw it as a necessary part of getting justice and closure – for others, it did nothing more than open up old wounds.

The quest to get answers is a very human instinct – a way to regain some semblance of control, to work out what went wrong or ask God why he could let such terrible things happen. Answers help us to make sense of the world.

But many of those who have suffered stillbirth or neonatal death find solace not in answers to scientific questions but in community – in the ability to be able to speak about what they have gone through and to know that they are not alone.

At times of great suffering, religious believers can turn to trite words in a well-meaning attempt to make things better. But phrases such as 'God works in mysterious ways' or 'God won't give you more than you can handle' just don't cut it.

Sitting with my friend who had suffered a miscarriage at her hour of greatest need, my place wasn't to provide answers or give platitudes but to weep with her.

In my experience, the Christian faith is profound because it doesn't suggest God promises life will be perfect. God himself is no stranger to deep pain; the incarnate Christ cried in anguish at the crucifixion: 'My God, my God, why have you forsaken me?'

I take solace in the belief that it is right in the middle of the most painful times that I need God the most.

C.S. Lewis – a writer and theologian who himself experienced tragedy – wrote: 'God whispers to us in our pleasures, speaks in our conscience, but shouts in our pains.'

GUVNA B

Knife crime, music and God

Over the Christmas period the Today *programme invites guest editors to join the editorial team. In 2019 one of the editors was George the Poet who was building an increasingly high profile for his spoken-word performance, so it seemed fitting to invite Guvna B, a MOBO award-winning rapper forging his own profile in music, to contribute that day's* Thought for the Day.

Guvna B is a very thoughtful man. When talking about his life he was open about the good things in his upbringing and the hurts and the problems that troubled him greatly. Help came in the creative expression he poured into his lyrics and his music. He had also begun to include ideas that stem from his faith, which was not always an easy thing to do in the world of rap.

In this Thought, *Guvna B tells his own story and reflects on the killing of Jaden Moodie, another teenager stabbed by a gang in the street. Like his music, the nature of the telling here is personal, direct, questioning and honest. It worked brilliantly on the day and got great feedback afterwards.*

31 *December 2019*

Knife crime is nothing new and it's an issue that has weighed heavy on my heart for as long as I can remember. Every time a young person loses their life to a blade, it pains me. Just recently, Jaden Moodie was deliberately struck by a car, stabbed, and left to die in cold blood. He was just 14.

Growing up I struggled to express my feelings externally after a close friend was stabbed to death, so it became a habit for me to do so internally. It resulted in me developing an apathetic attitude and I shielded myself from difficult conversations. I came to realise that isn't the best way to go about things. I thought I was dealing with my issues quickly but all I was doing was storing them at the back of my mind. By holding back, I began to grow bitter about all the unresolved and painful problems that I had never spoken up about.

Writing music was an unexpected outlet for me. I'd get lost in my own world and write unfiltered thoughts on how I was feeling. Making those thoughts rhyme allowed me to be creative in my pain. Every verse written felt like a giant exhale and release that I very much needed.

My art was the gateway to me getting in touch with my emotions. I started to become deeply affected by the examples of evil and injustice that surrounded me. Tragic events would play on my mind for hours – and days – on end. And the pain of others started to become my pain.

I began to ask questions. Why is this happening? How can it stop? What can I do to help? God, where are you in this?

I'm not sure I have the answers but I think God cares. With all my questions and 7 billion people in this world, it sounds weird I guess, but I still believe God sees me. He sees the individual. He sees the one, and I like that.

Racism, sexism, terrorism, and every other ism and schism was chucked in my face so often that I stopped seeing the one. What I mean by this is that each news story had lost its individual impact and I couldn't comprehend every headline as a real event that happened in a real place, to real people, with real lives.

When I started to picture my loved ones and family members in some of the horrible situations I read about, it changed my thought pattern dramatically. Seeing the one means to always put yourself in the shoes of the individual. And even though I ain't got all the answers, if I can do that, I know I'm moving in the right direction.

RHIDIAN BROOK

Remembering who we are

Rhidian Brook is a storyteller to his bones, and makes connections and offers insights that surprise, challenge and delight. He often talks in his Thoughts *about personal situations from his own family, as he does here – and the honesty of his self-questioning is engaging and helpful.*

Awareness around dementia has increased exponentially in the last five years, in line with the increase in statistics around the disease. In a survey by Alzheimer's Research UK in 2021, over half the UK public knew someone who had been diagnosed with the condition – usually a grandparent or parent. And their research suggested there's been a positive shift in understanding of the diseases that cause the condition, though fear persists.

It's that last observation that Rhidian taps into so skilfully in this Thought, *giving expression to what is still for many the unthinkable. And yet, I could imagine his Granny Sheila in her care home being well cared for, and I enjoyed following Rhidian's thought process to his poignant but ultimately uplifting message of solidarity in our human condition.*

7 February 2020

The news that the government have a plan to rescue the care system and provide dignity and security for the old and vulnerable is welcome. Unless you have to deal with the care system personally, it's hard to appreciate just how great the need is, and how profound the challenges being faced by the carers and the cared for.

My wife's mother has Alzheimer's and has just crossed the line from managing by herself to needing full-time care. There are practical challenges: how to pay for the care; can we move her closer to home? There are emotional challenges: are we abandoning her? Will she know any different? And then there are profound existential questions such as: is someone with dementia any less of a person for not knowing who they are? And what makes a person a person?

Entering the care home on my first visit, my prejudice and fear hits me as pungently as the smell of old age. It is like entering another country. A marginal and forgotten land, populated by a very fragile people, who seem to be just about getting through the day. The contingency of life – the utter dependency of these people – is overwhelming. And my desire to get away is powerful. I will never be like this, I tell myself.

But, the person we love is here. And after seeing Granny Sheila's light and clean room we join her colleagues for tea and play the memory game. There is enough self-awareness to laugh about this. A carer joins in and I notice that she remembers the name of everyone, including Sheila, who brightens at the recognition. And I feel shame for my initial reaction.

I know my reaction is fear. The very name dementia – 'deprived of mind' – is frightening. It raises fundamental questions: will anyone be there for me when I forget who I am? What makes me who I am? My memory? My capacity for thought? Will I know God? Or will I, like the psalmist, feel abandoned in 'a land of forgetting'?

Later, we look at old photos of Sheila when she was young. The same person but different. She doesn't recognise everyone – one day she might not recognise herself – but we remember for her. And it twigs: in this community, personhood is not based on someone's capacities. It's a gift bestowed upon people by others. Our minds – even failing minds – work relationally. As long as one is recognised as a person, one remains a person.

Another psalm speaks of people being held in the memory of God. 'Even in darkness, I cannot hide from you,' it says. Before we leave, I see a carer talking gently to a man whose head is sunk in his chest, holding his hand. It is a picture of absolute dependence. Which is, as the psalmist reminds us, the condition of all humanity – if only we would remember this.

ANNE ATKINS

The value of a life

This Thought for the Day *from Anne Atkins was one I'll never forget. Anne had wanted to explore how, as a society, we have yardsticks for evaluating the importance of one life against another. Different motivations in different eras, but all of them still recognisable. And, now, as we were beginning to live with a new deadly virus, fresh calculations emerged about the allocation of resources. Before leaving the house, she showed her script for approval, as she always did, to her beloved father.*

Not long before she was due to broadcast next morning she rang me to say she had just heard her father had died. She was adamant she wanted to deliver this Thought, *but she couldn't do it without including that news. She had rewritten a version of the end for me to hear. There wasn't long to decide and no time to warn anyone before she started.*

I listened to her get closer to the end as she delivered it on air, but I knew she was going to be all right. Her bravery in her steady voice was as moving as the news itself was sad. Her father David Briggs was an extraordinary man and much loved. But she wanted to do this for him and, amazingly, the subject she had chosen meant it could work. It was rightly praised in the press and on social media afterwards for being an 'extraordinary and moving' Thought for the Day. *It was indeed, and more.*

17 March 2020

A Nobel-winning professor, an elderly clergyman and a boy scout were in a plummeting helicopter, only two parachutes between them. The academic seized a package, said he was the cleverest man in the world and jumped. 'My child,' the priest said, 'I've lived long and I'm going to Heaven. You take the other.' 'Chill,' said the boy. 'The cleverest man in the world just jumped out with my rucksack.'

How can we possibly weigh one life against another? Already there's talk of focusing facilities on the fittest. Will we soon have to decide who's most important? When I heard Donald Trump had been tested I thought, the president will never be denied resources.

We already esteem importance, in our perceptions of history. We were taught the Black Death took a quarter of people: figures based on privileged urbanites. Now scholarship, factoring in the rural underclass, estimates 60 per cent of Europe. Most lost without trace or record.

One of my clergyman grandfather's first duties of 1918 was to bury 11 in one day ... victims, not of war but of 'flu. We know it killed more. But the trenches took the young men, and perhaps we missed them more.

Some years ago three generations were living in a vicarage that caught fire. The older ones were found and rescued: the children lost. My mother was distraught. What grandparents, she agonised, would want to be saved in place of the children? Older people are already saying they don't want scant resources at the cost of the young.

An impressive denial of self looks very different when decided by society. Women and children were rescued first from the *Titanic*. An extraordinary sacrifice of the strongest, influenced by centuries of Christianity. Now, they say, it would be young adults. Because they have more to give? Or are simply stronger to survive? Arguably the more we favour the weak, the more civilised we are.

No human life can ever be worth less than another's. Yesterday we heard centenarian Dame Fanny Waterman say she was asked to step down, aged 95, still with years to give. After I'd finished writing this script last night I read it to my father, as I always did for his approval; told him I loved him; and said goodbye. Five minutes after I reached my destination I got a call to say he'd died. A shock? Hardly, at 102. A loss? More than words can say. Last Thursday he was still helping me translate *Ænead* VI.

Society sometimes must evaluate, when not everyone can be saved. But all such evaluation is false.

Death equalises all. Not because it comes for all. But because the Pale Horse of plague and pestilence is the *enemy* of us all. The Last Enemy, wrote St Paul. Rage, rage, wrote Dylan Thomas.

Death is always an outrage. For fittest and weakest, richest and poorest, barely born or 102. Every one.

REV. JAYNE MANFREDI

Ebenezer and his nephew Fred

Jayne Manfredi is a fairly new voice on Thought for the Day. *Her Twitter biog includes the epithet* Holy Tomfoolery, *which sums up the way she talks about her family life – in glorious technicolour with just the right mix of caring and togetherness.*

Jayne is a Church of England ordinand at the Queen's Foundation, Birmingham. She enjoys a wide reputation on social media for having something to say, in her own singular voice. Her Stations of the Cross for a Global Pandemic, *using photographs from around the world to visualise Christ's journey to the cross, were very powerful.*

But perhaps more typical of her style is this Thought *in which, at Christmas, she uses some of the characters from* A Christmas Carol *to look back on the first year of the COVID pandemic, hiding nothing. She remembers the humour that, critically, kept her going in the darker days. Dickens would have approved of where she ends up.*

28 December 2020

My favourite book of all time is Charles Dickens's timeless classic *A Christmas Carol*. I love it so much that I read it every year and it's become a key part of my Christmas tradition. The transformation of Scrooge from wicked old covetous sinner to one who is redeemed and reformed, is a story that is steeped in all the things I treasure most about Christianity. Salvation. Forgiveness. Second chances. Good triumphing over evil. The ultimate promise that we are worth so much more than our worst moments.

The character who best illustrates all these things is not the haunted Ebenezer, but his indefatigably cheerful nephew Fred, who despite being faced with his uncle's rudeness and cold indifference to his persistent overtures at friendship, keeps doggedly trying again. To keep our good humour when we're confronted with indifference, despair, agony and sadness, has been one of the main challenges of the pandemic.

Dickens writes that 'there is nothing in the world so irresistibly contagious as laughter and good-humour.' My ministry is permeated in this assumption, and it has been both my greatest gift to others and my best coping strategy for surviving this past year. The losses, both collectively and personally, have been profound. In the midst of unimaginable agony and desperate pain, I had to dig deep to rediscover the truth that where humour resides hope soon follows.

I am a fond observer of the absurdities of life: a church service COVID-style, presided over by my rector enthroned in clerical robes and an unwieldy plastic visor, which he forgets to raise before trying to drink from the chalice. A school bus, full of teenagers with their faces pressed up to the windows, making rude gestures at me as I walk my dogs, all wearing masks, like a scene from a B-list horror movie. The Zoom meetings, an endless source for comedy, featuring the inevitable wi-fi glitches, which momentarily transform participants into contestants in a gurning competition. The people chatting away in blithe ignorance of their muted microphones. The surprise video-bombs from unexpected pets and toddlers. We laughed. We had to. What else could we do?

I am not an optimist by nature. To survive this cursed year of 2020 I've had to dredge up reserves of hope I didn't know I had. I have hope, like Ebenezer Scrooge, that this past year will, somehow, be redeemed. I have hope that shared laughter – even through tears – has the power to save us in all sorts of unexpected ways. I have hope that we are all worth so much more than our worst moments. I have hope.

REV. DR JANE LEACH

Naming a child

*What's in a name? A lot more than you might imagine, according to Rev.
Dr Jane Leach. Although she has had a distinguished career in academic
theology – culminating in her current post as Principal of Wesley House,
the Methodist theological college in Cambridge – Jane did the first of her
many degrees in history. She draws on both disciplines in this* Thought.

*When the Queen's granddaughter, Princess Eugenie, gave birth in
2021, the bookmakers had a field day taking bets on what name would
be given to her baby son. But the birth of the child prompted Dr Leach,
a forensic thinker with a real feel for people, to a deeper kind of thinking
about names.*

*Throughout her career Jane has specialised in pastoral and practical
theology that focuses on the varying social contexts in which people live. In
this* Thought *she throws new light on the significance that names carry in
our culture – how others can use names to claim power over us, or how they
can become tools for self-determination.*

15 February 2021

So the bookies are giving odds on the name that Princess
Eugenie will choose for her baby son, and whether or not the
Queen will like it … And whether or not you're interested in
royal baby names, the business of naming is a serious matter
– an act that expresses a bond and perhaps a hope. The hope
that the child will live up to something, or carry the memory of
someone, or simply that their name will be a good fit for this
unique person whose personality is yet to unfold.

Whatever their origins, our names are a deeply personal
matter. They abound with resonances of culture and family, and
of personal association and memory. Sometimes these are resonances we want to claim, and sometimes we want to distance

ourselves from them, and yet whatever name we embrace, we care about it being spelled correctly and pronounced correctly and that's why it's so easy to insult someone by refusing to learn to say their name. Kamala Harris must be very used to this by now, and she is not alone because naming – both the act of giving a name and the act of addressing someone by name – are acts of power.

We can claim power over the other in name giving – as enslaved people on plantations found their African names being supplanted by those of their owners – or we can empower others by seeking to hear and understand their names – the name Kamala (Comma-la) means lotus flower in Sanskrit – a plant that unfolds above the surface but has deep roots.

Many religious traditions recognise that naming is powerful because it's not just a social matter, it's also an existential one. In the biblical tradition names sometimes reveal the character of the players – like Jacob, which means cheat – who after a wrestling match with God was renamed Israel – a name that offered a different future to a man who had previously lived up to a bad name.

In the eighth century BC, as the prophet Isaiah addressed the plight of those in exile in Babylon who were living in a reality defined by others, he declared that the names of God's children are inscribed on the palms of God's hands, implying that whatever the names others call us, or even that we may find ourselves living up to, there is a deeper calling to pay attention to a name that belongs to us, that references our sacred value and unique identity.

For those, across the ages, whose opportunities for self-determination have been limited, this has been and remains a source of comfort and strength – the belief that our real names are known and are not forgotten; that our existence matters; that we have deep roots that one day may have the chance to flower above the surface; that there is hope that one day we will be heard.

PROFESSOR TOM MCLEISH

A little boy called Arthur

What can anyone say on Thought for the Day *when confronted with the news of yet another child callously killed by the adults who were supposed to love them? The names of these lost innocents haunt public memory like some terrible litany: Maria Colwell, Jasmine Beckford, Victoria Climbié, Baby P, Star Hobson and here – one grim December morning in 2021 – Arthur Labinjo-Hughes who died at the hands of his father and stepmother after what prosecutors called a 'campaign of cruelty' amounting to 'torture'. The NSPCC says at least one child a week is killed in the UK, most commonly by a parent or step-parent.*

Tom McLeish that morning avoided the temptation of repeating the gruesome details of the news reports, though the audio recordings of the six-year-old played at the trial clearly haunted him. Tom is Professor of Natural Philosophy in the Department of Physics at the University of York. He has an immensely wide background in the framing of science, theology, society and medieval history, and the theory of creativity in art and science. Yet despite all that learning he knows that the only response to the cruel murder of a child is lamentation.

8 December 2021

The morning scan of news features has for several days now been met with the delightful face of a fair-haired little boy called Arthur. And every day that delight is immediately frozen by a grip of horror as the wave of remembrance hits. It's the story we wish were not true – the events that a children's charity called 'horrendous, horrific, heart-breaking' but which soon find the well of language dry. Worse, he died believing – and we have it in his own words – that 'no one is going to feed me; no one loves me.'

In Arthur's case we know his name, his face, his story. All that breaks through our inured inability to respond emotionally or practically to most child deaths. According to the independent Institute of Health Metrics and Evaluation, about 15,000 children in the world under the age of six die every day – from preventable causes. But what is an appropriate reaction to the cruelty of which humans are capable? One reader of Arthur's story wrote: 'It brought back memories of my own abusive childhood. I have not cried like this for ages.'

Processing memories of suffering through lamentation is an ancient discipline, which has long connected the cruel death of children to the bigger stories of the communities in which they live.

A reading from Matthew's Gospel often used in Christmas services takes the much older words of the prophet Jeremiah to lament over King Herod's killing of all boys under the age of two, living near Bethlehem, to ensure that the infant Jesus would be among them: 'A voice is heard in Ramah, weeping and great mourning. Rachel weeping for her children, and refusing to be comforted, because they are no more.'

The cruel killing of innocent children is not, it seems, restricted to our own times, but is a shame that darkens every age and culture.

It is therefore something of a miracle that light ever shines in that depth of darkness. Yet Jeremiah moves from lament to hope, to a day when God's laws of love will be 'written on our hearts' rather than ignored in our books.

Perhaps our current shared cry of lament can renew a sensitivity to the still-unmet Millennium Goal to reduce global child mortality, to hope, and to action.

But for now, the 'cry in the wilderness' will for many be simply silence. For others, like the players of his favourite football club Birmingham City, it will be 'Arthur, we love you.'

BISHOP PHILIP NORTH

No neat and tidy endings

Philip North is a priest and bishop whose theology is traditional but who could not be more contemporary in the way he applies that faith, working to renew the Church in his work as Bishop of Burnley.

This Thought *was triggered by his realisation that he had no idea how the war in Ukraine could be brought to an end. But from that he launches into a philosophical exploration of what theologians call escha-tology – the part of theology concerned with the true end of human destiny – but he does so using only the language of the living room.*

It is an extraordinary piece of writing, which encompasses his grand-father's deathbed complaint, the Christian festival of the Ascension, and the human dislike of uncertainty and incompleteness. We all have a preference for neat and tidy endings – which he tells us we cannot have. Even on Thought for the Day. *But he does have a suggestion …*

27 May 2022

It's now almost exactly three months since the horrific conflict in Ukraine began. Part of the anxiety is that we still have no idea how or when it will end or who, if anyone, will emerge victorious. That sense of incompleteness gnaws away so that this terrible war has become a constant backdrop to so many aspects of our lives.

Human beings like neat and tidy endings. That's why so much enjoyment can be found in novels and films where every plotline is tied up and every mystery revealed. The trouble is that, in reality, there is rarely such a thing as resolution. Part of the human condition is living with uncertainty and incomplete-ness, with all the intense frustration that carries. I remember my grandfather in the last days of his life complaining bitterly that, because of his impending death, he would never see how things worked out for his family members. Well, he could have lived for a thousand years – and he would still have been making the same complaint.

Perhaps that's why the Feast of the Ascension, which Christians keep at this time of year, has always been such an attractive one, marked across the globe with such rejoicing. It offers that most satisfying thing of all, which is an ending. On Ascension Day Christians celebrate because the body of Jesus Christ has returned to be with the Father. He has gone ahead to prepare a place for us and so the story of his time on earth has concluded. All nice and neat.

Or is it? Because this is a feast that offers more than just an ending. It can also offer a way of living with uncertainty. He may have ascended, but Jesus hasn't left the world. Rather Christians believe he is present in a different way, present through the lives of his followers who are called to emulate his self-giving love. His hands are now the hands of those who follow him. It is exactly that combination of future hope and contemporary purpose that is giving so many Ukrainian Christians such strength right now.

Ascensiontide may be a time of joyful celebration for the churches. But it's also a season that can ask interesting questions for others in this uncertain and unpredictable world. If everything is contingent, provisional and transient, what can we depend on? Where can people go to seek security?

Maybe something which can appear fragile is the most dependable of all. Perhaps the thing we human beings can most fully trust is the power of self-giving love.

EPILOGUE

RABBI LORD JONATHAN SACKS

We've been through too much to go back

The last word must go to Rabbi Lord Sacks who sadly died in 2020. Over the decades his voice made an incalculable contribution to confirming the importance of faith in the public square and is much missed. He was eloquent and gently prophetic, he spoke with warmth as well as profound wisdom. Most of all he spoke from the heart of his own Jewish tradition but used language that would reach everyone; which is why so many of the six million daily listeners to the Today *programme felt they knew him personally. He was listened to with both respect and affection. One of his signature messages was that we must abandon our 'I' society and return to a 'We' society. In one of his last* Thought for the Day *scripts he was already urging people to begin thinking beyond the COVID pandemic to how society should be shaped for the future. How did We want to go forward? On his behalf, I leave it with you.*

15 May 2020

When the worst of the pandemic is over, what kind of future will we seek? Will we try as far as possible to go back to the way things were? Or will we try to create a more just and caring society? What impact does collective tragedy have on the human imagination?

The philosopher Hegel said that the one thing we learn from history is that we learn nothing from history. But the great prophets of the Bible who experienced tragedy, like Isaiah and Jeremiah, said in effect we must learn from history if we are to avoid repeating it. We have to use the pain we've been through to sensitise ourselves to the pain of others, the poor, the weak and the vulnerable – the widow, the orphan and the stranger.

Collective suffering can move us from I to We, from the pursuit of self-interest to care for the common good. Which will it be for us?

It's worth looking at the last two great tragedies in Western history, World War I and the Spanish Flu pandemic of 1918, and World War II. After 1918, nothing much changed. It was an age of individualism and inequality, of the Roaring Twenties and *The Great Gatsby*, wild dances and even wilder parties, as if people were trying to forget and put the past behind them. It was fun, but it led to the Great Strike of 1926 and the Great Crash of 1929, the recession of the 1930s and the rise in mainland Europe of nationalism and fascism. And a mere 21 years after the war to end all wars, the world was at war again. On that occasion, Hegel was right. People learned nothing from history.

The reaction to World War II was quite different. There was the 1944 Education Act that extended secondary education to everyone. There was the National Health Service and the birth of the welfare state. America produced the Marshall Plan that helped a ravaged Europe to rebuild itself. The result was 75 years of peace. People knew they had to build something more inclusive. When war or disease affects all of us, you learn to care for all of us.

I hope that's what happens now, that we build a fairer society, where human values count as much as economic ones. We've been through too much simply to go back to where we were. We have to rescue some blessing from the curse, some hope from the pain.

ACKNOWLEDGEMENTS

To my amazing team of stalwart *Thought for the Day* producers: Dan Tierney, Rosie Dawson, Phil Pegum, Norman Winter and, top of the shop, Amanda Hancox. Be proud of your work. I hope these scripts bring back some exciting, hairy and very good memories.

To our Production Co-ordinator for *Thought for the Day*, Rosemary Grundy. My wing-woman for over 20 years. Thank you for your tireless dedication, not least in helping source scripts for the book. I couldn't have done it without you.

To those in my early BBC days in Yalding House, London. My first editors Eley McAinsh, who trained me on *Thought*, the late David Coomes and John Newbury. And my first Heads of Religious Broadcasting David Winter and Ernie Rea. Thank you all for the advice, the support and the belief in me.

Respect to all the *Today* editors I worked with: Jenny Abramsky, Phil Harding, Roger Mosey, John Barton, Rod Liddle, Kevin Marsh, Ceri Thomas, Jamie Angus and Sarah Sands. Plus a special mention for assistant editor Ollie Stone-Lee.

My heartfelt thanks to successive Controllers of Radio 4 who kept faith with *Thought for the Day* and whose support has been absolutely vital: Helen Boaden, Mark Damazer, Gwyneth Williams and Mohit Bakaya.

Huge thanks to all the contributors over the years who have been part of the *Thought for the Day* journey, especially those who have been part of this retelling of where we've been and how we got here. You have been part of something very special, and that's what you will always be to me.

Thank you to the droves of listeners over the decades who wrote to say that you were glad we were there. You cheered us and kept us on our toes at the same time.

To all my family and friends who have put up with news bulletins and production calls at all times of day and night, however inappropriate. You are very wonderful people and deserve special praise.

During the writing of this book my darling mum, Brenda, died. She was a very special blend. She loved *Thought* and so wanted me to complete this book. It means a great deal to me to have done it. With thanks to my sister Anita and brother Stephen for being there in the months of loss. I have dedicated it to Mum and to our wonderful dad, Gerry. Together on another shore.

With thanks to Nell Warner at Ebury Publishing for giving me more time …

To Paul Vallely, my amazing husband, best editor, most honest and trusted opinion, constant support in all weathers. And to my boy Thomas, no longer a boy! You have always understood. My love to you both.